Eating In

Fay Maschler

BLOOMSBURY

First published in Great Britain 1987
Copyright © 1987 by Fay Maschler
This edition published in 1988

Bloomsbury Publishing Ltd, 2 Soho Square,
London W1V 5DE

British Library Cataloguing in Publication Data

Maschler, Fay
  Eating in
  1. Cookery, International
  I. Title
  641.5   TX725.A1

  ISBN 0–7475–0282 X

CREDITS
Edited by Vicky Hayward
Text designed by Paul Fielding
Illustrations copyright © 1987 by Chic Pix
Author's photograph on front cover by Ros Drinkwater

Phototypeset in Great Britain by
Butler & Tanner Ltd, Frome and London
Printed in Great Britain by
Richard Clay Ltd, Bungay, Suffolk

Eating out is a pleasure but also a career for Fay Maschler. What does she do when eating in?

Based on her recipe column for the *London Evening Standard* this book reveals the culinary inclinations of a working woman whose job is testing the cooking of others. The result is practical recipes, most of which are quick to shop for and quick to cook. Inspiration comes from celebrating what is in season or plenty, from the cuisines of different countries that now enrich eating out and eating in, from the pleasures and constraints of regularly preparing food for children, frequently feasts for friends and sometimes suppers for lovers.

Fay Maschler's column became a companion to all those who at the end of the day must get something on the table, but to whom convenience means comfort and delight rather than compromise. Meals are correctly regarded as high points in the daily round and there is advice on adventurous shopping, ways of approaching old standards to give them a taste lift, encouragement to the cook who feels more stale than day-old bread – and ideas as to how to put even *that* to good use.

Restaurant chefs are obliged to cook many of their dishes to order and their tips and ideas season the book which concludes with a chapter of chefs' recipes specially devised for the column.

Most followers of Fay Maschler's recipe column have bundles of yellowing cuttings stuck together with egg white and spotted with olive oil. Here is the complete collection neatly bound – over a year's worth of recipes to provide many years of sound meals.

CONTENTS

NOTE ON METRICATION

The metric and imperial measurements given in the recipes are, perforce, not exact equivalents, so it is important, particularly when measurements are more crucial, for example in baking, to follow one system or the other. Spoonfuls are level spoonfuls unless stated otherwise. If you are following metric measurements it is sensible to use a set of spoons sized as 5 ml, 10 ml and 15 ml (the equivalent of teaspoon, dessertspoon and tablespoon).

ACKNOWLEDGMENTS

The author and publishers are grateful to the following for permission to reproduce copyright recipes: W. H. Allen, Potato Gnocchi from *Pasta from A–Z*; Aurum Press, Preserved Sweet Peppers from *The Illustrated Book of Preserves*; British Trout Association, Trout in Newspaper from *Take Two Trout*; Jonathan Cape Ltd, 'One of the world's great sandwiches' from *The English Cookbook* by Victor Gordon and Gujerati Carrot Salad from *Eastern Vegetarian Cooking* by Madhur Jaffrey; Chatto & Windus, Grapes and Grape Tart and Grilled Goat's Cheese with Salad from *A Cook's Calendar* by Frances Bissell and Pumpkin Risotto from *The Pleasures of Cookery* by Frances Bissell; Sally Clarke, Spiced Plums, Nectarines and Peaches, Light Fish Broth with Chili and Fresh Coriander, Various Fish Wrapped in Wafer-thin Pastry with Spinach and Shallots, Tomato, Fennel and Basil Tart, Grilled Prosciutto Ham, Mozzarella Cheese and Basil 'Sandwich' and Marinated Chicken Salad; William Collins Sons and Company Ltd, Szechuan Bean Curd and Ham, Chicken and Noodles with Soya Egg from *Healthy Chinese Cooking* by Kenneth Lo; Conran Octopus Ltd, Pasta with Fried Eggs from *Pasta Perfect* by Anna del Conte and Stir-fried Beef with Vegetables from *Visual Delights* by Nathalie Hambro; Francis Coulson and Brian Sack, Sticky Toffee and Date Pudding; David & Charles, Damson Cobbler from *The National Trust Book of Traditional Puddings* by Sara Paston-Williams; Dorling Kindersley Ltd, Spaghetti with Chicken Livers and Lemon from *An Omelette and a Glass of Wine* by Elizabeth David; Ebury Press, Avocado Pie with Garlic Crust from *The Harrods Book of Entertaining* by Lady Macdonald of Macdonald, copyright © 1986 by Claire Macdonald of Macdonald and the National Magazine Company Ltd; Futura, Lemon Lentils from *Ismail Merchant's Indian Cuisine* and Pasta with Anchovies and Breadcrumbs from *The Classic Book of Pasta* by Vincenzo Buonassisi; Gill and Macmillan, Bacon and Cabbage from *Irish Traditional Food* by Theodora FitzGibbon; Victor Gollancz Ltd, Venison Steaks with Farthinghoe Sauce from *Good Food from Farthinghoe* by Nicola Cox; Grafton Books, Cinderella Soup from *The Cuisine of Paul Bocuse* by Paul Bocuse and Pasta with Potted Shrimps from *Perfect Pasta* by Valentina Harris; Macdonald, Nasi Goreng from *Easy Eastern Cookery* by Ranse

Leembruggen and Pigeon Breasts with Garlic from *Le Menu Gastronomique* by Jack Gillon; Macmillan London and Basingstoke, Pulled and Devilled Turkey from *English Food* by Jane Grigson and Pasta with Gorgonzola Sauce from *Classic Italian Cookbook* by Marcella Hazan; Michael Joseph Ltd, Pink Fir Apple Potatoes and Fennel Fritters and Fennel Baked with Parmesan from *Jane Grigson's Vegetable Book*; Anton Mosimann, Stir-fried Brussels Sprouts and Duck Breasts with Apples; Penguin Books Ltd, Ham in a Piquant Sauce, Chicken with Tarragon and Mushroom Soup from *French Provincial Cooking* by Elizabeth David, Walnut, Beetroot and Chicory Salad from *Summer Cooking* by Elizabeth David, Garlic Chicken from *Simple French Food* by Richard Olney (Penguin Books, 1983), copyright © 1974 by Richard Olney, p. 298, Tex-Mex Chili Con Carne from *A Taste of American Cooking* by Clare Walker and Keryn Christiansen (Penguin Books, 1986), copyright © 1986 by Clare Walker, pp. 85–6, and The Richest Brownies Known to Man from *Food as Presents* by Patricia Holden White, copyright © 1975, 1982 by Patricia Holden White; Claudia Roden, Pickled Lemons, Pickled Cauliflower and Red Cabbage and Kuku from *A New Book of Middle Eastern Food* by Claudia Roden; J. Sainsbury Plc, Prawn Pasta from *A Traveller's Tastes* by Josceline Dimbleby; the Savoy Hotel, London, Omelette Arnold Bennett; Carla Tomasi, Salmon Poached with Olive Oil and Rosemary, Tomato and Orange Soup Flavoured with Fresh Thyme, Roast Rack of Lamb with Mint and Honey and Little Mushroom Cakes; and John Tovey, Port and Claret Jelly.

INTRODUCTION

One day I idly mentioned to the editor of the *London Evening
Standard*, of which I am restaurant critic, that I thought the
recipes which were appearing in the paper had little relevance to
the lives of the readers – people who were busy at work and
probably had little time or opportunity to shop and cook, and
sometimes scant inclination to do so, but who were still faced with
getting something on the table at the end of the day.

The recipes should be seasonal, I said, quick and sparky and
they should take advantage of the ever-increasing availability of
interesting ingredients and some of the better pre-prepared foods.
They should reflect the changes in people's appetites and perceptions, their demand for healthy food, fast food and exotic food,
some of it inspired by what is available in restaurants, a subject I
felt I knew intimately. The recipes should take into account the
demands of children and their usually relatively undemanding
palates. Single people should not be ignored or presumed only to
want egg on toast. I became quite lyrical on the subject.

I was extremely taken aback some months later to receive a call
from the editor saying that I could start the recipe column in a
couple of weeks' time. That I enjoyed doing it so much also took
me by surprise for, in the hurly-burly of eating out as much as I
have to do, I supposed that my cooking had fallen by the wayside.
Once I started writing, however, all the recipes I felt I had in some
sense made my own over the years began to come back to me and
the evening meals for my three children became a new challenge.
Friends, both amateur and professional cooks, were immensely
generous with ideas and, although they will recognise themselves
through their recipes in the text, I particularly want to thank my
mother, Mary Coventry; my sister, Beth Coventry; David
Queensberry; Hazel Short; Nathan Silver; Simon Hopkinson;
Pierre Martin; and Ruthie Rogers.

An unexpected perk of doing the column was receiving copies
of new cookery books. Some of these I would review by quoting
a recipe and to those authors – and to many others – I have a debt
of gratitude.

I am unashamedly keen on spices and on oriental cooking of one
kind and another and, although I am influenced by restaurant
food, the converse is also true in that much of my own cooking

centres on preparing the sort of homely food you seldom find made by chefs. Careful cooking of traditional British dishes is something I like to promote, for in these days of so much primped and prissy food something like a meticulously well-made fish pie can be a real joy.

I am not the first to remark that shopping is as important as cooking, and that menus should be guided by what looks good that day in the butcher, fishmonger, grocer or supermarket. A well-stocked store cupboard is also important and to enjoy these recipes it would be as well to have on hand the following provisions: tins of anchovies, tuna fish, tomatoes, chickpeas, petits pois, one tin of consommé (for the spare rib recipe), extra virgin olive oil, sunflower oil, wine vinegar, sea salt, vanilla pods, a range of pulses, a range of dried pastas, risotto and basmati rice, polenta, couscous, cracked wheat (bulghur), sun-dried tomatoes in a jar, whole spices and a cheap coffee grinder in which to whizz them to order, good quality bitter chocolate, dried mushrooms, wind-dried sausage and rice vinegar (these last three available from oriental grocers), soy sauce, chilli sauce, a variety of mustards. I am not keen on dried herbs. In the freezer might sit puff pastry, tubs of chicken livers, kipper fillets, Canadian-style streaky bacon and extra packets of unsalted butter.

During the time of contributing recipes to the *London Evening Standard* I was also writing a book with my friend Elizabeth Jane Howard, published as *Howard and Maschler on Food,* and some of the recipes here also appear there. However, since this is the complete 'Eating In' collection, the volume that means that all the yellowed, stained and spotted newspaper clippings can be thrown away, the overlap seemed better than the omission of favourite recipes.

BÉCHAMEL OR WHITE SAUCE

This extremely useful sauce, the basis for a whole family of sauces and also for soufflés and croquettes has, in my view, the possibility of being much improved by the current availability of skimmed or semi-skimmed milk. They lighten the sauce and, of course, reduce the amount of fat. The recipe below is for use as a white sauce when an indigenous flavour is necessary. For other events, such as a soufflé base that will have flavouring ingredients added, there is no necessity to go through the milk steeping process. The risk of a floury taste will be obviated by cooking the butter and flour mixture very slowly for about 5 minutes. A squeeze of lemon juice at the end is also a help.

¾ pt (450 ml) milk (skimmed or semi-skimmed if possible)
1 small onion, peeled and stuck with 2 cloves
1 bay leaf
pinch of salt
6 black peppercorns
1 oz (25 g) butter
1½ tbsp plain flour
a squeeze of lemon juice

Put the milk in a small heavy-bottomed pan with the onion stuck with cloves, bayleaf, salt and peppercorns. Bring slowly to a simmer and keep it just below boiling – barely moving discernibly – for about 5 minutes. Remove from the heat and let stand for another 15 minutes. Warm the milk again and strain into a jug.

Clean the pan and then melt the butter. Add the flour and stir with a wooden spoon until the two are well blended. Cook over very low heat for up to 5 minutes then start to add the milk little by little, stirring after each addition until the liquid is fully incorporated, to avoid lumps. Continue adding the milk, beating well, until you have a smooth sauce, of the desired consistency for your recipe. Taste for seasoning and squeeze in a little lemon juice. Stir again.

MAYONNAISE

One of my childhood memories is of my mother sitting huddled in our freezing cold dining room dripping oil bit by bit into a bowl in which she was remorselessly stirring a mixture. A French friend of hers had told her that mayonnaise would only succeed if prepared in icy conditions and even then you could not be sure of its good behaviour. Probably in the late 1940s my mother was in a small minority of English women who made their own mayonnaise and the alleged uncertainty of the outcome must have enhanced a pioneering spirit. It was with sadness that much later in my life I read that mayonnaise is more likely to succeed if all the ingredients are at a fairly warm room temperature.

Mayonnaise made by hand and that made in a food processor are two very different substances but each have their role. You could say the same thing about mayonnaise made with olive oil and that made with vegetable oil. The electric method is quicker, and apparently more foolproof but, if you approach making mayonnaise with confidence and are sure to add the oil very slowly to begin with, it is hard to go wrong with the hand-made method. My own preference is for mayonnaise made by the bowl and wooden spoon method – particularly if the sauce is to be served separately – but do be sitting comfortably.

Flavourings and a choice of oils can be adjusted to suit the dish the mayonnaise is part of or accompanies.

SERVES 4-6   HAND-MADE METHOD

2 egg yolks, at room temperature
1 tsp Dijon or other French mustard, optional
½ pt (300 ml) olive oil or vegetable oil or a mixture
1 dsp wine vinegar or a good squeeze of lemon juice
salt and pepper

Put the egg yolks into a china or glass bowl. Beat them with a wooden spoon until they are well amalgamated and looking thick. If you wish to have a French mustardy flavour, add a teaspoon of Dijon or other mustard which seems to help the emulsifying process. Add the oil drop by drop, beating all the while, until the mixture looks viscous – almost like ointment, without any beads of oil in it. When you are sure it has 'taken' you can start adding the oil more sloppily, beating well after each addition. If you want to use less oil you can but two egg yolks will cope with half a pint. Season to taste with lemon juice or wine vinegar, salt and pepper. If you wish to thin the mixture but do not want to add more acidity in the form of lemon or vinegar, stir in a tablespoon or so of very hot water. Store mayonnaise covered in a cool place.

If the mayonnaise curdles, put another egg yolk into a clean bowl and add the curdled mixture drop by drop, beating all the time. Next time curb your impatience at the beginning.

FOOD PROCESSOR METHOD

2 egg yolks or 1 yolk and 1 whole egg
½ pt (300 ml) light olive oil or vegetable oil or a mixture
1 tbsp wine vinegar or a good squeeze of lemon juice
salt and pepper

Put the eggs into the bowl of the food processor using either the metal or the plastic blade. Using 1 egg yolk and 1 whole egg will give you a lighter, whiter result. Switch on the motor for about 30 seconds. With the motor still running, drip the oil on to the whizzing eggs through the funnel. Continue until the mixture thickens and the oil is all used. Season to taste with the lemon juice or vinegar, salt and pepper.

HOLLANDAISE

Hollandaise, basically an emulsion of egg yolks and butter, is not a tricky sauce if watched carefully. When making it, have a small jug of cold water by your side and any alarming thickening of the mixture speaking to you of scrambled eggs can be obviated by a dash of water whisked in. This also lightens the sauce, which is desirable. You can make your flavour base with either white wine or wine vinegar. Unsalted butter gives the purest and best result. If you wish to make considerable quantities of hollandaise, you can use an electric food processor or blender, but the result is somewhat less delicate. The qualities given below make enough sauce to accompany a dish for 4–6 people.

HAND-MADE METHOD

3 tbsp wine vinegar or white wine or a mixture
2 egg yolks
4 oz (120 g) unsalted butter
squeeze of lemon juice
salt

In a small saucepan boil the wine or vinegar or a mixture of the two until it reduces to about a tablespoonful. Pour it into a bowl which will fit into a saucepan of hot water without the base of the bowl touching the water or otherwise into the top half of a double boiler. Add the yolks to the reduction – making sure that it is not so hot that it will cook the yolks – and whisk together. Cut the butter into small cubes. Over simmering water whisk the butter in cube by cube, letting one melt before adding another. The mixture will thicken and mount in the pan. If it threatens to become too thick, add a splash of cold water and whisk in. Season to taste with lemon juice and salt. Hollandaise sauce should be served soon after it is prepared, though it will bide its time if kept over the hot water (the pan removed from the heat source) and whisked occasionally.

FOOD PROCESSOR METHOD

Put the wine or vinegar reduction and the yolks into the goblet of the blender or food processor. Melt the butter in a saucepan, taking care not to let it burn. When it is melted but not too hot, switch on your blender. Let the yolks and reduction whisk for 20 seconds and then add the melted butter in a thin steady stream. When the sauce thickens, switch off, decant into a warm dish and season to taste.

BEATING EGG WHITES

The optimum utensils for beating egg whites are a balloon whisk and an unlined copper bowl that has recently been rubbed with salt and lemon. However, since it is likely that you do not own this last vessel, you can mimic the effect of copper on egg foams by using a tiny pinch of cream of tartar. You can prepare perfectly satisfactory stiffly beaten egg whites without any aids, but you must ensure that your bowl and whisk are scrupulously clean. Any traces of fat will interfere with the foaming abilities of egg whites and thus you should avoid using a plastic bowl. The egg whites must also be free of fats, which are most likely to take the form of traces of yolk. If you spot any trails of yolk, try removing them with a half egg shell which has a usefully sharp edge.

Whisk the whites in a large bowl to accommodate their talent for swelling to eight times their original volume. Beat with a hand whisk, rotary beater or hand-held electric beater until the whites form peaks and the bowl can be turned upside down without the egg white plopping out. Do not overbeat as once the foam starts to lump there is no rescue service; nothing to be done but start again with new egg whites.

When making meringue add 2 tbsp caster sugar to every egg white used. If you are whisking by hand, add half your amount of sugar when the whites are stiff and beat some more until they are glossy. Fold in the remaining sugar carefully with a metal spoon.

If you are using an electric beater, you can add the sugar slowly but steadily once the white begins significantly to foam.

MAKING BREADCRUMBS

Flipping through this book, you will see that I am keen on breadcrumbs as an ingredient. Fried fresh breadcrumbs provide an oft-desirable crunchy texture contrast and if the original bread is a good loaf they will also contribute flavour.

Most of the recipes in this book will call for fresh breadcrumbs and by far the easiest way to make these is with a food processor. Tear the bread into chunks and whizz in the food processor, using the metal blade, until the bread is all in crumbs. If you have no food processor, use an ordinary grater and rub the bread against the larger holes, but this is laborious and you might scrape your knuckles which is infuriating.

To obtain dried breadcrumbs, dry out slices of bread in a low oven and then crumble them between your fingers. If you carry out the first process thoroughly the crumbs will keep for some time in a jar with a tight-fitting lid, so it is a good fate for stale bread.

Put from your mind for ever the thought of those bright orange crumbs sold in packets in shops.

GRINDING WHOLE SPICES

Ground spices are not only likely to go stale in your store cupboard; they also run the risk of being stale at the moment of purchase. If you like using spices in cooking – as I do – it is worth investing in a cheap coffee grinder which you keep for the purpose of grinding spices. Buy your spices whole in an oriental supermarket where they will be much cheaper than in those cutesy little bottles or jars in supermarkets and delicatessens. Keep the whole spices in jars with tightly fitting screw-on lids. When you come to use them, first heat whole seeds such as coriander, cumin, poppy, mustard, fenugreek, cardamom (removed from their husks) in a heavy-bottomed dry cast-iron frying pan. Don't burn them. Just heat them until they either jump and pop or start to give off a fragrance. Remove them from the pan. Let them cool and grind them in the coffee grinder. They are now ready for use in any recipe that calls for ground spices.

STOCKS

Anyone not absolutely new to the business of cooking will have heard the slightly irritating maxim about a good stock being the basis of sound cooking. It is almost irrefutable (although French chef Bernard Loiseau has recently had a go) but few of us have the time or inclination to have a serious stock-pot constantly simmering or indeed the kind of life that has as its detritus the appropriate bones and bits that are its foundation. However, the fact must also be faced that stock cubes are rarely a good substitute. They invariably have a salty chemical taste and in my view water, which at least takes on the flavours of what is cooking, is preferable.

It is always worth making fish stock if you have the trimmings, or at least a simple court bouillon for poaching the fish. Both these can be prepared quickly, for neither should simmer too long even if time is available. Chicken, duck and game stock should become a habit when you are left with a carcass, innards and trimmings and the resulting broth can always be frozen for the future.

I have given the method for making meat glaze from beef or veal bones because it is a curiously satisfying pastime, and the potent dark jelly that results keeps for weeks in the refrigerator and can be used to slip in teaspoonfuls under baked eggs or to liven up sauces and the *jus* of roast meat, poultry or game or to add to a dish of braised or glazed vegetables such as turnips, chicory or celery. Vegetable stock is the counsel of perfection for the basis of vegetable soups (and would sometimes be inappropriate), but it is quite a nice health-giving drink on the days you decide to do yourself good.

COURT BOUILLON

1 pt (575 ml) water
1 pt (575 ml) dry white wine or dry cider
1 tbsp white wine vinegar
2 carrots, scrubbed and sliced
1 leek, cleaned and halved
1 small onion or 2 shallots, peeled
1 dsp black peppercorns
a sprig of parsley and of fennel or dill if possible

Simmer all the ingredients for 30 minutes. Strain for use in sauces and soups or leave intact as a poaching liquid. A simpler, cheaper court bouillon can be made by using 2 pt (1.2 l) water, omitting the wine, and using 2 tbsp wine vinegar.

FISH STOCK

2–3 lb (1–1.5 kg) fish trimmings – heads, tails etc. can usually be begged or bought from wet fishmongers. Use also bones and prawn shells. Avoid the trimmings of oily fish such as mackerel.
1 onion, peeled and sliced
1 carrot, scrubbed and sliced
1 stalk of celery
1 leek, well washed and sliced in half
12 peppercorns
1 dsp white wine vinegar
1 glass of dry white wine
2–3 stalks of parsley or appropriate herbs
about 3 pt (1.75 l) water

Put all the ingredients in a pan, leaving out salt until you have decided the point to which you wish to reduce the resulting *fumet*. Simmer for 30–40 minutes. Strain through a fine sieve. Reduce by boiling if you want a more intensely flavoured stock. Freezes well.

CHICKEN OR DUCK OR GAME STOCK

The carcass of the bird, plus giblets (excluding liver), the neck and the feet if they are around
1 small onion, peeled and stuck with a clove
1 carrot, scrubbed and chopped in two
ends of leek and celery if around
pinch of salt
6 black peppercorns

Put all the ingredients into a heavy-bottomed pan with water to cover well.

Bring to the boil and then reduce to a simmer. Cook for anything up to 3 hours, skimming off any scum that forms. Strain and put into the refrigerator.

Remove any fat from the surface of the cooled stock before using.

NOTE. If you have some pork bones on hand – a couple of spare ribs would be good – add them in. This is how the Chinese make chicken stock and is why their soup bases taste so very good. It stops the stock being puny. Butchers will sometimes sell you chicken wings cheaply, which also add body to stock.

BEEF STOCK AND MEAT GLAZE

3 lb (1.35 kg) beef or veal bones cut up by the butcher
1 lb (450g) shin of beef, chopped into large pieces, optional
1 tbsp vegetable oil or lard
1 large onion with only the outer skin removed, leaving the inner golden skin
2 carrots, scrubbed and halved
1 leek, cleaned and halved
1 tomato, skinned
pinch of sugar
2 or 3 eggs for clarifying the stock

Try to make this when you are already using the oven. If not, turn on the oven to 200°C/400°F/gas mark 6. Put the oil into the bottom of the roasting pan and add the bones, the onion which you quarter, the carrots and leek. Place in the oven and roast the bones and vegetables, turning from time to time, for about 20 minutes or until you see evidence of browning. Remove from the oven and decant the bones and vegetables into a pot large enough to hold them. Add the beef shin if you have it. Pour off any oil from the roasting tin. Place the tin on a low heat on the stove and pour in enough water to cover the bottom. With a wooden spoon scrape at the sediment, incorporating it into the water and stirring until you have a brown liquid. Add this to the stock-pot, plus enough extra water to cover the bones. Add the skinned tomato and the pinch of sugar. Bring the liquid to the boil and then turn down to a simmer. Simmer for 3–4 hours with a lid half on the pan, skimming off any accumulated scum from time to time. Strain and leave to cool. When the fat has solidified on the top, carefully remove it. At this point you have a fine beef stock ready for use. If you want to make meat glaze, proceed as follows.

Measure your de-greased stock into a large saucepan. For each pint of liquid, you will need 1 egg white and the crushed egg shell. Keep the yolks for another dish. Put the egg white(s) and shell(s) into the cold stock and, while it is heating up, whisk with a balloon whisk. When the liquid becomes frothy and opaque and starts to rise as if to boil, stop whisking and remove the pan from the heat. The sediment in the stock will start to get trapped in the egg white crust that forms. Place the pan back on the heat and simmer the liquid gently for about 45 minutes. Line a sieve with muslin that you have wrung out in hot water. Holding back the crust as best you can, pour the stock through the sieve. You should obtain a clear liquid in the bowl beneath. If it still looks murky, carefully transfer the crust to your muslin-lined sieve and gently pour the stock through it again. Reduce the clear stock by boiling until you have about a tea cup of thick shiny liquid. Pour it into a small dish and place in the refrigerator. It will set to very firm jelly, pieces of which can be used as described above. If after a week or two, a mould forms on the jelly, scrape it off, re-boil the stock and pot again.

SIMPLE BREAD DOUGH

Baking bread is a highly satisfying occupation, one that many people feel is beyond them if they lead busy lives. For this reason the bread recipes in the text, such as Cornbread or Soda Bread, are quick-acting, although there is, of course, not much actual working time involved in making yeast-raised bread, just the time while it sits and proves itself. The recipe below makes a basic loaf or a base for the pizza and pissaladière recipes in this book. If you want to use wholemeal flour, substitute it for half to three-quarters of the flour quantity, making up the rest in white plain flour. Completely wholemeal loaves tend to be rather too heavily wholesome. Buy strong flour or all-purpose flour for best results. If making dough for a pizza, it is worth considering mixing in chopped spring onion or diced skinned green or red pepper for extra excitement. The quantities given below make a 1 lb (450 g) loaf or two large pizza or pissaladière bases.

1 lb (450 g) strong white flour sold for bread making. If you choose wholemeal flour see notes above.
2 generous pinches of sea salt
½ oz (285 ml) fresh yeast or 1 packet dried yeast
a scant ½ pt (15 g) of lukewarm water

Put the flour and salt in a large bowl. Pour enough of the warm water into a small bowl or cup to half fill it and crumble or sprinkle the yeast on top. Let it stand in a warmish place for 10 minutes. The yeast should bubble and froth and if it fails to do so – which is more likely to be the case with packet yeast which may be stale and have 'died' – chuck it out and try another packet. Make a well in the flour and pour in the yeasty liquid. Cover it with flour by pushing it down from the sides of the well. Add some of the warm water, stirring with a wooden spoon, and then some more until you see that the dough will probably stick together. Using your hands, make the dough into a ball and knead it a few times experimentally in the bowl. If it holds together take it out and on a worktop start to knead it, pushing the lump of dough away from you with the heel of your hand and then gathering it up and repeating, until you have an elastic texture and a smooth, faintly shiny lump of dough. Clean your mixing bowl. Wipe it lightly with oil and put the ball of dough in it. Cover with clingfilm or a plastic bag and leave in a warm place for a couple of hours or until it has doubled in bulk. Don't be tempted to speed up the rising by putting the dough in a really warm place – such as a low oven – as it becomes sour and yeasty.

When the dough has doubled in size, punch it down – an agreeable activity – and take it out of the bowl and knead again for a minute or two. If you wish to make a loaf, shape the dough to the appropriate shape and place it in an oiled 1 lb (450 g) loaf tin. If you are making pizza or pissaladière, divide the dough into two or four and roll into circles and place on baking trays or large tart tins. Cover the dough with a tea-towel and let it 'prove' for about 45 minutes. Heat the oven to 200°C/400°F/gas mark 6. When the heat is right, bake the dough. A loaf will take about 40 minutes. To test if it is cooked, turn it out of its tin and tap the base. It should sound hollow. Return it to the tin, top side down. Put it back into the oven. Turn off the oven and let the loaf do its final cooking in the cooling oven. To cook pizza or pissaladière, follow recipe instructions for timing.

PASTRY: SHORTCRUST AND SWEETENED

It is no myth that making pastry requires cool fingers and a light touch and some people are unarguably better at it than others. However, both recipes below are simple and should be achievable even by those with the coldest hearts and thus the warmest hands. Regarding puff pastry, a good brand of the frozen product seems to me perfectly adequate for our purposes. If you wish to make your own puff pastry, consult a fairly technical book that also has diagrams, for the folding and turning required is best demonstrated graphically.

SHORTCRUST
8 oz (225 g) plain flour
pinch of salt
2 oz (50 g) butter and 2 oz (50 g) lard from the refrigerator or 4 oz (100 g) butter
splash of iced water

HAND METHOD

Sift the flour and salt into a bowl. Cut your choice of fat into cubes
and then, using the knife, cut the fats into the flour. Now with
your cool and collected fingertips lightly rub the fat and flour
together until you arrive at the consistency of uneven crumbs.
Add the iced water gradually, using the knife to mix. When you
have a mixture that will obviously adhere, press the dough into a
ball with your fingers. Wrap the ball of dough in floured clingfilm
and let it sit in the refrigerator for about half an hour. This will
minimise shrinking when you come to cook the pastry.

FOOD PROCESSOR METHOD

Sift the flour and salt into the bowl of the food processor fitted
with the metal blade. Add the fats or fat and blend quickly. When
the flour and fat seem roughly amalgamated, pour the water slowly
and carefully through the funnel, stopping immediately when the
pastry forms a ball. Wrap the pastry in floured clingfilm and let it
rest as above.

RICH SWEETENED PASTRY FOR FRUIT TARTS

8 oz (225 g) plain flour
pinch of salt
2 tsp icing sugar
5 oz (150 g) chilled butter
1 egg yolk
1 tsp lemon juice
very little iced water in a jug

HAND METHOD

Sift into a bowl the flour, salt and sugar. Cut the cold butter into
small cubes and using a knife blade cut them into the flour. Rub
the fat into the flour using your fingertips – good pastry cooks do
not get floury beyond the first knuckle – until you have a texture
resembling uneven breadcrumbs. Stir in the egg yolk with a
wooden spoon. Add the lemon juice, which may provide enough
liquid to bind the dough. If not, add iced water judiciously until
the pastry can be gathered into a ball. Wrap in floured clingfilm
and chill for about 30 minutes. Roll out the pastry. Line your
baking tin or tart tin and chill again for 15–20 minutes before
baking. For open fruit tarts, it is best first to bake the pastry
'blind' – that is, covered with a piece of foil and some dried beans
for weight – for 10 minutes before adding fruit and baking again.

FOOD PROCESSOR METHOD

Sift flour, salt and sugar into the bowl of the food processor. Cut the cold butter into small cubes and tip in. Beat the egg yolk in a jug using a fork. Turn on the motor and, while the fat and flour are blending, add the yolk through the funnel. Add just enough iced water so that the pastry rolls into a ball. Stop the motor immediately and wrap the pastry in floured clingfilm and proceed as above.

NOTE. On page 249 there is another pastry method in the recipe for Grape Tart which is easy and gives good results for pastry-based puddings incorporating uncooked fruit.

FIRST COURSES

When faced with a formal, a three- or four-course, meal I always find the first course the most diverting, and not only because the appetite is at its keenest. Limited quantities and strictly marshalled flavours are appealing. No doubt this is why some restaurants offer only starters and desserts and why the bolder amongst us often order two first courses, even in conventional places.

At home a first course followed by cheese and good bread and a salad, if a salad is appropriate, can easily constitute supper. If you are vegetarian, feeding vegetarians or just in a non-meat-eating mood, then this is a sensible approach.

Many of the first courses here capitalise on the idea of the composed salad or 'salade tiède', as fashionable menus like to put it. Basically this means a foundation of interesting leaves dressed with a vinaigrette on to which you might put something warm: sautéed chicken livers or steamed wind-dried sausage or grilled goat's cheese. You could also just use fried, crumbled bacon or a poached or soft-boiled egg. Warm yolk dribbling into vinaigrette is a particularly nice sensation.

Remember that astute shopping at the delicatessen can provide a first course where none existed before: good quality salami, Parma ham to eat with figs or pears, fresh pasta that you dress simply with butter and herbs or oil and garlic, a tin of chickpeas that you can blend and turn into hummus flavoured with oil, lemon and sesame paste. Look also at the pasta, egg and cheese recipes for ideas that could well function as first courses. Some of the following, notably the pâtés, can be prepared ahead of time; nice to come home to.

COD'S ROE PASTE SERVES 4

Such wrongdoings are committed in the name of taramasalata – particularly in restaurants – that I shall not even use the word. David Queensberry, a great cook and coper, who gave me the recipe below, considers that paste is the correct description, certainly not pâté, a term he says Elizabeth David would deplore. Since the whole point of his method is that you should not use a blender or a food processor, which smashes up the little eggs and renders them a faceless emulsion, I am not sure he has hit on the right title, but never mind; it is the taste that matters and I know this to be excellent, unpadded as the paste is by bread, potatoes or anything else. It is worth noting that wine is a disaster with cod's roe as it gives any wine a most evil taste. Iced vodka is the best accompaniment if you can run to it.

about 8 oz (250 g) smoked cod's roe, i.e. in a piece, not from a jar
3 fl oz (90 ml) quality olive oil
fresh lemon juice, to taste
freshly ground black pepper

Scrape the roe from the skin and its membrane using a sharp little teaspoon. Discard any pieces that have gone hard and lumpy. Put the roe into a bowl and add the oil slowly, mixing all the while with a fork. Squeeze in lemon juice to taste and add a good deal of pepper but no salt. Serve in individual containers – egg cups are a thought – with hot toast.

SERVES 4 ## SMOKED SALMON PÂTÉ

Smoked salmon scraps can often be found at fishmongers, delicatessens, and supermarkets. The appearance may not be svelte, but the flavour is fine and they can be whirred in a food processor or blender into this easy pâté, which can be turned out of a small, straight-sided bowl. Because, to my mind, there is a certain monotony to the texture of pâtés and mousses, this one has three layers, which is less time consuming than it sounds.

8 oz (250 g) smoked salmon pieces
7 oz (200 g) curd cheese
lemon juice
freshly ground black pepper
1 tbsp chopped fresh parsley

In a food processor fitted with a steel blade, or in a blender, chop the salmon into small pieces. You could do this by hand, but making smoked salmon sandwiches might be a less tedious alternative. Remove about 2 oz (60 g) of the salmon. Add the cheese to the mixing bowl and run the motor until you have a smooth mixture. Flavour with lemon juice to taste (I like quite a lot) and freshly ground black pepper. Switch on for one more second. Remove half the mixture to another bowl and mix with the parsley. Lightly oil the base and sides of a small straight-sided bowl. Press in the plain smoked salmon and cheese mixture to make a smooth base. Add the smoked salmon pieces on top and distribute evenly, pressing them down lightly. Smooth on the salmon, cheese and parsley mixture, using a knife. Chill in the refrigerator for a few hours or overnight. To serve, run a knife round the pâté and unmould. Thinly cut, hot brown toast goes well with it. You could, of course, eat the pâté without chilling, but it would be unlikely to turn out so neatly.

CHOPPED LIVER   SERVES 4

Tubs of frozen chicken livers are a useful item to store. Chicken liver risotto, chicken liver kebabs – each liver wrapped with streaky bacon – sautéed chicken livers on toast are all excellent dishes. Chicken liver pâté, another idea, I am less keen on. When whizzed with butter and brandy, the livers become too rich and compact. I prefer the Jewish version of chicken liver pâté, chopped liver, in which hard-boiled egg lightens the mixture and chicken fat, if you have it, provides the succulence, indeed the *schmaltz*. The livers must be completely defrosted and, although they are usually well-trimmed, make sure there are no strings or green bits. If you do find any, cut them out as they impart bitterness.

2 oz (60 g) butter or chicken fat (available from Kosher butchers)
1 large onion, peeled and chopped
8 oz (250 g) chicken livers, fresh or frozen
3 stalks of celery, destringed and cleaned (optional)
2–3 hard-boiled eggs
salt and freshly ground black pepper

In the butter or chicken fat sauté first the onion and then the trimmed chicken livers. Cook until the livers are just pink inside, a matter of minutes but variable according to the size of the livers. If you want to include celery, which gives a nice crunch, remove any strings and dice it finely. I use an old hand-turned mincer to make chopped liver. It gives a light result. You could chop by hand or, as long as you have a fast trigger finger, use a food processor. Mince, or otherwise chop together, the livers, onion, eggs and optional celery. Season well and smooth into a pretty pot. Serve cold with hot toast. This can be made one day and eaten the next.

CARROT PÂTÉ   SERVES 4

One vegetable my vegetable-loathing son, Ben, will countenance is raw carrots. I think he actually quite likes them though he would sooner die than admit it. However, he would be particularly suspicious of this recipe. Don't you be, because despite the rather odd amalgam of ingredients it turns out to make a delicious first course. Serve with hot pitta bread.

2 oz (60 g) skinned almonds
8 oz (250 g) carrots
4 oz (120 g) ricotta cheese
1 tsp cumin seeds
4 rashers of streaky bacon
vegetable oil, as required
salt and pepper

TO SERVE: *hot pitta bread*

This is best made with a food processor using the steel blade, but
if necessary you can grate the carrots rather than chop them. Using
a food processor, chop the almonds quite roughly. Remove them.
Peel the carrots and chop them finely in the machine. Put the
ricotta in a bowl, break it up with a fork and add the carrots and
almonds. Mix well. In a heavy-bottomed frying pan, toast the
cumin seeds (without any oil) until you can smell their spiciness.
Add to the carrot mixture. Cut up the bacon finely and fry until
crisp. Drain and add to the mixture. Mix well again with enough
oil to moisten but not swamp, season and press into individual
small pots.

SERVES 4-6 ## COURGETTE PÂTÉ

My friend Hazel Short brought back this recipe from someone
who lives in Ibiza and who is a renowned cook. It is one of those
dishes that suffers not at all, and arguably improves, by being
cooked one day and consumed the next. It makes a delicious first
course or a light lunch and benefits from a sauce made by stirring
chopped, skinned, de-seeded fresh tomatoes into a vigorously
seasoned vinaigrette. If you fail to find fresh spinach use frozen
leaf spinach and chop it after it has cooked.

3 onions, peeled and thinly sliced
2 lb (1 kg) courgettes, trimmed and cut into thin slices
3 tbsp olive oil
1 heaped tsp cornflour
6 oz (175 g) fresh white breadcrumbs, squeezed out in a little milk
1 tbsp tarragon leaves
1 tbsp mint leaves
scrape of nutmeg
salt and pepper
3 eggs, beaten
1 lb (500 g) spinach
½ oz (15 g) butter

FOR THE SAUCE:
4 tomatoes, peeled, de-seeded and chopped into small dice
6 tbsp olive oil
2 tbsp wine vinegar
salt and pepper

Turn on the oven to 160°C/325°F/gas mark 3. Sauté the onions and courgettes in the oil until soft, mashing them with a wooden spoon or potato masher so that they are amalgamated. Stir in the cornflour. Remove from the heat and add the breadcrumbs, herbs, nutmeg, salt, pepper and beaten egg. Wash the spinach. Cook it in the water that clings to the leaves after washing, season and chop. Butter a large pâté dish or loaf tin. Put half the courgette mixture evenly into the bottom. Spread on a layer of spinach and then the remaining courgette mixture. Cook in the oven in a larger dish or tin containing hot water (a bain-marie) for 1 hour. Let cool and chill in the refrigerator. Remove for half an hour before serving. Slice the pâté and hand round the tomato vinaigrette separately.

STILTON TARTLETS SERVES 4-6

My sister, as any regular reader of my recipes must now know, works as the chef at Green's Champagne Bar in Duke Street, St James's. There Stilton is served and, as they adhere to the scooping method of service, Stilton is also left over there. These tartlets, served as a first course, though they would make an equally good savoury, were created as a way of using the 'walls' of the cheese. Most blue cheeses, I think, would work well in the recipe. The dried oregano in the shortcrust pastry is a good ruse.

1½ oz (45 g) butter
1 large onion or 2 smaller ones, peeled and very finely sliced
4 oz (120 g) Stilton cheese
6 eggs
½ pt (300 ml) double cream
salt and freshly ground black pepper
2 tomatoes, peeled and sliced

FOR THE SHORTCRUST PASTRY:
8 oz (250 g) plain flour
1 tsp dried mustard powder
pinch of salt
1 tsp dried oregano
2 oz (60 g) butter
2 oz (60 g) lard
about 2 tbsp ice-cold water

Turn on the oven to 180°C/350°F/gas mark 4. Make the pastry by sifting the flour with the mustard and a pinch of salt. Add the oregano. Rub in the fats until the mixture resembles breadcrumbs. Add the ice-cold water and mix, first with a knife and then with one hand. It might be necessary to add a little more water but don't overdo it or the pastry will be tough; add only enough water, really, to make it cohere. Let it rest, if possible, for 30 minutes wrapped in film. Roll out the pastry and line a tartlet pan or, should you have no suitable container, make one larger tart. Cover with foil and some dried beans and bake 'blind' for 20 minutes. Remove the pastry and lower the oven to 160°C/325°F/gas mark 3. Melt the butter and cook the onion gently until softened. Chop the Stilton roughly and add to the pan. Cook until melted. Quite a lot of oil will separate. Pour this away. Beat the eggs with the cream and season with salt and pepper. When the onion and cheese mixture has cooled a little, stir it in. Divide the mixture between the tartlet cases or pour it into the one case. Place a slice of tomato on each tart and bake for 30 minutes until golden brown. Serve with a little salad as a first course.

GRILLED GOAT'S CHEESE WITH SALAD

This happens to be a fashionable first course in French restaurants, but it also can make a quick and stylish supper at home. If you are embarking on a more formal meal, then you could serve your cheese and salad course combined in this manner. It will look as though you have gone to a lot of trouble, but what you have also accomplished is being economical in the cheese buying; there will not be a lot of little leftover wedges mocking you from the fridge or larder.

FOR EACH PERSON:
1 slice of good white or brown bread
1 Chavignol goat's cheese (often sold from a jar of olive oil) or other goat's cheese
black pepper
interesting salad leaves, e.g. frisée (curly endive), lamb's lettuce (corn salad, mâche), radicchio, watercress
vinaigrette made with good olive oil or walnut oil

Toast the bread. Put it in an ovenproof dish. Place the cheese on top. Grind on some black pepper. Grill for a few minutes until the cheese is lightly browned and bubbling. Serve with the dressed salad on the plate.

CHEESE PROFITEROLES

If you have any leftover goat's cheese or you feel like doing something more complicated than the grilled goat's cheese, you might like to try this recipe for cheese profiteroles, taken from the excellent book *A Cook's Calendar* by Frances Bissell.

2 oz (60 g) butter
¼ pt (150 ml) milk and water mixed
2½ oz (75 g) plain flour
pinch of salt
2 eggs
2 oz goat's cheese cut up into small chunks
cream cheese flavoured with herbs (optional filling)

Put the butter and mixed milk and water into a pan. Heat gently until the butter has melted. Bring to a strong boil, remove from the heat and tip in the flour and salt in one go. Beat vigorously until the mixture becomes a stiff paste and leaves the side of the pan. Stir in the eggs one at a time and keep stirring until smooth. Stir in the goat's cheese. Butter a twelve-tart tin and place a dessertspoon of the mixture in each case. Place in the top of a pre-heated oven 200°C/400°F/gas mark 6, and bake for 18 minutes. Switch off the heat, open the door slightly and leave in the oven for a further 3–5 minutes. Serve with a good green salad. You could, if you wish, slit the profiteroles before serving and slip in a teaspoon of a cold creamy, herby cheese mixture.

SERVES 4   BAGNA CAUDA

This Piedmontese dish is constructed rather along the lines of a fondue, but you use raw vegetables for dipping and a mixture of anchovies, garlic, oil and butter as the sauce.

It is important to prepare it in an earthenware pot which can be put on the stove over a heat-diffusing mat. Once you take the pot to the table you need a candle to keep it warm. You could, I suppose, renounce any peasant roots and use an enamelled cast-iron pan, but it would be a pity. In Italy this assembly is eaten in winter – not necessarily at mealtimes, just when you feel hungry – and traditionally on Christmas Eve. It is a good dish to share with friends.

Provide plenty of bread to intersperse with the vegetables and a robust wine like Barbera to help both the conviviality and the digestion. To complete the meal, when the vegetables have been eaten and there is just a glaze of sauce in the dish, break in some eggs and scramble them over a gentle heat, thus suffusing the creamy mass with the flavours of anchovy and garlic.

generous ¼ pt (150 ml) of olive oil
2 oz (60 g) butter
2 fat cloves of garlic, peeled and finely sliced
8–10 anchovy fillets, drained of oil and roughly chopped
raw vegetables, washed and trimmed as appropriate: carrots, cauliflower, red and green sweet peppers, broccoli, courgettes, celery, radishes, young spinach leaves, spring onions
4 eggs for scrambling (optional)

Heat the oil and butter slowly until the butter is melted and just begins to foam. Add the garlic, which should be in paper-thin slivers, and sauté briefly without letting it colour. Add the anchovies and cook, stirring assiduously until they dissolve into a paste. Taste and add salt if you think it is needed. Serve with a selection of vegetables cut as for crudités.

SERVES 4   MUSHROOMS À LA GRECQUE

This makes a good first course, or part of a first course, if you are feeding numbers and want to make a *meze* – a spread of little dishes. When I make these mushrooms, I reduce the liquid quite radically so that there is a strong and punchy sauce to be mopped up with French bread or crusty brown bread.

Should you want to assemble a selection of hors d'oeuvres, others that would go well with this one are fried aubergines (page 30), dolmades (stuffed vine leaves) or a rice salad, grilled peppers (their skins removed) marinated in olive oil; tabbouleh, a salad of cracked wheat and parsley (page 94), slices of smoked cod's roe and a mixture of chopped cucumber and yogurt flavoured with garlic and garnished with mint.

1 lb (500 g) tight-fisted button mushrooms
4 tbsp olive oil
8 tbsp water
juice of $\frac{1}{2}$ a lemon
2 cloves of garlic, peeled and slivered
1 heaped tsp coriander seeds
6 peppercorns, coarsely crushed
3 tomatoes, peeled and roughly chopped
bay leaf
thyme
salt and pepper

If some mushrooms are noticeably larger than the others, cut them in half or in quarters. Place them with the rest of the ingredients in a saucepan and bring to the boil. Simmer for 10 minutes until the mushrooms are cooked and then, with a slotted spoon, remove the mushrooms to a bowl. Boil the remaining liquid quite rapidly until you have just enough sauce left to cover the mushrooms and it looks oily rather than watery. Taste for seasoning and adjust if necessary. Pour the sauce over the mushrooms and leave to cool.

CELERIAC RÉMOULADE WITH ANCHOVY
TOASTS SERVES 4

I once had Alan Coren to dinner and, let me tell you, he is a picky eater. Much to my surprise, he loved the celeriac rémoulade and ate large quantities of it in favour, as I remember, of a particularly delicious home-made brawn. Celeriac is that knobbly beige root, tinging to green at the base, with some fronds *en brosse* at the top. You can cook it; I like it mashed in equal quantities with potato. But best of all I like it raw, grated and mixed with a mustardy mayonnaise for this rémoulade. Some recipe books tell you to blanch it but I think it is unnecessary and also, however careful you are, the process ends by thinning the mayonnaise. Accompanied by the spirited flavour of anchovy toasts, this makes a fine, substantial first course.

1 large celeriac, trimmed and peeled

FOR THE MAYONNAISE:
about ½ pt (300 ml) vegetable oil
2 egg yolks
1 dsp Dijon mustard
salt and pepper
squeeze of lemon juice

FOR THE ANCHOVY TOASTS:
1 × 2 oz (50 g) tin anchovies, drained of oil
2 oz (60 g) butter
3 slices of bread

Make the mayonnaise (a blender or food processor speeds things up) by dribbling the oil on to the well beaten egg yolks until the emulsion thickens. Flavour it strongly with mustard, salt and pepper and the lemon juice. Grate the celeriac and mix with the mayonnaise immediately, giving it no time to discolour. Taste and adjust the seasoning if necessary. Mash three or four anchovies into the butter. Toast slices of bread on one side. Spread the untoasted side with the anchovy butter and put under the grill, anchovy butter side up, until the butter is melted and the bread crisp. Cut into fingers and serve with the celeriac.

STUFFED MUSHROOMS
SERVES 4-6

Large flat mushrooms, the brown shaggy kind, sometimes as large as 4 in (10 cm) across, are often a bargain since many people prefer the hygienic look of button mushrooms. Sometimes you can buy a whole trug, for a knockdown price, so it is worth looking for bargains. Field mushrooms have more flavour than cultivated mushrooms (they are a completely different species), but they are also more difficult to find. For stuffing mushrooms, buy the caps as flat and wide as possible.

6 rashers streaky bacon, chopped
12 large flat mushrooms
4 hard-boiled eggs, shelled
2 thick slices of white bread
a little single cream or top of the milk
1 fat clove of garlic, chopped
1 tbsp chopped parsley
salt and pepper
2 oz (60 g) grated Gruyère or Lancashire cheese

Turn the oven to 200°C/400°F/gas mark 6. Fry the chopped bacon gently until the fat runs and the bacon is cooked. Pull off the mushroom stalks, chop and sauté with the bacon. With a fork break up the hard-boiled eggs to a crumb-like consistency. Whizz the bread in a food processor or blender to make crumbs. Moisten them with cream or milk. Mix the stalks, bacon, eggs, crumbs, garlic and parsley. Season well. Divide between the mushroom caps patting the stuffing into a mound. Sprinkle with cheese and bake for about 20 minutes.

MUSHROOM LOAVES SERVES 4

This makes a rich first course; follow it with something plain and possibly cold. Either field or farmed mushrooms, of any size, can happily be used.

4 round, soft rolls or baby Hovis loaves
2 oz (60 g) butter, and a little more for rolls
6 spring onions
¾ lb (375 g) mushrooms
splash of white wine (optional)
10 fl oz (300 ml) double cream
lemon juice
salt and pepper
4 bay leaves

Slice the top of the rolls and hollow them out carefully saving the crumbs for another dish such as the Stuffed Mushrooms (page 28), Pasta with Anchovies and Breadcrumbs (page 84) or Guilt-free Treacle Tart (page 256). Brush with melted butter and put in a hot oven to crisp. Clean the spring onions and chop finely. Wipe the mushrooms and slice them. Melt the butter in a heavy pan, add the onions and mushrooms and cook gently until the mushroom juices run. If you have wine to hand, add a splash and cook it almost away. Add the cream, simmer until you have a thickish sauce.

Season with lemon juice, salt and pepper. Fill the rolls with the mushroom mixture. Place a bay leaf in such a way that the lids sit on at an angle.

FRIED AUBERGINES WITH SKORDALIA

SERVES 4

Aubergines are good when glossy and tight in their skins. I first tasted them cooked in one of the ways I like them best in the house of a Greek friend: sliced, floured, fried and served with a garlicky sauce called skordalia. Mrs Karayiannis, the Greek woman who made them, had been very keen to own a Kenwood mixer so I had valiantly carried one, plus attachments, from London where they were alleged to be cheaper. She used it once for this sauce – generally made with a good deal of laborious pounding – washed it, carefully wrapped it in plastic and put it in a cupboard. I think it is sometimes paraded for friends.

1 large or 2 medium aubergines
salt
4 plump cloves of garlic
1 fat slice of stale white bread from a loaf
3 oz (90 g) ground almonds
¼ pt (150 ml) olive oil
pepper
lemon juice
seasoned plain flour
more olive oil or vegetable oil, for frying

Aubergine slices must be salted and left to bead with perspiration to remove bitterness and to stop them mopping up quantities of oil. So wipe the aubergine, trim off the calyx and slice into ¼ in (6 mm) slices. Lay in a colander and sprinkle with salt. Unlike Mrs Karayiannis you will probably want to use a blender or food processor rather than pestle and mortar for the sauce. Peel and crush the garlic cloves. Trim the bread of crusts, soak the crumb in water and squeeze it tightly in your hand. Put the garlic and bread into the machine for a brief whizz. Add the almonds and blend. Slowly add the olive oil, as if for mayonnaise, until you have a homogeneous thick sauce. Season with salt, pepper and lemon juice to taste. If it looks a bit porridgy, the texture and colour can be improved with a little milk or thin cream. Pile into a pretty bowl. With kitchen paper wipe the aubergines. Shake them in a bag with seasoned flour. Heat the oil to the depth of about ¼ in (6 cm) in a frying pan. Vegetable oil can be used for economy. Fry the aubergine slices, turning them once, until golden. Drain on kitchen paper. You will have to do batches, keeping them warm the while. Serve immediately with the skordalia sauce.

AUBERGINE WITH PESTO   SERVES 4

If you sometimes wonder what on earth you are going to make for dinner, then you will sympathise when I say that it was occasionally a struggle to devise a recipe for the newspaper each day. I have been known to appeal to friends, and the idea below was given to me by chef Simon Hopkinson whose cooking at Bibendum in the Fulham Road I admire very much. He says that the inspiration for it was a dish in a Japanese restaurant.

good handful of fresh basil leaves
2 cloves of garlic, peeled and chopped
pinch of sea salt
1 heaped tbsp pine kernels
2 oz (60 g) finely grated Parmesan cheese (freshly grated from a block if possible)
approx. 5 tbsp good olive oil
4 small aubergines or 2 larger ones
vegetable oil for frying

First you must make the pesto. This can be done fairly painlessly with a pestle and mortar, but it is a matter of moments if you have a good processor. With a pestle and mortar, pound the leaves, then add the garlic and a pinch of sea salt and pound some more. When you have produced a pulp, add the pine kernels and pound away. Add the cheese, thump some more and when all is well blended, start to add the oil, stirring until you have a cohesive sauce. With a food processor, just whizz everything together, but keep your finger on the button only long enough for the ingredients to amalgamate. Cut the aubergines in half horizontally. Heat the oil for deep-frying and fry the aubergine halves until golden. Remove with a slotted spoon, whereupon the cut surface will sink slightly, giving you a natural dip into which to spread some of the pesto. Prepare each aubergine half in this way. Heat the grill, slide the aubergines under and cook until the pesto is bubbling – a matter of minutes. Serve with a little green salad.

SERVES 4-6 # AVOCADO PIE WITH GARLIC CRUST

Lady Macdonald of Macdonald, owner with her husband, the High Chief of Clan Macdonald, of the Kinloch Lodge Hotel on the Isle of Skye, was one of the finalists in the picnic competition for restaurateurs, sponsored by Krug Champagne: the professional end of a competition for amateurs that we ran in the *London Evening Standard*. This recipe is taken from her book *The Harrods Book of Entertaining*. You could make this pie – I would – without gelatine, just laying avocado slices in the crust and garnishing with the chopped tomatoes.

4 tbsp white wine
4 tbsp powdered gelatine
2 avocados
juice of 1 lemon
dash of Tabasco
dash of Worcestershire Sauce
salt and freshly ground pepper
1 tbsp olive oil or sunflower oil
1 tsp wine vinegar
½ tsp caster sugar
6 tomatoes, seeded and chopped

FOR THE GARLIC CRUST:
6 oz (150 g) wholemeal breadcrumbs
2–3 oz (60–90 g) nibbed or flaked almonds
pinch of dried thyme or sprig of fresh thyme
3 oz (90 g) melted butter
2 cloves of garlic, finely chopped
salt and pepper

FOR THE GARNISH:
fresh parsley and chives

Mix together the ingredients for the crust. Press over the bottom and sides of a 9 in (23 cm) flan tin and bake at 200°C/400°F/gas mark 6 for 12–15 minutes until golden and crisp. Let it cool. Put the wine into a small saucepan and sprinkle the gelatine over. Heat gently, stirring, until the gelatine has dissolved completely. Halve and stone the avocados. Scrape out all the flesh and purée in a blender or food processor. Add the wine and gelatine, lemon juice, Tabasco, Worcestershire Sauce and seasoning. Blend until smooth. Pour into the pie crust and leave to set. Mix together the oil, vinegar, sugar and seasonings. Stir in the chopped tomatoes.

Spread in the centre of the avocado filling and garnish with parsley and chives. Serve in slices.

COURGETTE BLINIS AND THEIR GARNISH

SERVES 4

The basis for this idea came from the actress Mai Zetterling when I interviewed her on the subject of food for a magazine article. She was living part-time in France and experiencing a glut of courgettes in her garden. It can be a first course or main course, depending on how many blinis and their 'caviar' you want to eat.

1 lb (500 g) courgettes
salt
3½ oz (100 g) plain flour
4 oz (120 g) buckwheat flour (available at health food stores)
1 tsp bicarbonate of soda
1 tsp cream of tartar
1 egg
8 fl oz (250 ml) milk plus a little more
1 tbsp melted butter
pepper

FOR THE GARNISHES:
1 × 4 oz (100 g) jar Danish 'caviar' (lumpfish roe)
chopped raw onion
1 hard-boiled egg, finely chopped
5 fl oz (150 ml) soured cream
1 lemon
melted butter, to taste (optional)

Wash and trim the courgettes, but do not peel them. Grate them quite finely in a food processor or mouli-légumes, or on a hand grater if you have the patience. Lightly salt them and leave them in a colander or sieve, whereupon they will start to 'sweat' out some of the water you are trying to lose. To make the blini batter, sift together the flour, buckwheat flour, bicarbonate of soda and cream of tartar. Beat together the raw egg and milk and add the melted butter. Stir the liquid into the dry ingredients as if for pancakes but to achieve a thick mixture that drops fairly reluctantly from a spoon. In a clean tea-towel wring the grated courgettes quite toughly to squeeze out all the liquid. Mix the courgettes into the batter. Season with salt and pepper. Arrange the various garnishes – caviar, onion, egg and soured cream – in small bowls.

Quarter the lemon. Cook the courgette batter in spoonfuls on a lightly greased heavy iron frying pan or griddle, turning each pancake when bubbles break out on the surface. Keep hot in a napkin and serve with the garnishes. Extra melted butter separately is a wicked addition.

Courgettes prepared in the same way – that is salted and wrung out – can be sautéed briefly in a little butter or oil and seasoned with dill, salt and pepper, to make a delicate vegetable dish.

TOMATO SALAD

SERVES 2-3

You may think the method for tomato salad hardly worthy of a full recipe but, carefully made, tomato salad can be one of the nicest first courses. During the summer, when fresh basil is sold at the greengrocers and there are some tomatoes around that do not taste almost indistinguishable from the plastic boxes in which they are sometimes wrapped, it is well worth devoting some attention to the preparation.

The more fresh herbs you use, the merrier. Parsley is vital and I like to include a few fresh mint leaves. There are schools of thought about whether to peel or not to peel tomatoes. I was married to one of the not-peeling school, but one of the less profound results of separation has been the realisation that I prefer tomatoes plunged briefly into boiling water and peeled. I like the resulting infinitesimally cooked quality. If you buy those tiny cherry tomatoes, a good way to serve them is peeled but whole, dressed with single cream, chopped chives and freshly ground black pepper.

1 lb (500 g) fresh tomatoes, ripe and if possible not greenhouse-grown
salt and freshly ground black pepper
about 1 tsp sugar
2 tbsp finely chopped parsley
1 tbsp chopped basil
few chopped mint leaves
1 tbsp chopped spring onions or chives
1 tbsp wine vinegar or, better still, balsamic vinegar
3 tbsp virgin olive oil

Slice the peeled (or unpeeled) tomatoes. Lay the slices in a shallow dish. Sprinkle on some salt, pepper and sugar, then the herbs and spring onions or chives. Dribble the vinegar over the tomatoes and afterwards do the same with the oil. The point of the dish is almost to marinate the tomatoes. Therefore let it sit as long as possible before serving with hot bread and unsalted butter.

SALADE PAYSANNE SERVES 4

I was once commissioned to write a cookery book on gourmet food, a concept I struggled with for months before deciding it was not my style of cooking; my heart was not in it. One thing I did accomplish was persuading some chefs to give me their recipes. This one is from Bernard Gaume, a chef I admire greatly, who is at the Chelsea Room of The Carlton Tower in London's Cadogan Square. Chicken livers are more usually found frozen and a couple of the 8 oz (250 g) tubs are a sensible thing to have always in your freezer.

This is a fairly substantial first course and, accompanied by hot sesame-seed covered bread, can be a supper dish.

1 lb (500 g) raw spinach (try to find small, tender leaves)
1 hard-boiled egg
1 tsp Dijon mustard
salt and freshly ground black pepper
2 tbsp wine vinegar
6 tbsp walnut oil or olive oil
1 lb (500 g) chicken livers, defrosted if necessary
vegetable oil, for frying
juice of ½ a lemon
1 crisp eating apple such as a Cox's or Granny Smith

Wash and dry the spinach discarding any unappetising looking leaves. In a small bowl mash the egg yolk with the mustard, salt, pepper and vinegar. With a whisk make sure it is well amalgamated and then slowly whisk in the oil. Turn the spinach leaves in the dressing and divide between four plates. Pick over the livers and cut away any strings or green parts (they taste bitter). In a heavy-bottomed frying pan toss the livers in a little vegetable oil until cooked but still pink inside – a matter of minutes. Leave to rest while you peel and then grate the apple. Squeeze the lemon half over the grated apple. Divide the chicken liver among the four plates, scatter the shredded apple on top. Season with salt and pepper and serve.

FRESH WALNUTS

While poets might be wanly lyrical when their thoughts turn to autumn, I am as likely to think about a new jumper, or perhaps 'wet' walnuts. One of the virtues of food is that each season, however it gets you emotionally, brings compensations. As winter approaches, game, white truffles, mussels, Muscat grapes and, indeed, 'wet', or 'green', walnuts, the fresh new season nuts from France, can take your mind off the clocks going back.

These nuts are a fleeting pleasure and one not to be missed. They are new enough to be crushed in your hand and pliable enough to allow the slightly bitter skin on the nut to be rubbed off easily. If it proves obstinate and you are feeling perfectionist, pour boiling water on to the shelled nuts, leave for 2 minutes and drain: the skins will rub off in a trice. I am so keen on new season walnuts that I like to eat them with just the accompaniment of good brown bread, unsalted butter, some Maldon salt and quite a few glasses of wine.

If you happen to be the sort of person who makes bread, add some chopped nuts and perhaps also some chopped onion to the dough and make a loaf that is a treat to eat with a creamy cheese. In *Summer Cooking* Elizabeth David gives a recipe for a walnut soup, which you could adapt to a liquidiser or food processor, blending 6 oz (175 g) of walnuts and a fat clove of garlic with about 1½ pt (900 ml) of stock, heating the result with ¼ pt (150 ml) of single cream, and seasoning with salt and freshly ground black pepper. It has an alluring flavour.

When fresh walnuts are to hand, it is also the moment to lash out on a tin of walnut oil to make this wonderful first course salad. Make several, in fact, because once opened walnut oil does not keep well and it is expensive.

SERVES 4 ## WALNUT, BEETROOT AND CHICORY SALAD

2 plump heads of chicory
¼ lb (120 g) lamb's lettuce (sometimes called corn salad or mâche) or frisée (curly endive) if you can find them
2 large cooked beetroot
6 oz (175 g) 'wet' walnuts in their shells
1 crisp eating apple (optional variation)

FOR THE VINAIGRETTE:
salt and freshly ground black pepper
½ tsp Dijon mustard
pinch of sugar
1 tbsp white wine vinegar
3 tbsp walnut oil, or 2 tbsp walnut oil and 1 tbsp sunflower oil if you like a less assertive flavour

Trim the chicory and slice it diagonally into ½ in (1.5 cm) pieces. Wash the lamb's lettuce or frisée if you have managed to get hold of either of them. Mix the salad leaves. Make a vinaigrette by dissolving the salt, pepper, mustard, and sugar in the vinegar and whisking in the oil. Dice the beetroot, add to the greens, toss with the vinaigrette. Scatter the salad with the shelled and broken walnuts. Thin slices of a crisp eating apple is a thought as a variation in ingredients.

CONFUCIUS SALAD SERVES 4

That there are no new recipes under the sun is a truth any cookery writer worth her sea salt will acknowledge, but I feel that this particular example of combining cultures – East and West – is my own. It is part that restaurant cliché, a first course of a salad with bacon and croûtons; part a succumbing to that potent aniseedy flavour the Chinese like so much in their wind-dried sausages; part homage to Caesar, as in Caesar Salad. Thus ...

4 wind-dried sausages (obtainable in Chinese supermarkets)
a mixture of green salad leaves incorporating, if possible, young spinach
3 tbsp vegetable oil (preferably sunflower), and more for frying
1 tbsp red wine vinegar
salt and freshly ground black pepper
dry mustard powder
3 slices of sesame-seed covered bread or 3 slices white bread and 1 dsp sesame seeds

With a small sharp knife, trim the ends of the sausages and then slice them thinly on the diagonal. Wash and dry the salad leaves and heap them into a bowl. Prepare a salad dressing with the oil, vinegar, a pinch of salt, pepper and dry mustard. Assemble a steamer if you have one, or, failing that, find a metal sieve that fits snugly into the top of a saucepan. Boil water in the bottom saucepan and put in the sausage slices to steam. Cut the bread into small cubes and fry in vegetable oil until crisp and golden. If you are using white bread, fry the sesame seeds in the oil as well. Drain the croûtons on kitchen paper. Add the bread to the salad, then the sausage after it has been steamed for three to five minutes. Pour on the dressing, toss the salad and serve immediately.

I once suggested this salad as a dinner party first course to a man friend of mine and I hear he now serves little else. Wind-dried sausages have a particular elusive, addictive flavour and also the advantage of keeping well in the refrigerator; thus they can be always on hand to steam and serve with boiled rice for a quick meal.

SERVES 4 ## CHINESE NOODLE SALAD

If you share my passion for cold, spicy noodle salads made with those noodles which are just a transparent, shimmery thread-like texture, you will be pleased to follow the recipe below and then think up your own combinations. Bean-thread noodles look like skeins of brittle white hair and are available in Chinese super-markets. I often serve this as a first course when entertaining as it can be arranged to look so pretty and no one has yet failed to be delighted by the *sensation* of it. If you have some wind-dried sausages, they make a good addition.

8 oz (250 g) bean-thread noodles
3 tsp sesame oil or vegetable oil
2 oz (60 g) dried mushrooms
4 oz (120 g) cooked chicken, cut into fine strips, or 3 oz (90 g) sliced ham, cut into strips, or 8 oz (250 g) steamed prawns or steamed thin slices of wind-dried sausage
1 bunch of spring onions
½ cucumber

FOR THE SAUCE:
2½ tbsp soy sauce
1 tbsp wine vinegar
1 tbsp peanut butter
2 tsp sugar
1 tsp chilli oil
1 tbsp dry sherry
2 tbsp vegetable oil
1 clove of garlic, finely chopped
salt and freshly ground black pepper

Put the noodles in a large bowl and pour on enough boiling water
to cover them. Leave them to soften and 'cook' for about 4 or 5
minutes, then drain them. Toss with sesame oil or vegetable oil.
Pour boiling water on to the dried mushrooms and soak for about
10 minutes. Drain and cut into thin strips.

Prepare the chicken, ham or prawns. You could use a combination, but you do not want it to get too jumbly. Clean the spring
onions and slice them finely lengthways. Cut the cucumber into
matchsticks about 2 in (5 cm) long. Mix all the ingredients for the
sauce in a bowl. Taste and adjust for seasoning; it should taste
very strong as the noodles contribute their blandness. Mix half
the sauce with the noodles. Spread them on a large, shallow, pretty
dish. Arrange the other ingredients in rows. At the time of dividing
the salad between guests, add the rest of the sauce and toss the
salad together.

SALADE NIÇOISE   SERVES 4

There will never be agreement on what is a proper salade Niçoise.
It is one of those dishes that probably always depended on what
was to hand. Certain ingredients strike me as indispensable:
anchovies, black olives, hard-boiled eggs, tomatoes and, because
I like tuna fish, tuna fish. I prefer lightly cooked green beans to
lettuce and find the taste of peppers intrusive. So the list below is
arbitrary. If you think cos lettuce and artichoke hearts should be in
salade Niçoise, then you must put them there. What is completely
renegade is the hazelnut sauce taken from a recipe by Roger Vergé,
whose restaurant, the three-star Moulin de Mougins, is in the
appropriate part of France. Of course, you can also dress the salad
with just a fruity olive oil, wine vinegar, seasoning and fresh herbs.

¾ lb (375 g) thin French beans (haricots verts), cooked and cooled
3 tomatoes, quartered, or ½ lb (250 g) tiny cherry tomatoes
½ Spanish onion, thinly sliced, or bunch of spring onions, cleaned and
chopped
8 oz (250 g) boiled new potatoes
3 hard-boiled eggs, quartered
1 × 7 oz (200 g) tin of tuna fish, drained of oil or brine
1–2 oz (30–60 g) black olives
8 anchovy fillets, drained of oil

FOR THE SAUCE:
1 oz (30 g) shelled hazelnuts
4 tbsp chilled double cream
juice of ½ a lemon
1 tsp Dijon mustard
salt and pepper
2 tbsp chopped chervil or parsley

Assemble the salad as artistically as you are capable, handling the
tuna carefully so that it flakes into chunks rather than subsiding
into a mush. Either make a vinaigrette as outlined above or make
M. Vergé's sauce as follows: cut the hazelnuts into thin slices and
toast lightly in a small cast-iron frying pan over a brisk heat,
stirring all the while. They should not brown but remain pale.
Whisk together the chilled cream, lemon juice, mustard, salt and
pepper. Add the parsley. Pour over the salad and sprinkle with
the nuts.

SOUPS

I have to confess to ambivalent feelings about soup. I don't much like being greeted by soup at the beginning of an elaborate dinner; I feel drowned by it. However, if soup is the only course, as at lunch or supper, I relish it.

Homely soups based on vegetables seem intrinsically correct and potage bonne femme, which was invariably served in simple French restaurants in the good old days before *nouvelle cuisine*, is supper soup's personification.

The add-a-dash-of-cream or slosh-of-sherry school is not one where I am a pupil, but I do think pistou, a mixture of basil, pine kernels, Parmesan and olive oil (see page 45), can usefully be spooned into many vegetable soups. You can vary the basic herb; a mint version is excellent with tomato or carrot soup.

Liquidisers and food processors have made soups easy, too easy if it means allowing the consistency of the soup to become like emulsion paint. Have a light trigger finger on the blender motor and try to retain a nubbly texture. I sometimes whizz soups in two batches, leaving one rougher than the other, to give a smooth base into which to stir the half with more personality.

If you are serving soup as the basis of a meal, do not forget about croûtons as an addition. Fry cubes of bread in oil (olive oil for preference) in which you have heated, but not frazzled, slivers of garlic. Drain on kitchen paper and serve as soon as possible.

Careful reading of this book will reveal that I am not keen on the sort of stock cubes generally available in this country as a foundation for soup or sauce. Water is the preferable liquid; it lets the flavour of the vegetables or whatever is the main ingredient speak for itself.

If, however, you have a light home-made stock, that is a different kettle of soup.

AUTHENTIC FIRE ISLAND GAZPACHO   SERVES 4

I might have given you the Andalusian gazpacho or the Catalonian gazpacho or any other of the many variations of this summery chilled soup, but a friend assures me that all other gazpachos pale, or indeed pink, beside this recipe given to him by a married lady called Pat on Fire Island in 1965.

Unable not to fiddle with other people's ideas a bit, I have added the notion of croûtons as one of the garnishes. This liquid salad is particularly appealing on a hot day. Also, it is undeniably good for you.

2 green peppers, de-stalked, de-seeded and roughly chopped
4 tomatoes, peeled and quartered
2 cloves of garlic, peeled
1 stalk of celery, trimmed
1 large or 2 small cucumbers, roughly chopped
1 raw egg
1 × 1 pt (600 ml) tin or bottle of good quality tomato juice
2 fl oz (60 ml) olive oil
4 fl oz (120 ml) wine vinegar
pinch of salt
pinch of cayenne pepper

FOR THE GARNISHES
1 green pepper, cleaned and finely chopped
2 hard-boiled eggs, finely chopped
1 Spanish onion, peeled and finely chopped
2–3 slices of bread, cubed and fried until golden in olive oil

Using small amounts of tomato juice, blend together the first six ingredients in the list. Pour into a bowl, thin with 4 fl oz (120 ml) more of tomato juice and stir in the oil and vinegar. Season with salt and cayenne pepper. Decide on the consistency of soup that you like, and add more juice if necessary.

Chill thoroughly. Just before serving, prepare the garnishes and serve them in small bowls beside the soup for people to help themselves.

SERVES 4   POTAGE BONNE FEMME

The 'good woman' of this soup's title was presumably so named for her economical approach to cooking; this is one of the least expensive soups to make, but also one of the most satisfying.

If you leave out the carrots you have a vichyssoise, but they are a cheerful ingredient and contribute towards recreating the sort of first course that used to be served in nearly every simple restaurant and hotel in France. There the ingredients are sometimes not puréed in a blender nor even pushed through a mouli-légumes – the potatoes are just crushed against the side of the pan – but most people find an emulsion, albeit a knobbly one, more appetising.

2 large leeks or 3–4 skinny ones
1½ oz (45 g) butter
½ lb (250 g) carrots
1 lb (500 g) potatoes, peeled and diced
2 pt (1.2 l) water
salt and pepper
pinch of white or brown sugar
1 tbsp finely chopped parsley
2 fl oz (60 ml) double cream (optional)

Clean the leeks very thoroughly. To do this, trim them top and bottom, leaving a considerable amount of the dark green part intact. Slice through the dark green part with a sharp knife so that in washing the leeks you can check that all the grit is removed from between the layers of leaves. Shake the leaves dry and slice them finely. Melt the butter in a large pan and when it is beginning to froth, add the prepared leeks and carrots. Let them become glistening with butter and thoroughly hot. Add the prepared potatoes, water, a little salt, pepper and sugar. Cook at a simmer for about half an hour or until the vegetables are quite tender. Whizz in a blender or food processor, or put through the mouli-légumes. Return to the pan. Check for seasoning and add the parsley and the cream if you are using it. Serve in warmed bowls with hot French bread.

SOUPE AU PISTOU SERVES 4

The point of this soup is the pistou, made in Provence by hand with a pestle and mortar. I discovered that this was not so laborious to make when fresh basil was widely available. The result is infinitely nicer than a spoonful from a jar of Italian pesto and morally better than the same sauce made with a food processor!

Traditionally, this soup should be made in late summer when fresh haricot beans (the ones we buy dried) are in the shops in France. Since they are not sold here, you will have to resort to dried ones, which will have to be soaked, or, failing that, tinned beans – but only as a last resort as the texture is too squashy.

4 tbsp olive oil
2 large leeks or 2 medium onions, peeled and chopped
2 stalks celery, cleaned and chopped
2 large carrots, peeled and chopped
about 2 pt (1.2 l) hot water
4 oz (120 g) dried white haricot beans, soaked overnight and cooked
for 30 minutes, or 1 × 8 oz (250 g) tin beans
8 oz (250 g) courgettes, trimmed and chopped
6 oz (175 g) broad beans, fresh or frozen
8 oz (250 g) tomatoes
2 oz (60 g) dried pasta (optional)
salt and pepper and chopped fresh parsley

FOR THE PISTOU:
a handful of fresh basil leaves
2 cloves of garlic, peeled and chopped
2 tbsp pine kernels
2 oz (60 g) grated Parmesan or Pecorino cheese
about 3 tbsp olive oil

Pound the basil leaves in a pestle until smashed up. Add the garlic,
pound some more, add the pine kernels, keep pounding and then
add the cheese. When you have a cohesive mass, slowly stir in
olive oil until you have a sauce of just pouring consistency. Set
aside. Prepare the vegetables. Heat the oil and sauté the leeks or
onions, the celery and then the carrots. Add the hot water and the
haricot beans. Simmer for about 45 minutes then add the
courgettes, broad beans, the tomatoes, peeled and chopped, and, 10
minutes or so before you want to serve the soup, the pasta. Season
with salt and pepper and add the parsley. Serve with pistou sauce,
a dessertspoon of which is stirred into each individual bowlful.

SERVES 4-6   GREEN MINESTRONE

The image of minestrone has been ruined, I think, by the dolly-
mixture look of the tinned variety and the mish-mash that usually
gets served in its name in Italian restaurants – that is if it has not
come out of a tin as well. By omitting jarring colours and their
attendant flavours, ingredients like carrots and tomatoes, and
staying with what is young and green, you can make a sophisticated
soup, pleasing in appearance and taste. So good, indeed, is this
mixture that it can be the mainstay of the meal, to be followed by
just cheese and fruit.

In hot countries food is often deliberately served lukewarm on the grounds that you can taste the flavours better. I like this minestrone at that temperature with a visible sheen of Tuscan olive oil on top. Freshly grated Parmesan cheese rather than sawdust from packets is another important detail. The vegetables listed below are a guideline. Some can be omitted, others added, as long as you stick to the colour scheme. The hearts of globe artichokes, for example, are lovely if you can be bothered to prepare them.

8 oz (250g) asparagus
8 oz (250g) broccoli
a chunk of cauliflower
1 bunch of spring onions, trimmed and peeled
2 cloves of garlic, peeled and chopped
8 oz (250g) French green beans (haricots verts)
8 oz (250g) fresh broad beans
8 oz (250g) fresh peas in their pods
1 oz (30g) butter
4 tbsp virgin olive oil
salt and freshly ground black pepper
3 oz (90g) freshly grated Parmesan cheese

Prepare the vegetables, shelling the broad beans and peas, cleaning and chopping the rest into quite small pieces. Heat the butter and 2 tbsp of the olive oil in a large, heavy-bottomed sauté pan. Add the asparagus stalks (saving the tips for later), the broccoli, cauliflower, spring onions, garlic and green and broad beans. Toss them in the fat until glistening and beginning to soften. Add the peas. Add just enough water to cover and season with salt and pepper. When the vegetables are tender, but still crunchy, turn off the heat. Remove half the vegetables and whizz in a food processor or liquidiser until you have a none too smooth purée. Pour into a clean pan and bring to the simmer, adding more water if you want a thinner consistency. Add the remaining vegetables plus the asparagus tips. Stir and heat through. Taste for seasoning and for texture. You may wish to cook the soup for a few minutes more. Take off the heat. Serve in shallow plates with a trickle of oil on top and the Parmesan cheese handed separately.

THAI SOUP SERVES 4-6

Every now and then a prestigious chef lets slip a tip that sets you wondering . . . I was told about a product made in the Philippines and marketed by Knorr, a company that seems to make superior products for every market but the British one. It is a Tamarind Soup Base Mix (Sabaw ng Sinigang sa Sampalok) and can be found in most large oriental supermarkets. The packet instructions tell you to add two litres of water and any choice of vegetables, shrimps or fish that you fancy.

The instructions below are the ones given to me by a chef friend and they do have a sensational result. If you cannot find all the ingredients, do not despair – the sour tamarind taste in the base is good on its own as long as you have a few interesting items to stir in. Don't use 2 litres of water though; it dilutes the flavour too much.

1 packet Tamarind Soup Base Mix
$1\frac{3}{4}$ pt (1 l) water
1 bunch of fresh coriander, including the stalks
$1\frac{1}{2}$ inch (4 cm) piece of ginger root or a piece of dried galangal
1 × 14 fl oz (400 ml) tin coconut milk and $1\frac{1}{2}$ packets instant coconut powder, or, instead of both, 7 oz (200 g) creamed coconut
1 onion, peeled and sliced
2 sticks of lemon grasss
4 kaffir lime (also called curry) leaves
4 small fresh chillis, de-seeded and chopped, or more if you like things hot

Tip the soup base into a saucepan. Add the water. Bring to a simmer. While it is heating, cut off the coriander stalks, clean and chop. Peel the ginger root and chop, or slice the galangal. Add the coconut, onion and all other ingredients except for the coriander leaves. If you are using the creamed coconut, divide the block into small pieces and stir in bit by bit. Simmer for 30 minutes. Strain into a clean pan, heat again, add the chopped coriander leaves, taste for seasoning and serve in heated bowls. If you want to add prawns and thinly sliced vegetables such as spring onion, water chestnut or cucumber, do so after the soup is strained and cook just enough so that the crunch is retained.

SERVES 4   # CARROT AND MINT SOUP

This is a good summery soup served chilled with a swirl of cream; should the weather be chilly it can equally successfully be served hot. The flavour of orange marries well with carrots, despite the fact that they are both slightly sweet. Try to buy English carrots. Even the old fat ones, in fact especially old fat ones, have considerably more flavour than the anaemic Dutch variety.

1½ lb (750 g) carrots
1½ oz (45 g) butter
1 large onion, peeled and finely chopped
2 cloves of garlic, peeled and finely chopped
about 1½ pt (900 ml) water
1 tbsp fresh mint leaves
juice of 1 lemon
juice of 1 orange
salt and freshly ground black pepper
scrape of nutmeg
4 tbsp single cream

Peel the carrots and chop them up into fairly small pieces. Melt the butter and sauté the chopped onion, carrot and garlic until they are glistening and the onion is beginning to soften. Add water and simmer for about 15 minutes, until the carrot is tender. If you have a food processor or liquidiser, chop the mint leaves in this, using the steel blade, and then remove them. Strain the carrot mixture from the liquid, reserving the liquid in a bowl and purée in the food processor without cleaning any clinging pieces of mint from it. Dilute to the desired consistency with the reserved stock (you may not need it all) and the lemon and orange juice. Stir in the mint, and season with salt, pepper and nutmeg. Chill. When you serve the soup, swirl the single cream into it. Don't stir; aim for a marbled effect. If you have no food processor or liquidiser you can chop the mint by hand and purée the carrot either in a mouli-légumes or by pushing it through a coarse-grained sieve.

CINDERELLA SOUP   SERVES 4

Once, when I was staying in France, I went to dinner at the home of the mistress, so it was said, of someone referred to as the King of Beaujolais. 'Avez-vous des courges en Angleterre?' she asked me. 'Oui,' I said politely, not quite knowing what she meant, and was gratified – and vindicated – by the appearance of a pumpkin. It was both the basis and the tureen for the soup that was our first course. This enterprising lady had also done a *stage* in the kitchens of Paul Bocuse and the recipe was his. The method below I have adapted from *The Cuisine of Paul Bocuse*, but have added salt pork, which I remember well as one of the ingredients and which gives a necessary kick. Try this rather than sacrificing pumpkins to grinning Hallowe'en lanterns.

1 medium 3–4 lb (1.75–2.0 kg) pumpkin
4 oz (120 g) salt pork or piece of bacon
4 oz (120 g) toasted croûtons
2 oz (60 g) grated Gruyère cheese
salt and pepper
½ pt (300 ml) single cream
creamy milk

Turn on the oven to 180°C/350°F/gas mark 4. Cut off the top of the pumpkin to give it the shape of a soup tureen. Set the top aside. Remove all the pumpkin seeds. Chop the salt pork or chunk of bacon into cubes and fry them until they are lightly coloured and the fat begins to run. Make alternate layers of croûtons and cheese in the pumpkin shell with the salt pork or bacon dotted about. Add salt and pepper and fill with first the cream and then enough of the milk to come nearly to the top. Replace the 'lid' as tightly as possible. Place the pumpkin in a tin or gratin dish and cook in the oven for 2 hours. At the moment of service, using a spoon, mix the pumpkin flesh into the liquid. The combination with the bread should give a wonderful creamy texture. Correct the seasoning and ladle into hot bowls.

SERVES 4 ## MUSHROOM SOUP

This soup, the method for which is given by Elizabeth David in *French Provincial Cooking*, uses bread for the thickening agent. White bread is suggested, but I like the nuttiness of a slice of granary or wholemeal bread. The combination of that and the mushrooms give the soup a wonderful earthy quality and also, even if you use a food processor or blender, the mixture never quite reaches an emulsified state; a nice bitty texture remains. Home-made stock, even a vegetable stock, is preferable to a stock cube with its overbearing flavourings.

12 oz (375 g) mushrooms, preferably field mushrooms
2 oz (60 g) butter
1 thick slice of wholemeal bread
1¾ pt (1 l) light stock
1 fat clove of garlic, peeled and chopped
1 tbsp chopped fresh parsley
a little grated nutmeg
salt and freshly ground black pepper
3 fl oz (90 ml) cream

Wipe the mushrooms and trim the ends off the stalks. Only peel them if the skins are really felty. Chop them into small pieces. Melt the butter in a heavy-bottomed saucepan, put in the mushrooms and let them soften. Soak the bread minus its crusts in a little of the stock. When the juice starts to run from the mushrooms, add the garlic, parsley, nutmeg, salt and pepper, and cook for a few minutes more. Squeeze out the bread and add to the mushrooms. Stir until it is amalgamated. Add the rest of the stock and cook for about 15 minutes. Whizz in a blender or food processor. You should end up with a liquid the consistency of thin cream with little particles dotted in it. Re-heat the soup, add the cream, heat again and sprinkle with a little more chopped parsley. Taste for seasoning and serve.

PALESTINE SOUP SERVES 4

'What is the main, i.e. distinguishing, ingredient in Palestine Soup?' was one of our questions for the Mouton Cadet *London Standard* Great Competition 1986. The answer is Jerusalem artichokes. Some say the tubers are so called because when they came to this country from North America in the early seventeenth century, botanists recognised that they were girasols, plants whose flowers turn with the sun; from girasol it is not too far to Jerusalem and hence Palestine Soup. The French name, *topinambour*, is just as interesting: since the vegetable arrived in France at the same time as a party of Brazilian Tupi Tambo Indians, it got labelled with the same name. If you have never tried this unprepossessing vegetable, do. It has a marvellous subtle flavour. Try to buy artichokes not too tormented in shape and roughly of the same size; it makes them easier to handle. It was Escoffier who thought of the felicitous combination of toasted hazelnuts with puréed artichokes.

1 lb (500 g) Jerusalem artichokes
1 large onion, peeled and chopped
½ stick of celery, chopped
4 oz (120 g) butter
1 clove of garlic, peeled and chopped
2 rashers of bacon, chopped
1¾ pt (1 l) poultry stock or water
8 fl oz (250 ml) top of the milk, milk or thin cream
salt and freshly ground black pepper
2 tbsp toasted shelled hazelnuts, coarsely ground or finely chopped

Trim, wash and boil the artichokes in salted water for about 7 minutes, then plunge them into cold water and take off the peel. Alternatively, peel them raw if they are not too knobbly. Chop them into dice. Gently cook them with the onion and celery in half the butter, stirring occasionally, for 5 minutes. Add the garlic, bacon and stock. Simmer until all is tender. Either liquidise, whizz in a food processor or push through a mouli-légumes. Add the milk or cream and check for seasoning. Stir in the remaining butter and pour into a tureen or individual bowls. Scatter the nuts on top.

SERVES 4   ## PEASE SOUP

Finding a tin of pease pudding in my local supermarket reminded me of an interview I once did with the journalist Michael Bateman on the subject of his approach to cooking. He was very good on the business of getting something quickly on to the table after returning from work. The recipe below I tried to write in his style of delivery.

1 large onion, peeled and sliced
1 tbsp oil
1 tsp coriander seeds
1 tsp cumin seeds
1 fresh green chilli pepper
garlic, to taste
1 × 14 oz (430 g) tin of pease pudding
a few cupfuls of boiling water
Maldon salt and freshly ground black pepper

We assume you have just come home from work. Nothing is ready to eat. Before you take off your hat and coat, peel and slice an onion, making long strips, and set it to fry in a little oil in a heavy frying pan. Let it brown. Let it burn. You want it slippery; part sweet, part charred, caramelised. This is a reckless recipe. Throw in crushed coriander seeds and cumin seeds, the chilli pepper, finely chopped (include the seeds), and as much chopped garlic as you want. Mix it around aggressively. Spoon in the pease pudding – it will catch and burn a bit. Stir them angrily (you have just got back from work). Pour in a few cupfuls of boiling water. You should have put the kettle on as you came in. Scrape around the pan to release the flavours. Turn it all into a saucepan. Thin to the desired consistency with more water. Season with Maldon salt and freshly ground black pepper. Eat it when you like.

AVGOLEMONO SOUP SERVES 4

In a particular village that I like in Greece, there used to be holiday villas for parties of English people staffed by jolly, bouncy, upper-middle-class English girls, the likes of which we have got to know so well in recent years. In the summertime they would follow the sun; in the wintertime the snow. I remember listening to one of them as a local restaurateur attempted to convince her that this was the right place to bring the guests on the girl's night off. He reeled off the predictable list of specialities: moussaka, souvlaki, garides, bresaola, biftecki and so on.

'Oh super!' cried the girl.

'Yes,' he said in Greek, anxious to meet her demands, 'ke soupa.'

This is perhaps the most typical Greek soupa. Using the same technique, but with less stock or liquid, you can make egg and lemon sauce, ideal for chicken, fish, meat-balls or poached vegetables.

2 pt (1.2 l) chicken stock
1 heaped tsp rice or meat-balls (see below)
2 eggs
juice of 1 lemon

FOR THE MEATBALLS
8 oz (250 g) minced veal or lamb
2 tbsp fresh white breadcrumbs
1 onion, peeled and finely chopped
1 tsp chopped fresh dill, parsley or coriander
1 small egg (50–55 g/size 5)
salt and pepper

Heat the stock and check for seasoning. Add the rice and cook until tender. In a small bowl, beat together the eggs and lemon juice. Add a small cup of the stock to the egg and lemon and beat it in. Return this to the pan, whisking with a balloon whisk or similar over a low heat, until the soup is slightly thickened. Do not let it boil or the egg will curdle. If you want to make more of a meal of it, you can add meatballs as follows, omitting the rice from the soup. Mix together very thoroughly the ingredients for the meatballs. Form into small balls. Poach them in the chicken stock for 15 minutes. Remove the meatballs with a slotted spoon and place in a heated dish. Proceed with the egg and lemon method as above. Pour over the meatballs and serve.

EGGS AND CHEESE

It is to eggs that I turn when wondering what on earth to make for lunch or supper. They are a miracle of nature with their inherent ability to emulsify, foam, coagulate and, more pertinently, scramble, fry, poach, soft-boil, hard-boil and omelette. Some of the recipes in this section have evolved from last-minute improvisation when provisions were scarce on the ground.

Eggs take curiously well to Indian spices, as will be evident in the Dal with Crackling Eggs, the Scrambled Eggs Parsee Style, and Curried Eggs Stabbed with Almonds, which is quite unlike the usual egg curry.

Baked eggs are a great comfort if you happen to have some nice little something in the refrigerator or larder that you can slip underneath. This can be jelly from roasted meat, raw ham, wild mushrooms or a more quotidian item like a sliver of leftover ripe soft cheese. The slightly more elaborate cooking method required by baked eggs lifts them out of the snack class, the 'something eggy on toast' that Noël Coward favoured when at home.

Cheese is another source of quick gratification. Cheese on toast is not an ignoble thing, and it is a good way of using leftover hard cheeses. My mother-in-law makes a substance based on the principle of squashing used ends of soap into a cup. She grates the leftover cheese pieces, or chops them if soft, and mixes them together with either butter or cream or perhaps a little port. This is then pressed into a small jar and called Rita's Cheese. It can be quite nice, considerably better anyway than the noxious substance that results from false soap economy.

Frying a cheese and ham sandwich – as you do for 'croque monsieur' – always goes down well with children. Adults might appreciate the Grilled Goat's Cheese with Salad described in the section on first courses (see page 24). Well-bought cheeses with salad and good bread is to my mind a far better thing at a meal than micro-waved convenience food.

DAL WITH CRACKLING EGGS SERVES 4

This is a real Monday dish that I thought up one evening when faced with what you might call a Mother Hubbard situation. However, this particular Mother Hubbard always has some lentils, including the small orange variety sometimes called Egyptian lentils, that cook quickly to a sludge. In Indian shops they are called masoor dal. The idea of frying hard-boiled egg slices in spices resulted in eggs with a texture quite unlike eggs in any other form. Onions fried to a crisp and plain natural yogurt complete this actually rather delicious meal.

10–12 oz (300–375 g) orange lentils
2 onions
salt and freshly ground black pepper
1 tbsp vegetable oil
3–4 hard-boiled eggs
large pinch of garam masala or curry powder
small pinch of black mustard seeds (optional)
natural yogurt, to serve

Swill lentils about in a bowl of water to remove chaff and foreign bodies. Cover the drained lentils with fresh water so that there is about ½ in (1 cm) of water over the lentils in a saucepan. Bring to the boil. Peel and slice the onions, cutting from root to tip to make crescents. Watch the dal. It will cook to a mush in about 20 minutes but might need some additional water. The correct texture is rough volcanic mud. Season the dal with salt and pepper. Fry the onions in a little vegetable oil until brown and crisp. Set aside and keep warm. Clean the pan with kitchen paper. Slice the hard-boiled eggs thickly. Heat a little more oil in the pan, add a good pinch of garam masala or curry powder and the mustard seeds if you are using them. Fry until the seeds pop, add the egg slices and cook, turning them once or twice until a bubbly crust forms. Serve the dal garnished with the eggs and onion and a bowl of plain yogurt alongside.

SERVES 4   OEUFS SOUBISE

Making an onion sauce to accompany some roast lamb, or actually watching my sister make some onion sauce for that purpose, I thought about that comforting supper dish, oeufs Soubise, or hard-boiled eggs in onion sauce. The name comes from that of an eighteenth-century general who, after losing several important battles, retired and spent years perfecting his sauce. It is usually easy to assemble from what you might have on hand.

If, after sautéing the onions in butter, you crumble in a little piece of a stock cube you can then use a mixture of milk and water as your liquid, which makes the sauce less rich and heavy and hard on your heart. I used a vegetable bouillon I found in a health food store. It contains no monosodium glutamate, preservatives or colouring and has none of that synthetic kick of some cubes. A teaspoon in some boiled water even makes a rather nice, virtuous drink.

1½ oz (45 g) butter
12 oz (375 g) onions, peeled and chopped
1 tbsp flour
pinch of English mustard powder
¼ stock cube
¾ pt (450 ml) mixed milk and water
salt and freshly ground black pepper
grated nutmeg
6 hard-boiled eggs, cut in half lengthways
hot French bread, to serve

Melt the butter and sauté the onions gently until softened but on no account browned. Stir in the flour, a pinch of English dry mustard, the piece of stock cube, and keep stirring until the mixture is well amalgamated. Bit by bit add the mixed milk and water and proceed as if you were making a béchamel sauce. When you achieve a desirable creamy consistency, flavour with salt, pepper and grated nutmeg (you may not need all the liquid). You could at this point liquidise the sauce, but I prefer some texture in it. Arrange the eggs in an ovenproof dish, pour on the sauce and heat through in the oven. Serve with hot French bread.

CURRIED EGGS STABBED WITH ALMONDS   SERVES 4

I want to promote the idea of egg curry, but I have a friend who says he could never face such a dish again since he was served it every day for lunch at his boarding school in Singapore. However, this recipe, I feel sure, would alter his attitude. The almond slivers, inserted all over the eggs, give them an endearing hedgehog appearance and take away the possibly off-putting aspect of glassy eyes staring up at you, while the sauce, based on yogurt, a little cream and various spices, including delicious black onion seeds (available from oriental grocers), is nothing like that vicious red-brown oily gravy that you often find endemic to this dish. Serve basmati rice as an accompaniment, plus a poppadum or two for crunchiness and some sweetish chutney for contrast.

2 cloves of garlic, peeled and crushed
juice of ½ a lemon
8 hard-boiled eggs
1 dsp ground turmeric
3 oz (90 g) almonds, blanched and slivered
1 oz (30 g) poppy seeds
1 oz (30 g) sesame seeds
8 fl oz (250 ml) thick natural yogurt (the Greek variety is good)
2 fl oz (60 ml) double cream
1 tsp black onion seeds
2 dried red chillis, ground
salt and freshly ground black pepper

Mix the garlic cloves with the lemon juice. Roll the eggs in this and then in the turmeric. It might not adhere particularly evenly. With a sharp knife, prick the eggs and insert slivers of almonds all over.

Sprinkle on any remaining turmeric or garlic. Roast the poppy and sesame seeds in a dry iron pan and then pound them, crush them or whizz them in a clean coffee grinder. Heat together gently the yogurt and cream. Add the onion seed and chilli, and season. Stir until thick. Add a little stock or water to get a runny sauce, and then the eggs. Cook until the eggs are hot and the sauce somewhat reduced.

SERVES 4   EGGS GOLDENROD

It must be dismal to be an actor in a long run of a play that features the consumption of a meal. To have to eat the same thing every night, and twice on matinée days, with some semblance of enthusiasm is a harsh test of dedication. But it can be fascinating for the audience. In a play I saw called *So Long on Lonely Street* by Sandra Deer, the chief male protagonist had a dish prepared for him called Eggs Goldenrod.

After the black housekeeper had announced that this had been a favourite meal of his childhood, I spent the rest of the play wondering how it was made.

The play was set in Georgia in America and I found the answer later in James Beard's *American Cookery*. He describes it as 'a rather dreary recipe which once had great standing', but I think it is nice for the occasional supper, perhaps served alongside some good ham.

8 hard-boiled eggs
béchamel sauce, made from 2 oz (60 g) butter, 2 oz (60 g) plain flour
and about ¾ pt (450 ml) hot milk – enough to give a creamy texture
salt and freshly ground black pepper
pinch of cayenne pepper
1 tbsp chopped fresh parsley

Shell the eggs and separate the yolks from the whites. Chop the whites into small pieces. Mix the whites into the prepared béchamel and taste for seasoning. Using a wooden spoon, press the egg yolks through a sieve on to a plate. Season them with the cayenne pepper and mix in the parsley. Pile the egg white mixture on to the slices of toast and decorate with the sieved yolks. The effect should be that of goldenrod, or, as we might put it, mimosa.

SCOTCH EGGS   SERVES 4

Commercially made Scotch eggs are so horrid – a shrunken grey-rimmed egg rattling about in a case of pink sausage meat which in turn is gritty with orange crumbs – that it is easy just to dismiss them, whereas, carefully made and served fresh and warm, Scotch eggs can be experienced as a demonstrably good idea for a filling snack. With a home-made tomato sauce alongside and a salad, they make a fine supper.

If you cannot obtain good sausage meat – it often looks a dubious slurry – buy high quality sausages and take them out of their skins. This is facilitated by making a little slit in the skins and holding the sausages under the cold tap. Sunflower oil is the best frying medium.

4 eggs
12 oz (375 g) sausage meat
flour, as required for coating
salt and freshly ground black pepper
1 beaten egg
4 tbsp home-made dry breadcrumbs
sunflower oil or other vegetable oil, for frying

Boil the eggs for 6 minutes, then immerse them in cold water. Shell them carefully as the yolks wil not be rock hard. Divide the sausage meat into four. Roll the eggs in seasoned flour and then wet your hands, flatten a portion of sausage meat on your hand and coax it round the egg. It is not difficult. Dust each coated egg lightly with flour, turn in the beaten egg and coat with crumbs.

Either deep fry or shallow fry, but do it in two stages, once to cook the sausage thoroughly, the second time at a higher heat to crisp and brown the crumbs. Drain on kitchen paper and serve warm.

BAKED EGGS

One of the most enticing ways to cook eggs is to bake them gently in the oven in individual dishes – or, indeed, simmer them on top of the stove. The important point about baked eggs is to cook them so that the white sets but the yolk remains soft. To this end it is sensible to put together a bain-marie – that is, a pan containing hot water in which the cocottes or ramekins can sit. The recipe below is the master recipe for oeufs en cocotte à la crème, with some suggestions, but by no means a definitive list, for what you might tuck beneath the eggs.

½ oz (15 g) butter for each egg
1–2 eggs for each person
ground black pepper
1 tbsp cream for each egg

POSSIBLE GARNISHES:
a few mushrooms, chopped and sautéed in butter with some cream stirred in and a grating of nutmeg to flavour
a large tomato, skinned, chopped and de-seeded, tossed in a little butter
some thinly cut ham fried in a little butter

If you are using the top of the stove method, find a large pan to which you have a lid or cover and put in enough water to come about half way up the sides of the ramekins. Place the cocottes in the water in the pan, add the butter and set on a low heat until the butter is melted. Slip an egg into each cocotte. Season lightly and cover the pan.

After a few minutes, when the eggs have begun to set, pour on a tablespoon of cream, cover again and cook a few minutes more.

For cooking in the oven, turn the oven to 180°C/350°F/gas mark 4, set the ramekins in a baking tin with hot water and cook gently, uncovered, for about 10 minutes, adding the cream halfway through. When you take the ramekins from the pan, they will continue to cook the egg a little, so keep that in mind.

EGGS LUCULLUS SERVES 2-4

The usual response to a lettuce is to make a green salad but, let me tell you, it can also be very nice when cooked. When I cook peas, I always stir in strips of lettuce as they contribute a nice silky texture, and lettuce soup is a delicate first course. Pouring a hot dressing, such as bacon fat mixed with a little wine vinegar, on to lettuce wilts it in an interesting way. In this recipe you get three varieties of softness, the eggs, the mushrooms and the lettuce. If you can find oyster mushrooms or shiitake mushrooms, both now sold in supermarkets as well as Chinese stores, they will make this dish particularly good.

4 oz (120 g) mushrooms
1 round lettuce
1 oz (30 g) butter
1 small clove of garlic, peeled and slivered
salt and freshly ground black pepper
1 tbsp chopped fresh parsley
4 eggs
2 fl oz (60 ml) double cream
1 oz (30 g) grated Gruyère, Cheddar or Caerphilly cheese

Turn on the oven to 180°C/350°F/gas mark 4. Wipe the mushrooms with a damp cloth if they need it and slice them fairly thinly. Wash the lettuce if necessary and cut it into strips. Melt the butter, add the mushrooms and garlic and cook gently until they soften. Stir in the lettuce and cook only a few minutes until that, too, is listless. Pour off all the liquid, season the lettuce and mushrooms well and stir in the parsley. Spread the mixture in an ovenproof dish that will hold four eggs. Using the back of a spoon, make four indentations in the lettuce mixture and break an egg into each of them. Spoon the cream on top and then sprinkle on the cheese. Bake for 12–15 minutes, until the egg white is set but the yolks are still soft and the cheese melted.

OEUFS FLORENTINE SERVES 2-4

This is not a breakthrough recipe, just one of those tried and true ideas that sometimes one forgets about in the flurry of being cute and original. It is usually possible to make the dish from ingredients you have to hand, particularly if you choose to use frozen spinach, but fresh spinach is preferable. Fresh spinach can be cooked in the water that clings to its leaves after washing, then drained and left for a while before the final sautéeing in butter or oil.

1½–2 lb (750 g–1 kg) fresh spinach or 1 lb (500 g) packet frozen spinach (leaf or purée)
1½ oz (45 g) butter or vegetable oil
salt and freshly ground black pepper
scraping of nutmeg
4 eggs
1 tsp vinegar

FOR THE SAUCE:
1 oz (30 g) butter
1 tbsp flour
½ pt (300 ml) skimmed milk, or half stock and half single cream
2–3 oz (60–90 g) grated Gruyère cheese and
1 oz (30 g) freshly grated Parmesan, or
3–4 oz (90–120 g) grated Cheddar instead of both
salt and pepper

Turn on the oven to 200°C/400°F/gas mark 6. Cook fresh spinach in a large pan until wilted – a matter of minutes. Drain, let cool and squeeze out excess water with your hands. Follow packet instructions for frozen spinach. Chop the fresh spinach or frozen leaf spinach finely. Make the sauce by melting the butter, stirring in the flour and cooking over a gentle heat for a minute or two. Add milk or stock and cream, stirring conscientiously until you have a smooth sauce. Add the cheese, a pinch of salt and pepper and stir until the cheese is melted. Keep the sauce warm.

Sauté the spinach in the butter or oil and season with salt, pepper and nutmeg. Spread in a warm ovenproof dish and keep warm. Poach the eggs in simmering water into which you have put the teaspoon of vinegar. Drain them, lay them on the spinach and cover with the cream sauce. Sprinkle on the Parmesan or Cheddar cheese and give them a few minutes in a hot oven to bring everything to a satisfactory heat.

SERVES 3 ## PARSEE SCRAMBLED EGGS

The combination of chilli and eggs is particularly good and, even if you do not have all the spices mentioned below, just a little fried fresh green chilli stirred into eggs makes a dish substantially different to the usual breakfast assembly. Eggs prepared this way are served all over India, but the influence is from the Parsees, a Zoroastrian community that fled Persia in the eighth century because of Moslem persecution. Their cuisine, which benefits from few strictures, is especially inventive where egg dishes are concerned. Toast is the obvious accompaniment, but fried bread, although fattening, is more delicious.

3 tbsp vegetable oil or ghee or butter
1 onion, peeled and finely sliced
½ in (1.5 cm) cube of fresh ginger root, grated
1 small hot green chilli, de-seeded and cut into threads
¼ tsp ground turmeric
½ tsp ground cumin
1 tomato, peeled, de-seeded and chopped
6 eggs
salt and freshly ground black pepper
1 tbsp chopped coriander leaves

TO SERVE:
toast or fried bread

Heat the oil or fat in a sauté pan and fry the onion until golden. Add the ginger, chilli, turmeric and cumin and stir around. Add the tomato and cook gently for about 3 minutes. Beat the eggs lightly and season them. Add to the spicy onion mixture and stir over a low heat as you do for scrambled eggs. Just before they are ready, stir in the fresh coriander. Serve with toast or, as suggested above, with fried bread.

CROÛTONS OMELETTE SERVES 2

'What would you like in your omelette?' I said to a friend as I was hurrying to make some lunch before he left to catch a plane.

'Mushrooms?' he ventured. 'Bacon?'

When I admitted to having neither of these commodities on hand, he wondered out loud why I had asked the question in the first place. Determined, therefore, not to make an omelette *nature*, I used what was around and composed a filling of brown bread croûtons flavoured by garlic and quickly fried chopped spring onions. Though I say so myself, and my friend admitted it too, it was a successful combination. The crunch of croûtons provided edgy relief from the softness of egg, and because it was wholemeal bread, it also lent a nutty flavour. Had I had some Parmesan cheese, I would have tossed the croûtons in that, so I have added it to the instructions below. Parsley and chives I happened to have in the garden, but you could omit them without the recipe coming to harm.

4 eggs
2 tsp cold water
salt and freshly ground black pepper
few sprigs of parsley, chopped
1 small bundle of chives, finely chopped
2 slices of brown bread, cut into small cubes
vegetable oil
1 fat clove of garlic, peeled and chopped
1 oz (30 g) grated Parmesan
1 bunch of spring onions, trimmed and finely chopped
1½ oz (45 g) butter

I like to cook omelettes one at a time. If you are of this persuasion, break 2 eggs into a bowl, add 1 tsp cold water. Season with salt and pepper and add half the herbs. Beat lightly. Chop the bread into cubes.

Heat some vegetable oil in a small frying pan with the garlic and fry the bread, turning until you have croûtons crisp on all sides. Roll them in Parmesan cheese. Keep warm. In the same oil quickly fry the spring onions. Drain on kitchen paper and keep warm. Heat half the butter in an omelette pan. When it is foaming, add the beaten eggs. Push them and lift them, as you do with an omelette, and when set on the bottom and tacky on the surface, scatter on half the croûtons and onions. Fold over, tip out and serve with a little butter rubbed on top of the omelette to give it gloss. Repeat the procedure with the other two eggs. Alternatively, make one large omelette.

SERVES 2-3 # OMELETTE ARNOLD BENNETT

The Savoy Hotel was the scene of Arnold Bennett's novel *Imperial Palace*. When working as a theatre critic Bennett often dined at the Savoy where this dish was invented for him. It shows, I think, a proper English approach to what is essentially a French cooking mode.

Though you can simply make an omelette nicely *baveuse* – sloppy – cover it with smoked haddock mixed with Parmesan cheese, then some double cream and flash it under the grill, the following recipe taken from one of my favourite books, *The Adventurous Fish Cook* by George Lassalle, gives a lighter result. Also, were you to eat it late at night, and it is a good supper dish, then it will be more digestible.

12 oz (375 g) smoked haddock
1 pt (600 ml) mixed milk and water
¼ pt (150 ml) double cream
salt and freshly ground black pepper
4 eggs, separated
2 oz (60 g) Parmesan cheese, grated
1 oz (30 g) butter

Poach the haddock in the milk and water for 15 minutes. Let cool before removing any skin or bones. Combine the haddock with half the cream and season with pepper and salt to taste, depending on the saltiness of the fish. Beat the egg yolks and mix them and most of the Parmesan into the haddock mixture. Season, beat the egg whites until they are stiff and fold them into the mixture. Heat the butter in a large omelette pan and cook the mixture over a medium heat until the underside is lightly browned and the top still tacky. Turn the omelette on to a heated serving dish, folding it in half as you slip it out. Pour over the remaining cream, sprinkle with the remaining Parmesan and brown quickly under a hot grill.

SPANISH JERSEY OMELETTE SERVES 4

The price of Jersey potatoes at the beginning of the season compares not all that favourably with steak. However, so delicious are Jerseys that I feel they should be accorded the same respect you might have for any first-class protein, and pay what is necessary.

The phrase Spanish omelette is often the prelude to a jumble of ingredients imprisoned by egg. Green peas, red peppers, pink ham, beige potatoes all jostle for attention. A true Spanish omelette is made with only onions and potatoes fried in olive oil and mixed into the eggs and is all the better for its plainness. You could, of course, use any variety of potato, but preferably a fairly waxy one, for this dish. The result should be quite solid; a cake you can cut, rather than the sloppy approach of the French.

1 lb (500 g) Jersey new potatoes, scraped
3 tbsp olive oil
2 onions, peeled and chopped
salt and freshly ground black pepper
4–5 eggs

Cut the potatoes into quite small, evenly sized pieces. So, with a small potato cut it in half. Heat up the olive oil in a medium-size frying pan. Add the onions and potatoes, stir around and sprinkle

with salt and pepper. Find a saucepan lid that fits the pan, or very
nearly does, and cook the vegetables slowly in the oil, stirring from
time to time. When the potatoes are becoming tender, after about
15 minutes, beat the eggs in a bowl. Lift the cooked vegetables
from the pan, leaving behind as much oil as possible and stir them
into the eggs. If the pan is very encrusted, clean it, otherwise just
pour off enough of the oil to leave the base covered. Pour the egg
mixture into the pan. Cook gently, shaking it from time to time
until the base is set. Either turn out the omelette on to a plate and
slip it back into the pan upside down to cook the top, or (an easier
option) flash the omelette in the pan under the grill to brown the
top. Serve hot, warm or cold, in generous slices.

PIPERADE

SERVES 4

Doing a mammoth shop just before one Christmas I was tempted
by some red, green and yellow peppers, one of each colour pack-
aged together, almost like a child's beach game. I bought them,
thinking longingly of summer and intending to marinate them,
cut into strips, with olive oil and anchovies, but ended up making
instead that Basque dish piperade. Not a great fan of green
peppers, I nevertheless love this dish, creamy and soothing and a
reminder that warm weather will begin again. Most recipes do not
bother to state that you should skin the peppers, but it makes all the
difference, obviating the bitterness that peppers harbour. Slices of
jambon de Bayonne are the traditional accompaniment.

3 sweet peppers, preferably a variety of colours
1 large Spanish onion
4 large tomatoes
3–4 tbsp olive oil
1 fat clove of garlic, peeled and finely chopped
salt and freshly ground black pepper
pinch of dried oregano or thyme
5 eggs

Skin the peppers. Either grill them until the skin blisters, turning
them so it blisters evenly, or rotate them over a gas flame to the
same effect. A spell in the oven also facilitates peeling but does
not imbue the peppers with the pleasant charred undertones.
Leaving the peppers in a plastic bag to sweat as they cool makes
them easier to skin. Peel off the skins and slice the flesh into thin
strips, discarding seeds and the white pulpy parts. Peel and thinly
slice the onion. Skin the tomatoes by plunging them briefly into

boiling water. Chop them. Sauté the onion and garlic in the olive oil until the onion has softened and just begun to colour. Add the peppers and cook for 10 minutes. Add the tomatoes and cook for another 10 minutes. Season with salt and pepper and perhaps some dried oregano or thyme. Beat the eggs lightly. Stir them in and cook gently, stirring occasionally, until you have, in effect, scrambled the eggs. Serve immediately, remembering that the eggs will continue to cook in the pan.

TUMBET SERVES 4

This rather thumping sounding dish is a speciality of Majorca. It was one of the few truly indigenous dishes I was able to track down in restaurants and I liked its stance – somewhere between piperade and Spanish omelette. It is good supper food and stands up to waiting patiently for those late for a meal.

The breadcrumbs are an important element. Don't, whatever you do, use those bright orange ones that come in a packet. Should you have a food processor, fresh breadcrumbs can be made in a trice. Otherwise, you will have to resort to a grater, or drying the bread in the oven and crumbling it with your fingers.

2 green or red sweet peppers
3 large onions
4 peeled potatoes
2 courgettes
3 tbsp olive oil
4 eggs
salt and freshly ground pepper
½ oz (15 g) butter
1 cupful of fresh soft breadcrumbs

FOR THE TOMATO SAUCE:
1 lb (500 g) of peeled tomatoes or 1 × 14 oz (400 g) tin of tomatoes
a little olive oil
salt and pepper
1 tsp sugar
oregano or fresh basil

Pre-heat the oven to 180°C/350°F/gas mark 4. Make the tomato sauce. Cook the tomatoes in the oil with the seasoning and herbs until pulpy. Meanwhile, core and de-seed the peppers and cut them into strips. Peel the onions and cut into rings. Cube the potatoes. Wash and slice the courgettes. Fry these ingredients in the olive oil until the potatoes are almost cooked. Beat the eggs with a pinch of salt and pepper. Grease an earthenware casserole, or similar, with the butter. Coat it with breadcrumbs. Put in a layer of the vegetables. Pour over a little beaten egg and some of the tomato sauce. Repeat this process, finishing off with egg. Sprinkle the dish with more breadcrumbs and bake in the oven for 30 minutes until it is crusty and golden.

KUKU
SERVES 4-6

Picnics, even if pleasanter in theory than in practice, give a liberated 'Sing ho! for the open road' sort of feel. I have often taken this dish, which is from a recipe by Claudia Roden, on picnics and found it much enjoyed. It is not dissimilar to a quiche but it has no pastry and the inclusion of cinnamon in the spicing lends it the sort of exoticism that you seek – one preferable to ingesting an ant or a piece of gravel. If you have a strong-armed person in your party carry the kuku (an Iranian description of omelette) in the pan in which you cook it, or alternatively eat in your dining room and just manhandle it, preferably lukewarm, from the stove to the table. A green salad is the right accompaniment.

1 large onion, peeled and finely chopped
1 large leek, peeled, washed and finely sliced, or 4 spring onions, trimmed and chopped
2 tbsp vegetable oil
1 lb (500 g) minced beef
4 oz (120 g) chopped spinach (frozen will do)
salt and pepper
1 tsp ground cinnamon
6 eggs

Fry the onion with the leek or spring onions in 1 tbsp vegetable oil until they are soft. Add the minced beef and cook until it has changed colour and completely lost its rawness. Add the spinach, salt, pepper and cinnamon and cook gently. In a large mixing bowl, beat the eggs lightly. Add the meat mixture, which should not be too hot or it will start to cook the eggs. Clean the frying pan. Heat up the other tablespoon of vegetable oil and pour in the omelette. Cook over a gentle heat for about 15 minutes or until it is apparent that the eggs have set on the bottom and indeed most of the way through. Turn on the grill and slip the pan under that until the top of the omelette is golden. Serve lukewarm or cool. If you have used a heavy-bottomed pan, the kuku should be easy to slice like a cake, for it will have shrunk slightly from the sides in the cooking process.

GOAT'S CHEESE AND SUN-DRIED TOMATO SOUFFLÉ SERVES 4

Every now and then a product or an ingredient comes along that can cheer your cooking almost effortlessly. Sun-dried tomatoes packed in olive oil are one such item. They add a wonderful warm Mediterranean flavour to sauces and casseroles and have none of the stridency of tinned or tubed tomato paste. Enterprising delicatessens, supermarkets and grocers carry them. You can grow so attached to the flavour, you just want to spread it on toast. It revolutionises spaghetti with tomato sauce and combines beautifully with the flavour of goat's cheese in this soufflé.

Don't be afraid of soufflés. In my experience they are quite subservient.

2 oz (60 g) butter, and a little more for greasing dish
1½ oz (45 g) flour, and a little more for dusting dish
¼ pt (150 ml) milk
¼ pt (150 ml) single cream
4 eggs and 1 more egg white
4 oz (120 g) fairly strong goat's cheese
2 heaped tsp sun-dried tomatoes
freshly ground black pepper

Pre-heat the oven to 220°C/425°F/gas mark 7. Butter a soufflé dish and lightly dust it with flour (or grated Parmesan cheese if you happen to have some). Melt the butter, stir in the flour to make a smooth roux and slowly add the milk and cream until you have a thick béchamel sauce. You may not need all the milk and cream. Cook gently for as long as you can spare the time in order fully to cook out the taste of flour. A few minutes will do if you are in a hurry. Remove the pan from the heat and, one by one, beat in the egg yolks. Crumble the goat's cheese and stir in, followed by the sun-dried tomatoes and the pepper. Stir only enough to distribute them roughly. Whisk the egg whites until stiff. Add two tablespoons of the egg white to the béchamel and mix gently. Fold in the rest of the whites, taking care not to squash the bounce out of them. Pour into the soufflé dish and cook in the oven for 20–25 minutes. The top should be golden, but a bit of sloppiness in the centre is desirable.

CHEESE FONDUE

A friend who used to do a job as a chalet party girl in ski resorts tells me that the only time the guests did not fall asleep over their evening meal was when she served cheese fondue. Then people stayed lively and chatty and confessed to having a whale of a time. It seems, therefore, a good idea for a celebratory meal. Hand brushing hand as you stab for bread, cheek brushing cheek as you watch the kirsch flame over the crusty cheese at the bottom of the casserole could lead to all kinds of interesting consequences. Also that wodge of cooked cheese that you ingest must act as some kind of Thames barrier to alcohol.

If you do not have a fondue set, in other words you have not recently been involved in a wedding, improvise with a flameproof casserole, a spirit lamp or electric ring and some forks.

1 clove of garlic
12 fl oz (375 ml) dry white wine
1 tsp lemon juice
12 oz (375 g) Gruyère cheese
8 oz (250 g) Emmental cheese
1 heaped tsp cornflour
2 fl oz (60 ml) kirsch or clear fruit brandy or more white wine
freshly ground black pepper
a little grated nutmeg
2 baguettes
pinch of bicarbonate soda, in case the fondue separates

Rub the fondue dish with the peeled clove of garlic and pour in the white wine. Heat the wine slowly and add the lemon juice, which will help in the binding of the wine and cheese. Sprinkle in the cheeses, which you have coarsely grated, and slowly bring the mixture to the boil, stirring all the while. Dissolve the cornflour in a small glass of kirsch, brandy or white wine and when the cheese mixture has melted and become creamy, stir it in. The cornflour helps thicken the fondue and ensures a silky texture. Season with pepper and nutmeg and pass round pieces of crusty bread for dipping. If the mixture should separate and the cheese take on the look of chewing gum, a pinch of bicarbonate of soda usually, magically, works a transformation. When the cheese has been reduced to a crust on the bottom, splash in another bit of kirsch, set it alight and, when the flames have died down, divide 'the croûton' among the guests.

DESIGNER PIZZA

California is arguably where it started, with Wolfgang Puck of the restaurant *Spago* and Alice Waters at *Chez Panisse*, but now the designer pizza is everywhere in America. Gone are the pepperoni sausage, mushrooms, chopped green peppers and mozzarella cheese, to be replaced by tomato coulis, prosciutto, roasted red peppers, shiitake mushrooms, chèvre and virgin olive oil. Basil has ousted oregano. As you may have gathered, expensive and delectable toppings are the key to designer pizza, plus a thin, crisp (less fattening) bread dough base. Dedicated slimmers use tortillas. A fast food has been transformed into a fine food and it will happen here in London's restaurants once customers are prepared to pay for it.

The recipe below is only a guideline. Once you have grasped the concept, you can invent your own creations, incorporating all the fashionable ingredients such as radicchio, sun-dried tomatoes, yellow pepper purée, Peking Duck, enoki mushrooms, confit of garlic, ricotta, grilled aubergine, tapenade (olive purée) and so forth. Go carefully, though; balance is the essence. You can, and probably should, make your own pizza dough (consult the bread recipe) and a nice touch is to incorporate an ingredient like chopped spring onions into it. But you can do this even with a pizza dough mix and that is what I am advising here.

1 lb (500 g) pizza dough mix
14 oz (400 g) tin of tomatoes or carton of sieved fresh tomatoes
1 dsp olive oil
splash of red wine
salt and pepper
pinch of sugar
3 tsp sun-dried tomatoes or 1 dsp tomato paste
3 oz (90 g) prosciutto or other raw ham
1 tbsp chopped fresh basil or 1 tsp dried basil
2 cloves of garlic, peeled and finely slivered
6 oz (175 g) goat's cheese, crumbled

Pre-heat the oven to 250°C/475°F/gas mark 9. Prepare the pizza dough according to the packet instructions. Roll out thinly and line the pizza pan(s) or cake tins. Either drain the tinned tomatoes and put them into a saucepan or empty the contents of the carton of sieved tomatoes into one. Add the olive oil, a splash of red wine, salt, pepper and a pinch of sugar. Reduce over heat until you have a spreadable purée. Towards the end add the sun-dried tomatoes or, failing them, tomato paste. Taste for seasoning. Let cool. Cover the dough with the tomato mixture. Arrange the prosciutto slices prettily and scatter on the goat's cheese. Dot with the basil and garlic. Bake for 15–20 minutes or until the crust is crisp and gold.

PASTA, RICE AND GRAINS

Where a few years ago people might have had recourse to Spag. Bol. for dinner and left pasta pretty much at that, the recent wide availability of fresh pasta – some fresher than others, it has to be said – has brought about a quite different attitude to it. Now the fresh kind appears sauced and polished in all manner of ways until you start to wonder if its economical quality is not being over-played by your friends. Even children, who seem universally to adore pasta, can get glum if served it too frequently.

In the flush of enthusiasm about fresh pasta, it seems to me that the virtues of a good Italian brand of the dried kind have been overlooked. Dried pasta has an agreeable robustness – an integrity – and spaghetti, made only from strong flour, has a quite different effect to egg-based pastas. Macaroni cheese – the pasta dish of my childhood – also tends to be ignored these days but, carefully made according to the recipe in this section, it can be both nostalgic and delicious. The Greek version, pastitsio, is excellent for informal entertaining and responds well to being made one day and re-heated the next. It is no barmy Italian myth that different shapes of pasta taste different.

It is, however, the interaction of the sauce with the pasta shape that creates the pleasing discrepancies. Shells, for example, will cradle a sauce, spirals will trap bits. Try to match your pasta to its accompaniment. A crucial thing about pasta is the cooking time, and packet instructions always seem to over-estimate this, so start testing for *al dente* long before the manufacturers consider you should.

The same is true of rice dishes, but in a different way. It is important to choose the right sort of rice for the job. Risotto is best made with Italian risotto rice, often called Arborio, which cooks to a soothing texture with a little resistance at the centre. Otherwise, with the exception of making rice pudding, I use basmati rice as I find its scent when cooking irresistible and the texture the finest. 'Easy-cook' seems to me a daft appellation for rice as, once you understand the principle of soaking the grain, rinsing and then adding roughly the same volume of liquid for cooking, it is easy to cook anyway.

Couscous has been made gratifyingly easy to cook due to manufacturers' techniques of pre-preparation. No longer need you soak, drain, spread and fumble it about. Warm water, or even boiling water (see page 93), does the trick. If you have never tried polenta, get to know this grain which, with its bready texture and sunny golden colour, becomes a new accessory in your cooking.

SERVES 4 PASTA WITH FRESH TOMATOES AND BASIL

When fresh basil with its smell of summer is around, try this sauce, which is one of my favourites with fresh pasta. The point is its freshness and coolness in contrast to the hot pasta.

4 tomatoes or 2 beefsteak tomatoes, skinned and chopped
4 spring onions, cleaned and finely chopped
1 tbsp finely chopped parsley
10–12 fresh basil leaves, roughly chopped
3 tbsp good olive oil
1 tbsp red wine vinegar
salt and freshly ground black pepper

Mix together all the ingredients and at the moment of serving pour the cold sauce on to 1 lb (500 g) hot drained pasta.

SERVES 4 SPAGHETTI WITH HARLEQUIN PEPPERS

One of the jollier sights in greengrocery shops is shiny, waxy, peppers in red, yellow and green. Tempting as Snow White's apple, I feel they also should be treated circumspectly and not just tossed into dishes to provide that dash of colour that some recipe writers are so fond of promoting.

To eat peppers at their best, they should be skinned, which is a somewhat tedious process but one that pays off in terms of the flavour. To do this you can either grill them, turning them until the skin chars and blisters, or put them in the oven until the skin starts to bubble away like a badly painted wall. Put them in a plastic bag to steam for 5 minutes. You then scrape away the skin, holding the peppers under a running tap. You can, of course, make the recipe below with just one colour of pepper. My inclination would be to leave out the green.

3 large sweet peppers in different colours
5 tbsp extra virgin olive oil
1 onion, peeled and chopped
2 fat cloves of garlic, peeled and slivered
salt and freshly ground black pepper
pinch of sugar (optional)
1 tsp red wine vinegar
14 oz (430 g) spaghetti, linguine, taglioni or other pasta

Skin the peppers, remove the stalk and seeds and slice into strips. Heat the oil in a shallow, large pan and fry the onion gently. Add the garlic slivers and fry a little longer without letting the garlic brown. Add the pepper strips and cook gently for as much time as you can allow (up to an hour), so that they almost melt into the oil. Taste for seasoning and consider if they would benefit from a pinch of sugar as well as salt and pepper. Stir in the vinegar. Cook your choice of pasta until *al dente*. Drain, toss with the peppers and serve in a warmed bowl.

SPAGHETTI ALLA PUTTANESCA   SERVES 4

Pasta is the obvious quick, inexpensive meal. Indeed, the teenage son of a friend of mine recently persuaded his father who was looking after him that he deserved a meal in a restaurant on the grounds that he could not be expected to eat pasta again. But for its fattening qualities when put with a sauce and cheese, I would eat pasta at least once a meal and there are probably enough different recipes and varieties that you could do this for a year without repeating a dish. The one below has ingredients easy to assemble from any delicatessen. The name means whore's spaghetti, which may refer to its gutsiness or to its sustaining quality. Include the chilli; it makes all the difference.

3 tbsp olive oil and a dribble for cooking the pasta
2–3 cloves of garlic, peeled and finely chopped
1 small fresh chilli or 2 dried red chillis
5–6 anchovy fillets, drained of oil or brine and rinsed
4 oz (120 g) large black olives
1 tbsp capers
1 × 7 oz (200 g) tin of tomatoes
1 tbsp tomato paste
1 lb (500 g) spaghetti
salt and freshly ground black pepper
finely chopped parsley or dried oregano

In a sauté pan heat the olive oil and gently cook the garlic and chilli, chopped if you wish or whole if you plan to remove it. Chop the anchovies roughly and add them to the oil. Stir until they break up. Stone and slice the olives, add them to the capers, the tomatoes and tomato paste. Stir and break up the tomatoes and simmer the sauce while you cook the spaghetti in masses of boiling water into which you have put a pinch of salt and a dribble of olive oil. Drain the pasta, heap it into a warm bowl. Taste the sauce and adjust the seasoning. Pour the sauce on to the pasta. Mix in lightly and sprinkle the dish with a little dried oregano or some finely chopped parsley. Green salad, crusty bread and a bottle of robust Italian red wine are the only other requirements.

SERVES 3-4   # SPAGHETTI CARBONARA

My children are never happier than when I answer Spaghetti Carbonara to their question of 'What's for dinner?' I often say it on a day when I have been less than efficient about shopping for most of the ingredients are usually stock items in the refrigerator. I do not say it too often though, as you can see it is not the healthiest of dishes. I have noticed that some people feel fearful about getting it right. If you add some cream to the eggs it obviates the risk of them curdling, but even if they do – if the hot spaghetti 'cooks' them rather too well – the resulting grainy texture is quite pleasant. Try to get pancetta ham from the delicatessen or otherwise use thinly sliced smoked streaky bacon.

1 tsp salt
1 tbsp olive oil or other vegetable oil
4 smallish or 3 large eggs
2 tbsp double cream
2 tbsp grated Parmesan cheese
5 oz (150 g) streaky bacon or pancetta ham, thinly sliced
14 oz (430 g) spaghetti
freshly ground black pepper

Boil up a large pot of water for the spaghetti, salt it and add a spoonful of vegetable oil or olive oil to stop the strands sticking together. Beat the eggs with the cream. Stir in the Parmesan. Chop the bacon into small pieces and fry slowly in a heavy frying pan, only adding butter or oil if sufficient fat for cooking is not present in the bacon. Cook the spaghetti and when it is *al dente*, drain it and return it to the pan. Add the bacon and a little of the fat. Mix around. Pour in the egg mixture and toss carefully. This should be done off the heat. Grind on black pepper with the *brio* perfected by Italian waiters and serve on heated plates or in shallow bowls.

SERVES 4   # PASTA WITH FRIED EGGS

It is often possible to make more of a meal by adding a fried egg. Perching one on top of corned beef hash, or ratatouille or cheese on toast, to give some random examples, adds extra protein and the yolk of the egg becomes almost a little sauce. This recipe, from *Pasta Perfect* by Anna del Conte, a compendium of good ideas, expands the theme. The author says it has always been a favourite supper dish of her family. 'It is as simple as it is deliciously satisfying.'

4 tbsp olive oil
3 cloves of garlic, peeled and bruised
½–1 dried chilli, de-seeded and crumbled
4 eggs
salt
12 oz (375 g) ziti or bucatini (you could substitute linguine or spaghetti)
2 oz (60 g) Pecorino, Romano, Parmesan or mature farmhouse Cheddar cheese, freshly grated

Heat half the oil with the garlic and chilli in a large frying pan and sauté until the garlic is coloured but not brown. Remove and discard the garlic. Break the eggs carefully into the pan and cook over a low heat until the whites are set. Sprinkle the whites only with salt (not the yolks or they will harden). Meanwhile, cook the pasta in plenty of boiling salted water. Drain, then immediately add the remaining oil to the pasta and toss well. Mix in the cheese of your choice. Divide the pasta into four portions and put each portion on to a heated individual plate. Place a fried egg on top of each portion and serve immediately.

ANGEL'S HAIR SOUFFLÉ   SERVES 4–6

Angel's hair is a variety of pasta which, as you might imagine, is composed of extremely thin strands. For some reason you are rarely offered it in London restaurants, although it is very popular in the United States and often sauced lightly and creatively.

This soufflé recipe, which may sound improbable but is actually very good, comes from *Beard on Pasta* by the late James Beard, one of the great American cookery writers. You could use fried bacon in place of the prosciutto but it would be a pity. If prosciutto seems too extravagant, however, look for the cheaper coppa in a delicatessen.

4 oz (120 g) angel's hair pasta
6 egg yolks
3½ oz (100 g) grated Cheddar, Parmesan or Gruyère cheese
6 oz (175 g) finely diced prosciutto
dash of Tabasco sauce
freshly ground black pepper
8 egg whites

Heat the oven to 190°C/375°F/gas mark 5. Cook the pasta according to the packet instructions – it should cook very quickly so test before the given time – and drain. Beat the egg yolks. An electric hand whisker is best for this. Keep going until they are thick and butter coloured; 5 minutes is no exaggeration. Stir in the cheese, prosciutto, Tabasco and pasta. Season with a few turns of the pepper mill. In a large clean bowl beat the egg whites until they hold their shape in billowing peaks. Stir a large spoonful of the whites into the yolk mixture and then fold in the rest of the whites gently but thoroughly. Pour the mixture into a buttered 3 pt (1.8 l) soufflé dish and smooth the top. Draw a circle with your finger on top of the soufflé about 2 in (5 cm) in from the rim. This will make the centre rise higher than the sides. Bake in the oven for 15–20 minutes.

SERVES 3-4 ## PASTA WITH GORGONZOLA SAUCE

This idea came from Marcella Hazan, one of my favourite writers on the subject of Italian cooking. It is worth searching out really good and freshly cut Italian Gorgonzola for this recipe. Other blue cheeses, such as the dismal Danish blue, will not give the correct combination of creaminess and piquancy that makes this such a delicious, supple dish. Now that freshly made pasta is so easy to buy, try to find either tagliatelle or fettuccine newly made rather than buying the boxed variety.

4 oz (120 g) Gorgonzola cheese
6 tbsp milk
1½ oz (45 g) butter
salt and freshly ground black pepper
12 oz (375 g) fresh pasta or slightly less dried pasta
2½ fl oz (75 ml) double cream
1–2 oz (30–60 g) freshly grated Parmesan cheese

Using a shallow enamelled iron pan or other flameproof dish that can later hold all the pasta, mash together over a low heat the Gorgonzola, milk, butter and salt and pepper to taste. A wooden spoon is the best implement. Cook for about a minute until the consistency is creamy. Turn off the heat. Cook the pasta, timing it according to whether it is fresh or dried. Seconds before the pasta is done (*al dente*), turn on the heat under the cheese and stir in the double cream. Add the drained pasta and toss it in the sauce. Sprinkle with the Parmesan cheese and serve on warmed plates.

NICE MACARONI CHEESE   SERVES 4

I call this nice macaroni cheese because I have had, and no doubt
you have had, the horrid variety; mean, pallid and gluey. However,
as with many dishes associated with childhood or institutions,
there is a punitive way of making it and an enticing way of making
it. The key to the latter, as indeed the key to any good recipe, is
the quality of the basic ingredients. If you use freshly grated
Parmesan cheese, farmhouse Cheddar, sweet-cured streaky bacon,
a splash of white wine in the sauce and unsalted butter in the roux,
you will end up with perhaps not a sophisticated or startling
dish but a jolly nice supper. Don't go too fancy; don't go using
prosciutto in the macaroni. It would be like casting Sophia Loren
against George Cole.

8–10 oz (250–300 g) macaroni (wholewheat if you wish)
1 tbsp oil
6 rashers of sweet-cured streaky bacon
1½ oz (45 g) butter and more to grease dish
1 onion, peeled and finely chopped
2 level tbsp flour
¾ pt (450 ml) milk
a splash of white wine
6 oz (175 g) grated farmhouse Cheddar cheese
2 oz (60 g) freshly grated Parmesan cheese
pinch of English mustard powder
pepper
1 tbsp fresh breadcrumbs
1 large beefsteak tomato, sliced

Boil the macaroni in masses of water into which you have put a
spoonful of oil until the pasta is tender; about 10–15 minutes.
Drain. Chop the bacon and fry it until fairly crisp. Drain on
kitchen paper and then mix into the macaroni. Melt the butter
and fry the onion gently until softened but not browned. Stir in
the flour and cook for a minute or two. Gradually add the milk,
then the wine, stirring until you have a smooth sauce. Add the
Cheddar cheese and half the Parmesan. Stir off the heat until the
cheese is melted and add a good pinch of mustard. Season with
black pepper. Fold the macaroni into the sauce. Turn into a
buttered shallow baking dish. Arrange the sliced tomato on top.
Scatter on the crumbs which you have mixed with the remaining
Parmesan. Heat through in a hot oven until the top is crisped.
Serve with a green salad as an accompaniment.

SERVES 4 ## PASTA WITH ANCHOVIES AND BROCCOLI

The pronounced flavour of broccoli contrasts well with that of
anchovies. The way they use this combination of flavours as a
pasta garnish in Apulia is with garlic and no cheese. In other parts
they might add grated Parmesan and, in still others, some chilli,
the last version being the one I favour. You can use spaghetti or
any pasta shape – bows might be nice. Make sure you do not
overcook the broccoli as it is then apt to turn a depressing wet
mackintosh colour.

1 lb (500 g) broccoli, divided into small florets
4 fl oz (120 ml) olive oil
4–6 anchovy fillets, drained of oil
2 cloves of garlic, peeled and thinly sliced
½ fresh chilli, finely chopped or 2 small red dried chillis
1 oz (30 g) butter
freshly ground black pepper
14 oz (430 g) spaghetti or other pasta

Bring a large quantity of water to the boil and boil the broccoli
florets for a minute or two, keeping them green and crisp. If you
like, as I do, to cook the stalks, slice them thinly on the diagonal
first. They add yet another texture. Drain the broccoli and keep
it warm. Cook the anchovy fillets and the garlic slivers in the oil,
stirring and mashing until the anchovies disintegrate. Add the
chilli and the butter and stir some more. Turn the broccoli gently
in this sauce and grind on some black pepper. Meanwhile cook
the pasta, drain and pour on the sauce. Mix carefully and serve,
perhaps with an extra dribble of oil.

SERVES 4 ## PASTA WITH ANCHOVIES AND
BREADCRUMBS

There has been a rash of pasta cooking books in the last few years,
presumably reflecting our enthusiasm for the stuff. *The Classic
Book of Pasta* by Vincenzo Buonassisi numbers the recipes and
goes up to 653, which is a recipe for pasta with roast game (giving
you the choice of boar, venison and roe buck). This seems to me
to be taking something Too Far, but many of the recipes, like the
one for pasta with anchovies and breadcrumbs from which this is
adapted, are agreeably simple.

6 anchovy fillets, drained of oil
2 cloves of garlic
6 tbsp olive oil
1 lb (500g) pasta (linguine maybe)
2 slices of stale white bread

Chop the anchovies roughly. Crush the garlic and heat it in half the olive oil but do not let it brown and cause bitterness. Remove the garlic and cook the anchovies gently until they fall apart and meld with the oil. Cook your pasta and when it is almost ready crumble the bread into the remaining oil in another small pan and fry until crisp and golden. Drain the pasta, place in a warmed bowl, pour on the anchovies and then the breadcrumbs. If you have some parsley to hand, chop a handful and sprinkle on because the combination of colours is good.

PRAWN PASTA   SERVES 4

Josceline Dimbleby has contributed several books to the excellent cookery list distributed by Sainsbury's supermarkets. Of *A Traveller's Tastes,* she said 'More than any of the others, this book is part of my life.' As a child she lived in various places abroad and since then she has become an enthusiastic and hopeful traveller, for whom food and recipes are both discoveries and a means of reliving experience. This recipe was chosen in part for its speediness; it is ideal for a quick supper. Buy the book for other astonishingly inventive and evocative ideas.

1 large bulb of fennel
6 tbsp virgin olive oil
4 cloves of garlic, peeled and cut in slivers
salt
12oz (375g) pasta shells
$\frac{1}{4}-\frac{1}{2}$ nutmeg
8oz (250g) peeled prawns
freshly ground black pepper

TO SERVE: grated Parmesan cheese

Chop the fennel into small pieces, reserving any leafy bits. Put 3 tbsp of the olive oil in a frying pan. Heat over medium heat and add the chopped fennel. Fry gently for about 10 minutes, then add the sliced garlic and cook for another 2–3 minutes. Remove from the heat and keep on one side. Bring a pan of salted water to the boil and add the pasta shells. While the pasta is cooking – it will take 12–15 minutes – grate the nutmeg into the frying pan of fennel and garlic. Add the remaining 3 tablespoons of olive oil and the prawns and season with a little salt and plenty of black pepper. Stir in any reserved fennel leaves. When the pasta has cooked, drain it and empty it into a heated serving bowl. If necessary, very gently re-heat the contents of the frying pan, and then turn it into the pasta, mixing well. Serve immediately, with grated Parmesan cheese if you like.

PASTA WITH POTTED SHRIMPS

Perfect Pasta, by Valentina Harris, from where I took the idea of using potted shrimps as a quick, easily purchased sauce, contains some good ideas. The shrimps should be at room temperature.

FOR EACH PERSON:
3 oz (90 g) pasta, preferably conchiglie or farfalle
1 small carton of potted shrimps
2 tbsp double cream

Cook the pasta in plenty of boiling water. When it is tender, drain and decant it into a warmed bowl. Mix in the potted shrimps and 2 tbsp double cream to moisten. Serve before the butter from the prawns is completely melted.

SERVES 4   ## FRESH PASTA WITH SMOKED TROUT AND FISH EGGS

4 oz (120 g) smoked trout
1 lb (500 g) fresh pasta
¼ pt (150 ml) double cream
4 tbsp fish eggs, such as caviar, lumpfish roe (known as Danish caviar)
or salmon eggs

Put four plates to warm. Skin and bone the smoked trout and carefully flake the flesh. Set aside. While you set to boil a large pot of water for the pasta, reduce the cream slightly in a small pan over medium heat. Cook the pasta until it is *al dente* – if it is fresh this should be only a matter of a minute or two, otherwise consult the packet but test the pasta some time before their suggested limit. Add the smoked trout to the hot cream and mix carefully with the drained pasta. Divide between the plates and crown each heap with a tablespoon of fish eggs. A pepper-mill should be at the ready.

PASTITSIO SERVES 6

Here is the Greek version of lasagne. Pastitsio often numbers among the offerings in Greek restaurants where it sits in its tin, solidly and patiently, growing ever cooler as the day wears on. It is infinitely nicer made at home, but on a hot day eating it warm rather than piping hot is nevertheless a good idea.

The trick to the dish is to cook the meat sauce enough to bubble away any excess liquid. This way the pie can be sliced into neat, compact squares. Try not to omit the seasonings of cinnamon and nutmeg. They contribute to a Middle Eastern authenticity. The correct macaroni to use is the variety like long fairly narrow-gauge tubes, but if you cannot find it, use the elbow-shape macaroni.

2 tbsp olive oil
2 onions, peeled and chopped
2 fat cloves of garlic, peeled and finely chopped
1 lb (500 g) minced beef or minced veal
4 fl oz (120 ml) milk
1 × 14 oz (400 g) tin of peeled tomatoes
2 tbsp tomato paste
a splash of red wine
1 level tsp ground cinnamon
1 heaped tsp oregano
salt and pepper
béchamel sauce made from 2 oz (60 g) butter, 2 oz (60 g) flour and about 1¼ pt (750 ml) skimmed milk
4 oz (120 g) grated Cheddar, Gruyère or Parmesan cheese
1 lb (500 g) macaroni
2 eggs, beaten
pinch of ground nutmeg

In the olive oil fry the onion and garlic until softened. Add the meat and cook, stirring until thoroughly browned. Add the milk and bubble it away (a technique that enriches the meat). Add the tomatoes, tomato paste, wine, cinnamon, oregano, sugar, salt and pepper. Simmer until you have a thick sauce. Into your béchamel sauce, stir half the cheese. Turn on the oven to 400°F/200°C/gas mark 6. Boil the macaroni in masses of salted boiling water until just done (*al dente*). Stir two tablespoons of the béchamel sauce into the meat sauce. Whisk the eggs and the nutmeg into the remaining béchamel, which will be used for the topping. In a rectangular baking tin or similar size ovenproof dish, make a thin layer of meat sauce. Add a layer of macaroni and continue this way, ending with a layer of noodles. Pour on the béchamel topping. Scatter on the remaining cheese and bake for about 45 minutes until puffy and golden. Pastitsio is at its best made and cooked one day and heated up the next.

SERVES 4 SPAGHETTI WITH CHICKEN LIVERS AND LEMON

Elizabeth David's *An Omelette and A Glass of Wine*, a compilation of articles written by Elizabeth David over the last thirty years, is a fascinating record of one writer's passionate perceptions on a subject that affects us all but is rarely accorded such elegance, erudition or asperity.

The recipe below comes from a chapter entitled 'Mafalda, Giovanna, Giulia', which gives some authentic Italian, and specifically Tuscan, dishes. I hope that in condensing it somewhat I have not misplaced Elizabeth David's effect – to lure you into cooking.

1 lb (500 g) spaghetti
5 oz (150 g) chicken livers
4–5 cloves of garlic, peeled
salt
3 oz (90 g) raw ham or coppa
3 fl oz (90 ml) olive oil
freshly ground black pepper
grated rind of 1 lemon
5 eggs
6 oz (175 g) grated Parmesan or Pecorino cheese
sprinkling of fresh nutmeg

Cook the spaghetti *al dente*. While it is cooking, clean and chop the livers, crush the garlic with a little salt (using less garlic if you prefer) and cut the ham into fine strips. Warm the olive oil, throw in the chicken livers and the ham, the garlic, salt, freshly milled pepper and the coarsely grated lemon peel. The cooking of all these ingredients should take scarcely three minutes. Now, in a big bowl, beat one whole egg and four yolks. Add the grated cheese and a sprinkling of nutmeg. When your spaghetti is ready, drain it and turn it into a big, deep, heated dish. Quickly pour the egg mixture into the sauté pan containing the chicken livers. Mix everything together thoroughly but away from the heat. Now amalgamate the sauce with the pasta, turning it over and over, as if you were making a salad. Serve on warm plates.

HAM, CHICKEN AND NOODLES WITH SOYA EGG

SERVES 4

The basis for this recipe and the notion of a soy-cooked egg came from one of Kenneth Lo's many books on Chinese cooking, *Healthy Chinese Cooking*. Since most of us have eggs around and conceivably some leftover chicken or ham, it seemed like an idea easy to assemble on the spur of the moment. A soya egg is also something you could drop into other areas of your cooking. The colours of this dish are particularly pretty – the yellow noodles, pink ham, beige chicken and mahogany egg scattered with the green and white of spring onions.

If you cannot buy Chinese egg noodles, Italian ones would suffice, but the colour is not so good. Nor is the richness of flavour. This is often served as a welcoming dish for a Chinese birthday party; the Chinese believe that eggs represent reproduction and continuity.

soy sauce, as required
4 hard-boiled eggs
4 spring onions or more, to taste
12 oz (375 g) Chinese or Italian egg noodles
2 pt (1.2 l) chicken stock (use stock cubes if necessary)
1 tbsp cornflour
4 oz (120 g) cooked ham, cut into matchsticks
8 oz (250 g) cooked chicken, cut into thin strips
freshly ground black pepper

Put about 1 in (3 cm) of soy sauce in a small pan and heat and turn the hard-boiled eggs in this until they take on a rich colour, a matter of quite a few minutes. Leave them in the pan with the heat off. Chop the cleaned spring onions finely. Cook the noodles according to the packet instructions. Drain. Heat the stock in a fairly large saucepan. Put the cornflour in a small bowl and mix until smooth with a couple of tablespoons of the stock. When the stock boils, stir in the cornflour mixture, and add the noodles and a splash of soy sauce for flavouring. Simmer for a few minutes. Divide the noodles and stock between four bowls. Place a soya egg on top of the noodles in each of the bowls. Make a heap of ham and a heap of chicken alongside the egg and scatter over the spring onions. Grind on some black pepper and serve. Take a bite at the egg with every few mouthfuls of noodles mixed with the chicken and ham – a nice contrast of textures.

SERVES 4 ## POTATO GNOCCHI

One of the perks of recipe writing is being sent cookery books. One that arrived recently is *Pasta from A–Z*, originally published in Italy, which has merit in its uncompromising Italianness. Indeed, should you be holidaying in Italy with scope for cooking, it would be a handy book to have along as some of the ingredients and pasta shapes referred to are more easily available there than here.

Here is the recipe for gnocchi made with potatoes rather than semolina. Though gnocchi might not spring to mind when the word pasta is mentioned, they are worth making for their extra-comforting quality and the grace with which they underline a sauce, be it a home-made tomato sauce or some pesto from a jar.

2 lb (1 kg) baking potatoes
salt and pepper
pinch of ground nutmeg
1 egg
10 oz (300 g) plain white flour

Boil the potatoes in their skins, peel and mash them. Season with salt and pepper and nutmeg. Heap them on to your work surface and make a well in the centre. Break in the egg and add a little of the flour. Begin to mix, gradually incorporating all the flour. The result should be a soft dough that does not stick to your fingers. Break off a piece of the dough and on a floured surface, roll it into a long thin sausage. Chop this into 1 in (3 cm) pieces and repeat the process with the rest of the dough. Roll each piece gently down the prongs of a fork to make indentations. Cook batches of the gnocchi in a large quantity of boiling, salted water; drain them with a skimmer as they rise to the surface. Keep them in a warm dish with some melted butter in a low oven while you cook the rest. Serve with a sauce of your choice.

SERVES 4-6 ## RISI E BISI

Risi e Bisi (rice and peas) is one of the definitive dishes of Venetian cooking. Traditionally it was offered to the Doges on the feast day of St Mark, the patron saint of the city. When peas are fresh, young and sweet, it is one of the nicest, simplest, dishes imaginable. I remember once interviewing a rather sophisticated art dealer about the food he liked and asking him that predictable question 'What is your favourite dish?', thinking it would be some elaborate confection utilising rare ingredients. He replied, 'Rice and peas.'

In Venice the dish is made not exactly as a risotto nor really a soup, but of a consistency that requires it to be eaten with a spoon. Try to find Arborio rice, which will contribute the correct texture, and if you have the time and energy make a stock with the pea pods to moisten the rice. The ham is optional, but does make it more of a meal.

1 onion, peeled and finely chopped
1 oz (30 g) butter, and a little more for serving
2 oz (60 g) raw ham, preferably pancetta or coppa, otherwise streaky bacon
2 lb (1 kg) peas in their pods
salt
1½ pt (900 ml) chicken or veal stock, or a mixture of stock and the water from boiling the pea pods
14 oz (430 g) Italian risotto rice
2 tbsp chopped fresh parsley, preferably the flat-leafed variety
freshly ground black pepper
2 oz (60 g) freshly grated Parmesan cheese

Sauté the onion in the butter until softened, then add the chopped ham and stir round for a few minutes. Add the shelled peas and a pinch of salt and turn around in the butter. Add 1¼ pt (750 ml) of stock, cover and simmer for about 10 minutes. Add the washed rice, the parsley and the rest of the stock. Cover again and cook slowly until the rice is tender but retains a bite. Check the seasoning, adding more salt if necessary and some freshly ground black pepper. Stir in half the cheese and a dab of butter. Serve, handing the rest of the Parmesan cheese separately.

RISOTTO WITH DRIED MUSHROOMS   SERVES 4-6

Whatever some magazine recipes might tell you, a risotto is *not* cooked rice mixed up with the contents of little foil-covered bowls that have been living in your fridge, made exotic by the addition of a tin of sweetcorn and some chopped red pepper. To make a good risotto you need patience, good stock and Italian risotto rice, often called Arborio rice. This is smaller and stubbier than ordinary long grain or basmati rice and has the quality of turning out slightly sticky, but retaining a chewy kernel, which gives texture to the assembly. I find a carefully made risotto so seductive that I like it in its simplest form using just rice, butter and oil, stock and grated Parmesan cheese, but it has to be admitted that the dried mushrooms and their liquid make it more of a dish. If you want to make a plain version, the instructions still hold.

1 oz (30 g) dried mushrooms (porcini are excellent)
1¾ pt (1 l) light chicken stock
1 onion or 3 shallots, peeled and finely chopped
3 tbsp vegetable oil
2 oz (60 g) butter
14 oz (430 g) Italian risotto rice
1 oz (30 g) freshly grated Parmesan cheese
salt (if necessary) and freshly ground black pepper

At least half an hour before cooking time, soak the mushrooms in lukewarm water. Drain through a sieve lined with kitchen paper and keep the liquid. Soak them again if you think they need to be softer or cleaner. Bring the stock to simmering point. In a heavy-bottomed pan sauté the onion or shallot in the oil and half the butter until soft. Add the rice and stir until it is absorbed. Continue for about 10 minutes, adding a ladleful of hot stock each time the rice dries out. Now add the mushrooms and ¼ pt (150 ml) of the mushroom liquid. As this becomes absorbed, add more mushroom liquid bit by bit until it is finished. If you need more liquid to finish cooking the rice, use stock or hot water. Mix in the rest of the butter and the Parmesan. Taste for saltiness and grind on some black pepper. Turn into a hot serving dish and offer more grated cheese separately.

SERVES 4-6 # NASI GORENG (FRIED RICE)

This recipe comes from a book called *Easy Eastern Cooking* by Ranse Leembruggen. Ranse was born in Bangkok in 1945 while his parents were laying the Kuala Lumpur–Bangkok railway under Japanese rule. He started cooking after the family had moved to a jungle village in Malaysia where, with wok and brazier, he fed immigrant workers. The story takes an unlikely turn when he was sent to relatives in Scotland and to a job as an apprentice welder in a Glasgow shipyard. Soon he was feeding the dockers. Since then he has trained as a chef and now has three restaurants. Nasi Goreng is usually a favourite of anyone who likes Indonesian food. The method below produces authentic-tasting results (I would increase the number of prawns). Serve it with prawn crackers, which, when you buy them, look like chips of plastic, but puff up miraculously on frying.

2 eggs
pinch of salt
3 tbsp vegetable oil
4 oz (120 g) onions, peeled and diced
1 clove of garlic, crushed
8 oz (250 g) minced beef
2 rashers streaky bacon, diced
½ tsp chilli powder
1 tsp paprika
1 tbsp soy sauce
1 tsp brown sugar
1 tsp tomato ketchup
1 lb (500 g) cooked rice
1 oz (30 g) cooked prawns

FOR SERVING (OPTIONAL):
cucumbers
tomatoes
fried onions
prawn crackers

Beat the eggs with a pinch of salt. Using 1 tbsp of oil, make a flat omelette. Set aside and keep warm. Heat the remaining oil, fry the onions and garlic until soft. Add the beef, bacon, chilli powder, paprika, soy sauce, brown sugar and ketchup and sauté over high heat until the meat is cooked. Add the rice and prawns and stir well until the rice is heated through – about 8 minutes. Transfer to a warm dish. Slice the omelette into thin strips and scatter on top. Garnish, if liked, with cucumbers, tomatoes and fried onions – and the prawn crackers.

COUSCOUS MADE EASY SERVES 4-6

Making roast chicken one Sunday lunch, I wanted to use as a stuffing something to hand and found some couscous. Late as usual in the preparations, I poured some boiling water on to the grains, thinking that all would come all right, light and free from lumps, after it had been baked inside the bird. In fact the grains swelled beautifully after only minutes of soaking and were nearly 'cooked'.

Most cookery books that would have you fool about wetting and separating and spreading out and steaming the grains twice are suffering from a hangover from the days when couscous was not so effectively pre-prepared. It is now almost an instant food. A real Tunisian or Moroccan couscous accompanied by a stew takes time and patience and a long list of ingredients. This is a simplified, no doubt inauthentic, version, but one sympathetic to the needs of the working person.

1 chicken, jointed (unless you want just a vegetable stew)
spices e.g. ground cumin, coriander, cayenne, ginger or cinnamon
salt and pepper
2 tbsp olive oil
2 large carrots, peeled and cut into large chunks
1 × 14 oz (400 g) tin of chickpeas
1 lb (500 g) couscous
2 courgettes
2 tomatoes
3½ oz (100 g) frozen broad beans or peas
1 tbsp raisins (optional)
1 bunch of fat spring onions
harissa or chilli sauce

Rub the chicken joints with your choice of spices plus salt and pepper. Place in the bottom of a large pot into which you can fit a metal sieve or colander, or use a steamer. Add water to cover and olive oil. Add the carrots and drained chickpeas. Set to simmer on the stove. Put the couscous in a large bowl and pour on boiling water to just cover. Let it swell and when cool, rake through with your fingers, pinching out any lumps. If you think it can absorb more water, add some. Put the couscous to steam in a sieve or colander over the stew. After about 40 minutes add the sliced courgettes, sliced tomatoes, broad beans or peas, raisins (if used) and spring onions. Simmer until the chicken is done, about another 15 minutes. Season. Tip the couscous in a heap on to a large serving dish. Mix in a little butter. Serve the stew separately. Mix a little of the broth in a bowl with harissa or chilli paste and hand round to those who want to spike the dish a bit.

SERVES 4-6   # TABBOULEH

Nodding, as sometimes I do, in the direction of healthy eating, I assemble this Lebanese dish to have on hand should I want to snack, or, as the Americans put it, graze. It is a good stand-by in your refrigerator since it keeps well for a couple of days, but it also constitutes a delicious first course for a meal and can look pretty when served with crisp lettuce leaves as scoops.

Bulghur or burghul, cracked wheat, is sold in delicatessens,

Middle Eastern groceries and health food shops. It is important to get the substance that looks like tiny grains and not an English variety of cracked wheat that is flaky. If you have no luck finding it, couscous will do almost as well. With its hefty quantity of parsley tabbouleh is a great source of iron and Vitamin C. Mint adds freshness and lemon sharpness. Once hooked, you can become addicted. The quantities below are a guideline only. Feel free to dabble with the proportions. Middle Eastern recipes were never precise. But they are always generous.

4 oz (120 g) cracked wheat
1 bunch of spring onions, trimmed and finely chopped
2 large tomatoes
3 oz (90 g) fresh parsley, washed and finely chopped
3 tbsp finely chopped fresh mint (less if dried)
3 tbsp lemon juice
3 tbsp olive oil
salt and freshly ground black pepper

TO SERVE: *lettuce leaves*

Pour cold water on to the cracked wheat to cover and leave to soak and swell. Drain in a sieve and then squeeze out what water you can with your hands. If the grains still seem waterlogged, spread them on a clean tea-towel, but this is the counsel of perfection. Put the cracked wheat in a bowl, add the spring onions and mix energetically. Plunge the tomatoes into boiling water for a minute. Remove them, peel off the skins and dice the flesh, discarding the pips and juice. Add the chopped tomato, parsley, mint, lemon juice, olive oil, and salt and pepper to taste. Mix and taste to see if you wish to emphasise any flavour. Leave a while for the flavours to develop and serve on individual plates or heaped on to a pretty dish. Leaves of iceberg, cos or Webb's lettuce should be offered alongside.

POLENTA SERVES 4-6

An Italian country kitchen's polenta was 'more than food, it was a rite'. So writes Marcella Hazan in *The Classic Italian Cookbook*. It was made daily in an unlined copper kettle, the *paiolo,* which was always kept hanging at the ready on a hook in the centre of the fire place. Marcella Hazan continues, 'The hearth was usually large enough to accommodate a bench on which the family sat, warming itself at the fire, talking, watching the glittering meal stream into the boiling kettle encouraging the tireless stirring of the cook. When the polenta was done, there was a moment of joy as it was poured out in a steaming golden circle on the beechwood top of the *madia*, a cupboard where bread and flour were stored.' There is a great scene along these lines in the film *Tree of Wooden Clogs*.

This solid porridge of cornmeal can be served hot with butter and cheese, or, after it has cooled and hardened, it can be cut up and fried, grilled, deep fried or baked. It accompanies well any roast meat or grilled chops and sausages. It is particularly good as a foil for game birds. Fried polenta, which obtains a crust, is to my mind the most interesting form. The instructions are below. Grilled polenta can make a wonderful snack when spread with Gorgonzola or any ripe strong cheese. Buy the coarse variety of corn meal for the most gritty result. Most health food shops and enterprising supermarkets stock it.

salt
12 oz (375 g) coarse grained corn meal
vegetable oil for frying

Bring about three pints of water to the boil in a large solid saucepan and add a good pinch of salt. Reduce the heat so that the water is simmering and add the corn meal in a steady, thin stream. While adding it, stir with a wooden spoon in a clockwise direction. This may sound cabalistic, but it is evidently important. Continue stirring for about 20 minutes. When the polenta begins to lurch away from the side of the pan it is done. Pour on to a large plate or other cool surface, let it get cold and set, then slice into pieces about ½ in (1.5 cm) thick for frying. The traditional method is with a tautly held thread. Fry in hot vegetable oil until a crust forms, turning once.

If you want to eat plain boiled polenta, serve from the pot with generous additions of butter and Parmesan cheese.

FISH AND SHELLFISH

Few can have escaped noticing that fish is held to be good for you. From mothers and school teachers promising it will make you brainy, to government health reports remarking on its lack of cholesterol and presence – sometimes – of beneficial oils, fish has had a good press. The modern style of French cooking, concentrating on freshness and immediacy, has given fish new clout in the main course section of menus.

An encouraging sign, in London anyway, is the increase of fishmongers and of wet fish counters in supermarkets. Should you be one of those mythical housewives, or househusbands, who are reported to be nervous of handling fish, all I can say is that it is worth getting over the fright and that your fishmonger can be your friend. If you really do not like a fishy stare or a network of bones, he or she will behead and fillet fish for you.

Fish dishes in restaurants tend to go from the sublime to the cor blimey, from steamed fillet of turbot to deep-fried fish and chips, with little middle ground. Home is therefore the place to explore the middle ground, the soupy dishes such as bourride and clam chowder, good versions of old standbys like cod with egg sauce, fish pie and fish cakes and the homely but nourishing species such as herrings.

Eating in is also the time to make affordable such dishes as sashimi and gravad lax that always are wildly priced on restaurant menus.

A supply of canned fish, such as anchovies and tuna and frozen items such as kipper fillets, means that fish dishes can be prepared at whim. Salt cod, another good store-cupboard buy, is a twenty-four-hour whim. Fish is also amenable to quite vigorous spicing and the Fish Steaks au Poivre recipe in this section will convince any doubter that fish is just as bully for you as beef.

BOURRIDE SERVES 4

There are many people who will tell you that it is not possible to make a good bouillabaisse in England as the correct varieties of fish, such as 'rascasse', are almost impossible to buy. What is also missing, of course, is the Mediterranean sea nearby. However, there is no reason why one cannot produce an authentic and delicious version of another Provençal fish dish, bourride. All it requires is a firm white fish and firm affection for garlic. The sun-coloured sauce for bourride is based on the garlicky mayonnaise aïoli. If you can persuade your fishmonger to give you some heads and tails for the stock, it can only improve matters.

2 lb (1 kg) white fish, such as bass, bream, grey mullet, cod, halibut; choose one variety or a mixture

FOR THE AÏOLI:
4 cloves of garlic
salt
2 egg yolks
½ pt (300 ml) extra-virgin olive oil

FOR THE COURT BOUILLON:
4 pt (2.4 l) water
fish trimmings
1 onion, peeled and thickly sliced
1 carrot, peeled and cut into chunks
a piece of fennel or ½ tsp fennel seeds
bay leaf
parsley
piece of orange peel
¼ pt (150 ml) white wine
salt and pepper
1 small French loaf, cut into slices and baked in the oven or toasted

Make the aïoli by crushing the garlic cloves with a little salt, stirring them into the egg yolks in a bowl and adding the oil very gradually, as you do for making mayonnaise. The result should be as thick as ointment. Prepare the court bouillon by simmering together the water with fish heads or trimmings and the seasonings detailed above, for about 15 minutes. Strain and poach your fish in this liquid, brought to the simmer until cooked. Timing depends on the choice of fish and its thickness, but it is unlikely to take more than 15–20 minutes. While the fish is cooking put the aïoli, reserving 2 tbsp, into a bowl which will fit into a pan with hot water in it, or into a double boiler if you have one. Remove a ladleful of fish stock and whisk it into the aïoli while it is over simmering water. Add another ladleful and stir for five minutes until you have an only slightly thickened sauce. Spread two slices of toast per person with a dab of the reserved aïoli. Place in a shallow warmed serving dish. Lay the fish on top and pour the sauce around. Serve with the remaining toast.

SERVES 3-4   ## CLAM CHOWDER

Clam chowder is a Yankee dish often eaten as a meal in itself rather than just a soup. New Englanders feel very strongly about what should and what should not be included as ingredients and my heart goes out to a certain Maine legislator named Seeder who, in 1939, introduced a bill to make it illegal to add tomatoes to the pot. I think cooked tomatoes add little to any dish, except *perhaps* tomato sauce, and this soup, traduced by any canned version, is best when it is just a combination of clams, salt pork, potatoes, onions and milk.

There is nothing like the selection of clams you find in the States available here, and even though some are appearing in fishmongers, a tin of clams in their juice works fine in the recipe below. Find whole clams, not minced ones.

4 oz (120 g) salt pork or a thick slice of gammon or bacon, diced
a little vegetable oil
1 onion, chopped
3 potatoes, peeled and cut into $\frac{1}{2}$ in (1.5 cm) cubes
1 pt (600 ml) milk
1 × 7 oz (200 g) tin of clams
$\frac{1}{2}$ tsp dried thyme or fennel seeds
salt and freshly ground black pepper

TO SERVE: *chopped fresh parsley*
a little double cream (optional)
pinch of cayenne pepper (optional)
crackers, such as water biscuits

Fry the salt pork in a little vegetable oil until it is cooked and the fat is crisped. Remove the pork. Fry the chopped onion until soft, then add the potatoes, milk, juice from the tin of clams, thyme and pepper. Taste for salt before adding any. Simmer until the potatoes are tender. Stir in the clams and the pork and simmer again until they are heated through. An optional garnish is a swirl of double cream sprinkled with cayenne pepper. In any case try to have some chopped parsley for sprinkling over because the colours of the chowder – the creamy milk, the beige clams and the rosy pork – are enhanced by a flourish of green. Serve in heated bowls with crackers as an accompaniment.

FISH STEAKS AU POIVRE SERVES 4

I contributed this recipe, among others, for an article called 'Lightning Food' in the first edition of the foodie glossy *À La Carte*. In some readership survey they later conducted, this way of preparing fish as you might do steak emerged as being particularly popular.

It is quick and mildly impressive and, surprisingly, the flavour of the fish can stand up to the nitty-gritty of black peppercorns. I once very successfully treated a large fresh tuna steak this way, but you seldom find that in the fishmongers and it is expensive when you do. Cod is my recommendation. I think cod is under-rated. Try to obtain steaks rather than fillets.

4 cod steaks or steaks from other firm-fleshed fish such as halibut or haddock
sea salt
2 heaped tbsp whole peppercorns (black or mixed black and white)
1 tbsp plain flour
2 tbsp vegetable oil
2 oz (60 g) butter

FOR THE SAUCE:
$\frac{1}{2}$ pt (300 ml) good stock (veal stock if you have it)
$\frac{1}{4}$ pt (150 ml) white wine or a squeeze of lemon juice
a nut of butter or $\frac{1}{4}$ pt (150 ml) double cream

Trim the fish if necessary to present nice, neat steaks. Sprinkle them with sea salt. Crush the peppercorns coarsely; putting them in a plastic bag and smashing them with a rolling pin is an effective method. Mix with the flour. Press this mixture into the fish steaks, covering them as evenly as possible. Heat the oil and butter in a frying pan or sauté pan and cook the steaks carefully, turning once. When the fish is almost cooked – a knife winkled in next to the bone reveals opacity almost right through – pour in the stock down the side of the pan (i.e. don't douse the fish). When the fish is quite cooked, remove it and keep it warm. To make the sauce, add the wine or lemon juice to the pan and boil it energetically until about a cupful of liquid remains. Taste for seasoning and either use the sauce as it is, with a nut of butter whisked in, or add the cream and continue to boil, stirring, until you have a rich, well amalgamated sauce. Check again for seasoning and pour the sauce around, not over, the fish. Plain boiled potatoes or rice are suitable accompaniments.

INDIAN BARBECUED FISH
SERVES 4

This spicy barbecue sauce is particularly good with fish, but it could also be used with chicken. If so, the meat should be allowed to marinate in it for longer. The optimum way of cooking the fish is over charcoal, but if this is not practical just line a grill pan with foil and cook the fish under the grill. The spices given below need not be adhered to meticulously; they are a guideline. If the array of individual spices seems daunting, use 1 level tablespoon garam masala from a recently purchased tin.

1 dsp ground coriander
2 tsp ground cumin
½ tsp turmeric
1 tsp cinnamon
1 tsp fennel seeds
1 tsp black onion seeds (kalonji) optional
1 onion, peeled and roughly chopped
4 cloves of garlic
1 in (3 cm) square peeled piece fresh ginger root (more if you like the flavour)
1 small green chilli, de-seeded, or pinch of chilli powder
juice of 1 lemon
½ pt (300 ml) plain yogurt
2 lb (1 kg) fish; choose either one large fish, several smaller fish or fish steaks e.g. cod
salt and freshly ground black pepper

TO SERVE: *lemon quarters*
raw onion rings
chopped fresh coriander, optional

Grind the spices if you are starting with them in their whole form. In a liquidiser or food processor whizz together the onion, peeled garlic cloves, ginger root roughly chopped, fresh chilli, lemon juice and 2 tbsp of the yogurt. Add the rest of the yogurt and spices, season with salt and pepper and blend again. Cut slits in the body of whole fish. Rub the marinade into the fish, both inside and out for whole fish, and leave covered by the rest of the marinade for about 2 hours. When it comes to cooking, shake off the excess marinade and grill over a medium heat until the flesh is opaque and the skin crisps. One of those sandwich-shaped metal contraptions makes grilling fish on a barbecue much more satisfactory. Season. Serve with lemon quarters, onion rings and, if possible, chopped fresh coriander.

FISH PLAKI   SERVES 4–5

Fish is so much the darling of the *nouvelle cuisine* chefs that there is little these days, in restaurants anyway, between fish in batter as in a chippie and steamed fillets surrounded by some nancy little sauce in high-priced shrines to gastronomy. This Mediterranean method of cooking fish has a welcome robustness. If you are a lover of Greece, as I am, you will probably have encountered fish cooked in this matter with the almost unavoidable, but poignantly summery, mélange of tomatoes, onions, garlic, lemons and olive oil. Any firm-fleshed white fish takes readily to this treatment, but given the price of varieties like halibut and turbot, cod is perhaps most to the point. This is also an amenable dish to varying degrees of temperature; it can be served hot, cold, when the juices turn to a nice jelly, or lukewarm – as in Greece.

1½ lb (900 g) firm-fleshed white fish, preferably in steaks
1 lemon, squeezed and sliced afterwards
salt and pepper
3 tbsp virgin olive oil
2 onions, peeled and finely sliced
2 cloves of garlic, peeled and slivered
4 tomatoes, peeled and sliced
fresh parsley or dill or mint
5 fl oz (150 ml) white wine
pinch of sugar

Sprinkle the fish with some of the lemon juice and season with salt and pepper. In the olive oil, soften the onions and garlic. Add the tomatoes, parsley and white wine. If you are using anaemic-looking tomatoes, put in a pinch of sugar. Cook until the sauce is somewhat reduced and tastes good, using your judgement about more lemon juice etc. Oil a baking dish. Lay in the fish. Pour on the sauce and arrange slices of the squeezed lemon on top. Cook in a moderate oven, 180°C/350°F/gas mark 4, for about 45 minutes.

SERVES 4   ROASTED FISH WITH ANCHOVY SAUCE

Fishmongers need our support if they are not to end up filleted, battered, crumbed and frozen. A whole fish is easy to cook and turns out much more festive than the googly-eyed creature might imply. Choose sea bass if you are feeling flush, but the cheaper grey mullet, red bream or haddock actually stand up better to the quite forceful anchovy sauce. It couldn't be easier and yet is mysteriously good. It goes well also on boiled vegetables, for example celeriac or celery or kohlrabi, is not unthinkable with boiled chicken and makes a change from the tuna fish sauce with veal, as in vitello tonnato.

1 whole fish, weighing about 2–3 lbs (1–1.5 kg)
fresh herbs: fennel, dill or parsley
1 bay leaf
1 slice of lemon
salt and freshly ground black pepper
a little olive oil

FOR THE SAUCE:
2 oz (60 g) butter
1 × 2 oz (50 g) tin of anchovy fillets, drained of oil·
½ pt (300 ml) double cream
freshly ground black pepper

Have the fishmonger clean the fish, leaving on the head and tail. Turn on the oven to 220°C/425°F/gas mark 7. Using a small sharp knife, make three diagonal slashes on each side of the fish, cutting practically down to the bone. Tuck herbs and the bay leaf, plus a slice of lemon, into the body cavity. Rub salt and freshly ground black pepper into the surfaces of the fish, making sure that some topples into the slashes. Trickle olive oil over the fish and place in a roasting pan. Put into the pre-heated oven. An average-size fish should be cooked in approximately 25–30 minutes. The cuts in the sides will enable you to see if the flesh is opaque to the bone. To make the sauce, melt the butter in a frying pan or sauté pan. Add the anchovies and stir around until they break up and more or less disintegrate. Add the cream, bring to the boil and stir. Add some freshly ground black pepper and taste to see if the sauce could stand the addition of another anchovy. The flavour should be robust. Carefully lift the fish, whose skin should be brown and crisp, on to a serving dish and serve the sauce separately. Plain boiled potatoes are the best accompaniment.

SASHIMI   SERVES 4

If the idea of eating raw fish gives you the willies – but, think, have you eaten oysters? – then this recipe is only of academic interest. But if you have eaten sashimi or sushi in Japanese restaurants or had salads garnished with thinly sliced raw fish, and wished you could recreate the dishes at home for much less money, here is how.

What you must have is a fishmonger on whom you can rely to sell you only the freshest fish. Aim to buy two or three varieties of fish to achieve a contrast in colour and texture. The pink of salmon is pretty. Endeavour also to find small tins of powdered

Japanese horseradish called *wasabi* (available in oriental super-markets) or, failing that, fresh ginger root, for both serve a digestive function as well as being complementary flavours.

12 oz (375 g) fillets of fresh fish: choose from salmon, bream, halibut, turbot, trout, sole or whatever else looks good
1 large Japanese radish (daikon) or mouli, or a selection of interesting salad leaves
2 tbsp wasabi or 2½ in (6 cm) piece of fresh ginger root
5 fl oz (150 ml) light soy sauce (shoyu or tamari)

Trim the fish fillets of any bits of skin or bone and put them in a colander. Pour boiling water over them and then immediately plunge them into cold water. This does not cook the fish, but it does blitz any surface bacteria. Using an exceedingly sharp knife, cut the fish into slices, either thickish or thin according to preference. *Aficionados* prefer the thick and, be assured, raw fish does not have a fishy flavour. Grate the cleaned radish, or wash and dry the salad leaves. Arrange a heap of radish or salad on four pretty plates or in four bowls. Arrange the slices of fish as aesthetically as possible on, or beside, the salad. Mix the wasabi with a little water to form a paste. Wait 10 minutes for its pungency to develop and put a teaspoonful beside the fish in each of the plates or bowls. Divide the soy sauce between four shallow bowls. Each diner mixes the wasabi to taste into the soy and dips in the fish slices lightly. If you are using ginger, peel the root and grate it into the soy sauce.

SERVES 4

POACHED FISH BALLS WITH EGG AND LEMON SAUCE

I once contributed this recipe to an article on the joys of mince, but it was not used. One of the joys of mince is that it is quick to cook. Another is that it is relatively cheap, another that it is receptive to varied flavourings. Minced fish might strike you as an odd commodity, but in the part of North London where I live they sell it and, should you fail to find it, you can simply buy equal quantities of each of two kinds of white fish (no oily varieties) and chop them in a food processor or mincer.

As when making gnocchi or dumplings, consigning the mixture in spoonfuls to simmering liquid seems to require an act of faith, but be assured that the egg white and Matzoh meal between them will hold the balls together. If you cannot buy Matzoh meal, use very fine breadcrumbs. I once made this for a Jewish friend on the grounds that it resembled gefilte fish. I don't think it does much, but he seemed to like it and said he was touched.

1 lb (500 g) minced fish
2 egg whites
2 level tbsp fine Matzoh meal
1 heaped tsp finely grated ginger root
1 heaped tsp finely chopped fresh parsley or coriander
salt and freshly ground black pepper

FOR THE STOCK:
1 onion, peeled
1 carrot, peeled
½ tsp fennel seeds, or a piece of fennel root
a little lemon juice
a little white wine

FOR THE SAUCE:
2 egg yolks
juice of ½ lemon

Add the stock ingredients to a large pan of water and bring to a simmer. Mix the fish with the egg whites, Matzoh meal and seasonings, adding more meal, which has a binding but not ponderous effect, if necessary to produce a consistency that can be formed into balls. Using a dessertspoon, slide balls of the fish mixture into the water. Poach for about 10 minutes, never letting the water get much beyond a shudder. Meanwhile mix the egg yolks and half the lemon juice in a bowl. Remove ½ pt (300 ml) of stock from the pan. Whisk 2 tbsp of it into the yolks. Pour the rest into a small heavy pan. Add the yolk mixture and stir over low heat until slightly thickened. Taste and add more lemon juice if you like an overt citron flavour. Remove the fish balls with a slotted spoon. Place them in a warmed serving dish. Slice the carrot from the stock thinly and put a round of carrot on each fish ball. Pour the sauce around, or serve it separately.

BETH'S FISH CAKES SERVES 4

These are the fish cakes my sister sells like hot cakes at Green's Champagne Bar and Restaurant in Duke Street, St James's. Fish cakes are enjoying a vogue at the moment – probably entirely due to her – and some true devotees maintain that they should only be accompanied by tomato ketchup. A gutsy tomato sauce or a parsley sauce is served at Green's.

I think a tartare sauce would also go well. Assuming you are making it yourself, which of course I assume you are, mix into $\frac{1}{4}$ pt (150 ml) mayonnaise, 1 tbsp each of chopped capers, gherkins and parsley, one finely chopped shallot and lemon juice, salt and pepper to taste. A mixture of fish, as below, is good, but if necessary just go with haddock or cod.

8 oz (250 g) fresh cod fillets
8 oz (250 g) fresh haddock fillets
milk to cover fish
1 onion, peeled and chopped
a little oil
a little butter
8 oz (250 g) potatoes, boiled and mashed with pepper, salt, nutmeg and 2 oz (60 g) butter
1 tbsp chopped fresh parsley
2 eggs
a little plain flour
fresh breadcrumbs
vegetable oil

Cook the fish in milk to cover until it flakes easily (about 5 minutes). Sauté the onion in a little oil and butter until it is soft. Mix the drained fish, onion and mashed potatoes together. Add parsley and season with a little salt and pepper. Add one of the eggs and mix well. Shape the mixture with your hands into four or six flat cakes. Flour them lightly. Beat the second egg in a shallow plate. Coat the cakes with beaten egg, then with bread crumbs. Fry in hot vegetable oil until golden brown and well heated through.

SERVES 4-6   # FISH PIE

This is one of those dishes that has the potential for horror or for delight. Badly made, with a gluey sauce and top-heavy with lumpy mashed potato, it will just confirm the undesirability of fish in some people's minds. With a bit of thought, for example using some smoked fish as well as white fish, adding some prawns for colour and for their image of luxury, mashing the potatoes with generous amounts of butter and hot milk and seasoning them well, fish pie can be a treat. It is also a good dish to make when entertaining: timing is not crucial and, for some reason, fish pie is not served all that often.

12 oz (375 g) smoked haddock (try to buy Finnan haddock)
12 oz (375 g) fresh haddock or cod
¾ pt (450 ml) milk
about ½ pt (300 ml) water
1 oz (30 g) butter
1½ oz (45 g) flour
salt and freshly ground black pepper
squeeze of lemon juice
4 oz (120 g) peeled prawns
2 hard-boiled eggs, sliced
chopped fresh parsley
1½ lb (750 g) potatoes, boiled and mashed with plenty of butter and hot milk

Pre-heat the oven to 190°C/375°F/gas mark 5. Put the fish in an oven dish large enough to hold it in one layer. Pour on the milk and water. The fish should be more or less covered. Cook in the oven for about 20 minutes or until the fish flakes away easily from the skin and bones. In a heavy-bottomed saucepan make a roux with the butter and flour. Stir in enough of the fish poaching liquid to make a sauce with the consistency of double cream. Season with salt, pepper and lemon juice. Carefully fold in the flaked fish, the prawns, hard-boiled eggs and parsley. Pour into a pie dish and cover with the mashed potato. Plough the expanse of potato with the prongs of a fork. Dot with butter and bake in the oven for half an hour or until the potato is lightly browned.

BAKED COD WITH EGG SAUCE SERVES 4

If you have done time in any British institution, be it school, the services or a hospital, you have probably had a gloomy version of this dish which, when reasonably painstakingly made, can be one of the highlights of our indigenous cuisine. Fresh cod has a lovely flavour and if you make your béchamel with milk in which you have steeped flavourings, the sauce will be as good as any fancy French number. A few plainly boiled potatoes are a fitting accompaniment and, since bacon goes well with both cod and eggs, I might garnish the plates with a couple of crisply fried rashers of unsmoked streaky bacon.

4 cod steaks
1 oz (30 g) butter
splash of white wine
salt and freshly ground black pepper

FOR THE SAUCE:
½ pt (300 ml) milk (skimmed if you wish)
1 small onion, peeled
1 bay leaf
2 cloves
a few black peppercorns
1 oz (30 g) butter
1 oz (30 g) plain flour
2 hard-boiled eggs, finely chopped
1 tsp anchovy essence
1 tsp finely chopped parsley
salt and pepper

Turn on the oven to 180°C/350°F/gas mark 4. Wrap the fish loosely in foil, encasing the butter, white wine and a seasoning of salt and pepper (if you have no white wine use lemon juice). Place in an ovenproof dish in the pre-heated oven for 30 minutes.

During that time make the sauce. Put the milk into a heavy-bottomed saucepan with the onion, bay leaf, cloves and pepper-corns and bring to a just shuddering heat. Let it steep for at least another 10 minutes. In another pan, melt the butter and stir in the flour. Cook for a few minutes. Strain in some of the flavoured milk, stir until smooth and then add some more. You want to end with a thickish sauce as you will dilute it further with the juices from cooking the fish.

Near the time of serving, pour off the juices from the oven dish, stir them into the sauce and then add the chopped hard-boiled eggs, the anchovy essence and the parsley. Stir gently and taste for seasoning. Jettison the fish's foil wrapping and pour the sauce over the cod steaks in their hot dish.

SERVES 4   COD WITH BACON AND MUSHROOMS

Cod and bacon are a good combination and this a quick and simple supper dish. I have never understood why cod is not more highly prized (could it be the name?) for the flavour is excellent and, just as important, the texture is appealing, with firmer flakes than you find with some of the classier species like halibut or turbot. Try to find cod steaks cut to a thickness of about 1½ in (4 cm). Use back bacon and, if you can find them, field mushrooms.

about 2 lb (1 kg) cod steaks
salt and freshly ground black pepper
a scraping of nutmeg
4–6 rashers of lean back bacon
¾ pt (450 ml) milk
8 oz (250 g) mushrooms, trimmed (peeled only if necessary) and sliced
1 oz (30 g) vegetable oil or butter, for frying
¾ oz (25 g) butter
¾ oz (25 g) flour
2 tbsp double cream (optional)
2 tbsp finely chopped fresh parsley

Set the oven to 160°C/325°F/gas mark 3. Rub the cod with a little salt, pepper and nutmeg and arrange the steaks in a single layer in a shallow ovenproof dish not much bigger than the assembled pieces of fish. Arrange the bacon on top. Pour on the milk – enough to come to a depth of about ¾ in (2 cm). Bake for 30 minutes. While the cod is cooking fry the sliced mushrooms in oil or butter, according to preference. Check the fish to see if it is cooked through. If so, remove it and the bacon to a warm serving dish. In a small, heavy-bottomed pan, melt the ¾ oz (25 g) butter, add the flour, stir well to make the basis of a roux. Use the fish-cooking milk to make a smooth sauce. Finish it with cream if you are using it. Season and sprinkle in the chopped parsley. Pour the sauce round the fish and scatter on the fried mushrooms. Serve with plain boiled potatoes.

HERRINGS IN OATMEAL   SERVES 4

When dwelling on the subject of herrings, which I hope you will for a minute, it would be salutary to think about what has happened to oysters. Once so plentiful that they were considered food for the poor, now they are prized and extremely pricey. One herring apparently lays at least ten thousand eggs and so you would think they were exempt from the fate of the oyster, but over-fishing has already affected the shoals and so one day they, too, may join the ranks of luxury ingredients. Before they do, cook them in this homely but delicious manner. It is the way Scots cook herrings. A further incentive might be the fact that herrings are very good for you. It is not only the highly unsaturated oil. They feed on plankton, full of nutrients. As one cookery book rather sweetly puts it, 'The herring, like most fish, are the cattle of a vegetation other than our own.'

4 fresh herrings
salt and pepper
2 oz (60 g) coarse oatmeal
4 rashers back bacon
FOR THE MUSTARD SAUCE:
2 egg yolks
2 tsp Dijon mustard
a little chopped fresh parsley
2 oz (60 g) butter

Slit the herrings along their bellies and clean them out. Skin side up, press firmly on the back-bone. Turn the fish over. You should be able easily to pick off the bones, rather like undoing a zip. Season them well. Press them into the oatmeal until they are well coated. Fry the bacon gently until the fat runs, then fry the fish in the bacon fat (you may need extra oil) until they are crisp on both sides. Season. Serve the fish and bacon together (the flavours marry well) with mustard sauce. In a bowl mix the egg yolks and mustard and chopped parsley, if available. Melt the butter gently. When it is just melted, not madly hot, stir it into the yolks as if making mayonnaise. Use immediately – a very useful little sauce.

SERVES 2   ## MACKEREL WITH GOOSEBERRY SAUCE

I read recently that mackerel are champion for the condition of your heart. Eat mackerel as often as possible and the fishy oils therein will protect you from attack. Well, I am not wild about mackerel unless it has just been pulled from the sea, but goose-berries contrast well with the often over-rich quality of the fish that others, I now realise, construe as its benefit.

Buy fish that can look you straight in the eye and are almost iridescent in colour. Grill them without fudging the first blast of heat which gives a crisp skin. A mackerel weighing about 1 lb (500 g) will feed two as a first course, one as a main course.

4 oz (120 g) butter
1 tbsp chopped fresh parsley
juice of ½ lemon
1 tsp Dijon mustard
2 mackerel, gutted and washed
FOR THE SAUCE:
1 lb (500 g) gooseberries
sugar, to taste
1 egg or 3 tbsp double cream

Make the grilling butter by mixing together 3 oz (90 g) of butter, the parsley, lemon juice and mustard. Prepare the sauce. Top and tail the gooseberries. Melt 1 oz (30 g) butter in a heavy-bottomed pan and add the gooseberries. Cover and cook gently until they fall apart and are cooked through. Taste for tartness and add sugar if you wish, but take care not to over-sweeten. Either mash, sieve or whizz in a food processor and then stir in the egg, beaten, or the cream. Make your grill very hot. With a sharp knife make three diagonal slashes on the mackerel down to the bone. Work a little parsley butter into each slash. Grill for a minute and then reduce the heat somewhat. After 4 minutes, baste the fish with the melted butter in the grill pan. When the fish is opaque, turn over and repeat the slashing, anointing, grilling process. Serve the fish with the sauce handed separately and the remaining parsley butter as a pat on top of the fish.

'LEG' OF MONKFISH SERVES 4–6

I suspect that there are few discoveries left to be made about cooking. There was a time when monkfish (otherwise known as angler) went unappreciated in this country and was therefore relatively cheap. Now it is every restaurateur's darling, not least of all because its firm flesh is claimed by some to resemble lobster. Alan Davidson, in his book *North Atlantic Seafood*, quotes a supplier at Billingsgate talking about a restaurant owner. 'If Mr X comes down and orders two whole lobsters and forty pounds of angler tail, I know what's on the menu that evening and it isn't angler.' However, rather than pretend monkfish is lobster, it seems to me preferable to enjoy it for its own virtues, even if it is more expensive these days. The tail of monkfish vaguely resembles the shape of a leg of lamb and the French often serve it roasted, as a 'gigot de lotte'. Prepared this way it will convert anyone who thinks fish is sissy.

1 tail of monkfish, weighing about 2–3 lb (1–1.5 kg)
2 cloves garlic, peeled and cut into fine strips
4 tbsp good olive oil
4 tomatoes, peeled and sliced
1 onion, peeled and cut into fine crescents
1 tsp fennel seeds (optional)
1 small lemon, sliced
7 fl oz (200 ml) white wine
salt and freshly ground black pepper
chopped fresh parsley

Set the oven to 220°C/425°F/gas mark 7. Skin the fish scrupulously, removing all the membrane, which, if left, will cause the
fish to curl up in the oven. With a sharp knife, slip the chips of
garlic into the flesh, dotting it about until the surface is fairly well
covered. Heat the olive oil in an ovenproof dish. Turn the fish in
the hot oil lightly to brown it. Scatter around the fish the tomatoes,
onions, fennel seeds and lemon slices. Pour the white wine over
the fish. Season thoroughly with salt and freshly ground black
pepper. Cook in the pre-heated oven, basting from time to time
with the pan juice, for 35–40 minutes. Serve on a heated plate with
the mixture from the pan poured around. Sprinkle with chopped
parsley.

SERVES 8   # BAKED WHOLE SALMON

Whatever salmon farmers say, wild salmon does taste better, unless
perhaps it is just some 'Born Free' spirit that continues to hover.
The idea of cooking whole fish often alarms people because deep
down they know they neither possess a fish kettle nor really want
to. This method allows you to use your familiar roasting tin and
ensures that the fish will stay moist. Serve salmon with hot new
potatoes, hand-made mayonnaise and a cucumber salad dressed
with rice vinegar (available from oriental supermarkets).

1 whole salmon
1 oz (30 g) butter
4 spring onions, trimmed
2 carrots, peeled and roughly chopped
a wedge of fennel
3 sprigs of parsley
1 tsp dill weed
salt and whole peppercorns
5 fl oz (150 ml) white wine

Ask the fishmonger to clean the salmon but leave on the head and
the tail. At home check that any loose scales have been scraped
off and give it a rinse in clear water. Turn on the oven to
200°C/400°F/gas mark 6. Line a roasting tin with greaseproof
paper, letting enough hang over the rim to provide a handle for
lifting out the fish later. Smear the butter over the paper. Lay on
the salmon and dot the vegetables, herbs and flavourings around.
Pour on the white wine and enough water to just come level with
the fish. You may need to coil the fish to fit it in. Cover the pan
with foil, pinching it well in around the sides. Put in the oven and

bring to a simmer. Simmer for 10 minutes. The whole process should take about 20 minutes. Remove. Let sit with foil intact for 5 minutes, then remove it. Let cool and serve the fish, ideally, lukewarm.

GRAVAD LAX SERVES 4-6

This Scandinavian treatment of fish, usually salmon, which involves marinating it in a mixture of sugar and salt, had a great vogue in restaurants some years back. It appealed to customers as a diverting change from smoked salmon and, because it was foreign, seemed glamorous. For these reasons restaurateurs seemed to feel it was perfectly all right to charge a price quite out of proportion to that of the raw material or the work involved, which is minimal.

The preparation takes only a few minutes and the fish manages the rest of the process by itself until it is ready in 2–3 days' time. The sugar and salt pickle also works well on humbler fish such as herring, but the first time try a tail piece of salmon, a cut sometimes sold a little more cheaply than the main body of the fish.

1 piece of salmon, either a tail-piece or a whole small salmon or salmon trout, weighing $1\frac{1}{2}$–2 lb (750 g–1 kg)
1 heaped tbsp sea salt
1 rounded tbsp sugar
1 tsp coarsely ground peppercorns
a little brandy (optional)
1 rounded tbsp dill weed, chopped if fresh

FOR THE SAUCE:
mayonnaise, preferably home-made
German mustard
sugar
dill weed
dash of vinegar

Bone the fish which will give you two kite-shaped pieces, or, if you have bought a small salmon or salmon trout, clean, bone and behead it. Ask the fishmonger to do this if you are unsure about it. You can also remove the skin now and use it as a wrapping around the fish while it is marinating, spreading the seasoning between the skin and the fish. Mix together the salt, sugar and pepper. If you wish, moisten with a little brandy. Put some of the mixture plus a third of the dill weed into a dish that holds the fish quite snugly, lay on it the first piece of fish, skin side down. Spread on more pickle, more dill weed and sandwich with the other piece of fish, skin side up. Scatter on the remaining pickle and dill. Cover with a double layer of aluminium foil and then weight down with tins or a brick. Leave in the fridge for at least 24 hours, turning once. To serve, remove the skin, slice thinly or thickly according to preference and drain away all the brine that has accumulated. Mix together the ingredients for the sauce. Hand round rye bread or accompany with boiled new potatoes, and serve with the sauce.

SKATE AU BEURRE NOIR

SERVES 4-6

Hazel Short, who has helped me look after my household for the last five years, said I should give this recipe because not everyone knew about it and when she had made it for her boyfriend he had been most enthusiastic. The thing that skate has got going for it, apart from its interesting, slightly gelatinous texture, is that, almost uniquely among fish, it is all the better for not being sparklingly fresh. A faint maturity is desirable. The usual test of bright eyes and firm gills is not applicable in any case since skate is sold in 'wings'. Beurre noir, which is butter cooked until it is not really black but a dark, nutty brown, is a useful technique (sauce seems a slight exaggeration) that can be applied to almost anything bland, for example brains or fried eggs.

4 wings skate, totalling about 2 lb (1 kg) in weight
2 oz (60 g) butter
2 tbsp red wine vinegar
salt and pepper
1 dsp capers
finely chopped parsley

FOR THE COURT BOUILLON:
2 tbsp white wine vinegar
1 carrot, sliced
1 onion, peeled and sliced
10 peppercorns
salt
sprig of parsley

In a large shallow pan put enough water to cover the skate and add all the flavouring ingredients for the court bouillon. Put in the fish and bring slowly to the boil. After one eruption of bubbles, lower the heat to achieve just below simmering point. Cook the fish for 10–15 minutes until the flesh is opaque down to the main bone. You can do this in the oven if you feel happier about it. Drain the fish thoroughly and arrange on a warm serving dish. Melt the butter in a frying pan and, watching like a hawk, cook it until it goes a deep brown. Pour it over the fish. Put into the hot pan two tbsp red wine vinegar, season it, swirl it around and let it bubble for a few seconds. Pour that over the fish. Scatter over the capers and chopped parsley and serve immediately. Boiled potatoes are the best accompaniment.

FILLETS OF DOVER SOLE IN A LETTUCE LEAF

SERVES 4-6

The quest for good local produce is the proper concern of any restaurateur. It will be a welcome day, in London anyway, when that does not end in meeting the truck from Rungis, the main wholesale market in Paris.

A fascinating account of the relationship of a country restaurant to its suppliers is contained in *Cooking in the Country* by Tom Jaine. Jaine is the stepson of George Perry-Smith, who started the seminal restaurant The Hole in the Wall in Bath and was one of the founders of the admirable Carved Angel in Dartmouth. This recipe comes from the second part of the book, which reveals some of the secrets of the Carved Angel.

Having read the book, which will comfort the country lover who dwells inside every city-dweller, you may well wish to read the newsletter from which it grew. It is published as *The Three Course Newsletter* and subscription details are given in the Bibliography.

4 oz (120 g) shallots
5 fl oz (150 ml) white vermouth
outer leaves of a Webb's lettuce
1¼ lb (600 g) Dover sole
salt and freshly ground black pepper
2 oz (60 g) butter

Turn on the oven to 300°C/150°F/gas mark 2. Chop the shallots and put them in a pan with the vermouth. Reduce the liquid by half by boiling. Blanch the outer leaves of the lettuce very briefly in boiling water, drain and refresh under a cold tap. Spread them on a board. Skin the fillets and score before rolling each of them, skin side inside. Season them. Place each little fillet on a lettuce leaf and fold over to make a parcel. In a small flameproof dish, lay out the shallot and vermouth reduction and put your parcels on top. Cover with foil. Bring to cooking temperature on the top of the stove and then cook in the oven for about 5 minutes. Remove the parcels to a warmed dish in a warm place. Bring the cooking dish back to the top of the stove. There, shuffle in a few pats of butter, taste, season with lemon juice and pour over the fillets.

TROUT IN NEWSPAPER

SERVES 2

Every foodstuff seems to have its own fan club or marketing organisation. Recently the British Trout Association, a body 'committed to high standards of production of fresh, smoked and processed rainbow trout, coupled with humane farming techniques', published a recipe booklet called *Take Two Trout*. As well as a large selection of recipes there are notes on buying, cleaning and filleting the fish, which they admit is nowadays most likely to be farmed rather than caught in the wild. My experience of farmed trout has only convinced me of the theory that life must be a struggle in order to be worthwhile, or indeed rewarding in flavour, but this simple method of cooking the fish caught my eye. Of course by far the tastiest results are obtained by using the *London Evening Standard*.

Serve the fish with the sauce suggested below or a cold cucumber, garlic and yogurt sauce or a hot cucumber sauce made of a béchamel into which you stir steamed, puréed cucumber.

2 trout
2 slices of lemon
salt and pepper
fresh herbs to taste, such as parsley or dill weed
yesterday's London Evening Standard *(outside London you must improvise)*

FOR THE SAUCE:
1 oz (30 g) butter
3 oz (90 g) sliced mushrooms
1 clove of garlic, peeled and finely chopped
1 tbsp anise-based drink such as Pernod or Ricard
2 tbsp double cream
salt and freshly ground black pepper

Turn on the oven to 180°C/350°F/gas mark 4. Tuck a slice of lemon into each cleaned trout and season inside and out with salt, pepper and herbs. Wrap each fish in three sheets of newspaper, tucking in the ends to make a neat parcel. Run under the cold tap until sodden. Cook until the paper is dry, about 15–20 minutes. Using scissors open the package and unwrap, lifting away the skin of the fish. Melt the butter and cook the mushrooms and garlic until the mushrooms are softened and the juices run. Add the Pernod or Ricard. Bubble it hard and then stir in the cream and keep stirring until the sauce is amalgamated. Season and serve around the paper-free trout.

'ONE OF THE WORLD'S GREATEST SANDWICHES'

That was the description given by wine merchant Simon Loftus to this idea, which I first encountered in a booklet called *Feasts* by Victor Gordon. He has since written a fascinating cookery book, *The English Cookbook*, where I notice he repeats the recipe, obviously keen, just as I am, that as many people as possible should be apprised of this excellent combination of ingredients. *Feasts* was divided into months and festivals and Bacon du Bedat – the correct title of this sandwich – came under February. I am quoting below from both renditions of the instructions for what could be one of the quickest, but also most satisfactory suppers ever:

> Any roisterer lingering in the Yorkshire Grey towards closing time in the early fifties was liable to be swooped up by Bill du Bedat and borne along Piccadilly to a basement club near Simpson's, there to consume bottles of, by that time, superfluous Chablis and du Bedat's favourite sandwich – smoked salmon and bacon combined.

The addition of mango chutney has genteelised or gentrified it. Victor Gordon suggests 'ardent spirits' as an accompaniment. Apparently du Bedat also used the sandwich to eat along with heroic quantities of pink gin.

FOR EACH PERSON:
2 slices of hot toast or 1 slice for an open sandwich
butter
smoked salmon
mango chutney
hot, crisp, streaky bacon
cayenne pepper

For each person, lightly butter 1 piece of toast, cover it (thickly) with smoked salmon, spread the salmon (thinly) with chutney, cover the chutney with bacon, sprinkle cayenne pepper on the bacon and surmount with another piece of lightly buttered toast. Equally good as an open sandwich, in which case the single piece of toast should be medium-thick instead of medium-thin.

SERVES 4-6 ## KEDGEREE

Kedgeree was what happened when the English met the Indian dish khichri, originally a mixture of lentils, rice and spices and, incidentally, delicious made in that austere way. The additions of smoked haddock, hard-boiled eggs, curry powder or turmeric, cream or whatever else you happen to believe is appropriate or necessary, is just proof of how dishes can evolve fortuitously.

In my household kedgeree has become an institution for breakfast on Christmas Day. It not only gets the day off to a satisfactory start – important given the *tension* of the whole event – but most of the constituent parts can be prepared the night before to be assembled on the morning. This makes it a good dish for any time of year and breakfast, lunch or supper. Finnan haddock, which is the fish smoked on the bone, is infinitely preferable to dyed fillets. And, of course, basmati rice is preferable to boil-in-the-bag, prefluffed or that notorious American brand.

12 oz (375 g) smoked haddock
milk to cover fish
8 oz (250 g) basmati rice
1 tbsp vegetable oil
2 oz (60 g) butter
2 onions, peeled and thinly sliced
1 dsp ground turmeric
3 hard-boiled eggs
salt and freshly ground black pepper

Put the haddock in an oven dish, add enough milk nearly to cover the fish and cook in a medium oven (180°C/350°F/gas mark 4) for about 20 minutes or until the fish flakes easily. Remove any skin or bones and keep the fish-flavoured milk. Cook the rice, using the method you have found best. In the oil and butter fry the onion until golden. Add the turmeric and cook it gently for a few minutes. Add the haddock and rice and mix gently until the rice is coloured a rich saffron yellow. Use some of the milk to moisten the mixture and more butter if you like richness. Scatter the dish with chopped hard-boiled eggs. Taste for seasoning and be generous with the pepper.

KIPPER FILLET SALAD SERVES 4-6

In the late sixties this dish became a cliché of the bistros that were opening up all over the place and at dinner parties, which was the way some of us felt constrained to enjoy ourselves. So commonplace was it – not cooking the kippers seemed sort of *daring* at the time – that I stopped making it despite the fact my husband used to say plaintively that he liked it. However, it is good and quick to do and, though no one would be fooled by the idea that raw kippers served with brown bread and butter are somehow like smoked salmon, they have virtue, especially if you use a good olive oil to dress them.

When you buy the packets of kipper fillets moan loudly to whoever will listen about the unnecessary addition of the artificial colour Brown FK. As Jane Grigson says it would be interesting to meet that mythical idiot housewife who will only buy spherical watery tomatoes and needs to be lulled into buying kippers by their dark brown dye.

8 kipper fillets
1 large onion, peeled and sliced into thin rings
2 tbsp lemon juice
olive oil, for dressing
freshly ground black pepper

Rip the silvery skin off the kipper fillets and then slice the fillets on the diagonal into strips about $\frac{1}{4}$ in (6 mm) wide. Place them in a shallow dish and scatter half the onion rings on top. Pour on lemon juice. You may need more to ensure that all the pieces will affected by the juice. Leave it in the fridge for a few hours turning occasionally. Drain off the juice. Pour on olive oil, enough to dress the kipper pieces generously. Scatter on the remaining onion rings – you then have two textures of onion – and grind on black pepper enthusiastically. Serve as a first course with brown bread and butter.

BRANDADE OF SALT COD SERVES 6-9

This was a dish traditionally eaten on Fridays in France, most particularly in and around Nîmes, in the Languedoc. With the advent of refrigeration and fast effective transportation, salt cod, once a most important ingredient in the diet, has been largely forgotten or scorned. However, it has a flavour and a texture all its own, one worth including every now and then in your cooking, be it served as part of 'un grand aïoli', the fish, eggs and vegetables served with a heavily garlicked mayonnaise, or in a Portuguese style, for example with potatoes, hard-boiled eggs and olive oil, or in the way I like best, as a brandade.

The cod should be soaked for at least twenty-four hours and I find the mode of leaving it in a bowl of water under a dripping tap the most effective. However, if you don't want to do that, just change the water regularly. Brandade, once very labour intensive, has been made easy, like so many other dishes, by the food processor.

2 lb (1 kg) dried salt cod, soaked as above
about 1½ pts (900 ml) milk, to cover fish
1 clove of garlic, crushed
¼ pt (150 ml) olive oil
¼ pt (150 ml) thin cream or some of the milk from above
black pepper, and salt, if necessary
bread, as required
a little oil, for frying
a little butter, for frying

Simmer the soaked cod in milk for about 8 minutes. Turn off the heat and let it sit for a further 10 minutes. Remove the cod and pick away skin and bones. Roughly cut up the fish and process it in a food processor until you have a purée. You may need to switch on and off and scrape down the sides of the bowl. Turn into a bowl and stir in the clove of garlic, pushed through a garlic crusher. Heat the oil and the cream or milk in two small pans until they are warm, not hot. Beat the oil and cream alternately, bit by bit, into the salt cod, almost as if you were making mayonnaise, until you have a creamy cohesive mass. Grind on some black pepper and add salt if necessary (it shouldn't be). Fry triangles of bread in a mixture of oil and butter and poke them in around the dish of brandade.

SERVES 4-6 # CAVIAR AND BLINIS

Caviar and the much cheaper black or red Danish 'caviar' (lumpfish roe) need blinis. Here is a simplified recipe for these pancakes, using some buckwheat flour but not yeast as the raising agent. Serve the blinis with soured cream, some melted butter and whatever fish egg you can run to. Smoked cod's roe perhaps?

6 oz (175 g) plain white flour
2 oz (60 g) buckwheat flour
1 tsp cream of tartar
1 tsp bicarbonate of soda
pinch of salt
scant ½ pt (280 ml) skimmed milk
1 egg
1 tsp sugar
1 tbsp melted butter

Sift together the dry ingredients except for the sugar. Beat the milk, egg and sugar. Stir in the melted butter. Slowly add the milk mixture to the flour mixture as if you were making pancakes, aiming for smoothness. Leave to stand for 15 minutes. Cook in spoonfuls on a greased griddle or heavy iron frying pan. When bubbles appear at the top of the blinis, turn them and cook the other side. Do them in batches and keep them warm in a napkin.

JANSSON'S TEMPTATION   SERVES 4

Jansson sounds to me as though it might be a fairly common name in Scandinavia and most people, I think, would be seduced by this easily assembled fish. Potatoes and cream, spiked with the agreeable savouriness of anchovies, lend it soothing qualities. You could, if you were so inclined, track down Swedish anchovies, which are really cured sprats, but the contents of those familiar small rectangular tins sold in every supermarket work fine. There are those who soak anchovies packed in oil in warm water or milk before using them and those who don't. I am of the second persuasion. In any case the cream has an ameliorating effect on the flavour.

2 oz (60 g) butter
2 lb (1 kg) potatoes
2 × 2 oz (50 g) tins of anchovy fillets (do not drain off the oil)
3 onions, peeled and thinly sliced
freshly ground black pepper
½ pt (300 ml) whipping cream

Turn on the oven to 220°C/425°F/gas mark 7. Using a scrap of butter, butter a shallow ovenproof dish. Peel the potatoes and cut them across the length of the potato into slices about ¼ in (6 mm) thick. Cut these slices, again lengthways, to give matchsticks of potato. Open the tins of anchovies, remove the fillets and pour the oil into a little bowl. Divide each fillet lengthways. Place half the

potato sticks into the prepared dish and cover with half the onions.
Arrange the anchovy strips in a lattice pattern on top. Cover them
with the rest of the onion slices and then spread the remaining
potato on top. Grind on some pepper (add salt, if you need it, at
the time of eating since the anchovies might well donate enough).
Dribble the anchovy oil over the top and pour on half the cream.
Dot with the rest of the butter and bake in the pre-heated oven
for 15 minutes. After that reduce the heat to 190°C/375°F/gas
mark 5 and cook for about another 35 minutes, by which time the
potatoes should be tender and turning a golden brown. Pour on
the rest of the cream and keep at a low heat until you are ready to
serve. Adding the cream in two stages corrects the tendency of
the sauce to look curdled. A green salad is what you need as
accompaniment.

SERVES 3 TUNA FISH SALAD

From the ages of twelve to fifteen I lived in Connecticut. Although
those are supposed to be formative years the experience has
become a blur, but I do remember the terribly good sandwiches
in the drug stores. I liked the BLT (bacon, lettuce and tomato),
egg salad and tuna salad. A key ingredient in those days was
Hellman's mayonnaise, a commodity which, like tinned salmon or
cream of tomato soup, strikes me as having a valid existence quite
separate from the original that it is emulating. You can use bought
mayonnaise or make your own (a matter of minutes in a blender
or food processor) in this tuna fish salad, which I now quite often
eat on lettuce leaves as a first course or as a light meal. The process
may seem so simple as hardly to merit the description recipe, but
with the crunch of celery and the bite of spring onions, it is more
than a sum of its parts.

1 large tin of tuna fish, packed in brine for preference
2 tbsp mayonnaise
2 large sticks of celery, cleaned and cut into fine dice
4–5 spring onions, trimmed and finely chopped
squeeze of lemon juice
dash of Tabasco sauce
salt and freshly ground black pepper

TO SERVE: *lettuce leaves, for a salad, or wholemeal toast, for sandwiches*

Drain the tuna of its oil or brine and place in a bowl. Break up the
chunks with a fork. Add the rest of the ingredients and mix well,

but without smashing all the texture out of the fish. Serve either on lettuce leaves or as a sandwich filling with wholemeal toast.

Americans also make tuna-noodle casserole with tuna, cooked noodles, hard-boiled eggs, sautéed mushrooms and finely chopped onion baked in a white sauce with fried breadcrumbs scattered on top. I give it to you only as a thought. It never much appealed to me.

CRAB WITH GINGER AND SPRING ONION SERVES 2

This is a highly popularised version of the dish of the same name that you encounter in Chinese restaurants. I have adapted it in part because of the difficulty in getting hold of live crabs, which should really be the starting point, but also because when I made it at home I wanted to steam the crab rather than fry it in oil for reasons of calories. Really the steaming is just a way of heating the crab through and the flavour of the dish lies largely in the dipping sauce. If you cannot find rice vinegar, use white wine vinegar and perhaps an extra pinch of sugar. This is a perfect light supper for two, possible to assemble in ten minutes. When buying fresh crabs, ask the fishmonger to open them, to check that there is plenty inside them. It follows that heaviness is a desirable quality in a crab.

1 large fresh crab in its shell
1 × 2 in (5 cm) piece fresh ginger root, peeled and cut into matchsticks
1 bunch of spring onions, trimmed and sliced lengthways

FOR THE DIPPING SAUCE:
4 tbsp soy sauce
2½ tbsp rice vinegar, or 2 tbsp white wine vinegar
1 tsp sugar
1 clove of garlic, peeled and crushed
a few drops of chilli oil or chilli sauce (optional)

Wrench off the crab claws and legs. Bang them with a mallet, enough to crack the shell all over. Open the body of the crab and take out the undesirable parts if the fishmonger has not done it. These are the 'dead men's fingers', easily recognisable by that graphic description, and the stomach with its attached organs, which will come away if you press down on the mouth part of the carapace or upper shell. If in doubt, though it is fairly self-evident, consult a good seafood cookery book. With a small teaspoon, scoop out the rest of the brown crabmeat and then rearrange in the shell with some strips of ginger and spring onion. Put the shell, open side up, in a steamer basket, surrounded by the cracked claws and legs. Strew ginger and spring onion on top, leaving some to add to the sauce. Bring water to the boil vigorously under or in the steamer and set the crab, covered, on top. Meanwhile mix the ingredients for the dipping sauce, adding the strips of ginger and chopped spring onion lengths to it. As soon as the crab is hot, serve with the dipping sauce and plenty of paper napkins.

MUSSEL AND POTATO SALAD

If you have never tackled fresh live mussels there are a few things worth knowing, one being that you should waste no time in getting to grips with them; they are a reasonable and delicious source of protein. Mussels should be used the day you buy them. They must be thoroughly scrubbed, but with the large English variety with their encrusted shells I do not think it is necessary to scrape off every single barnacle. In this recipe you do not see the shells. Tug off the byssus, the thread by which the mussels cling to stones or wooden poles or whatever. Discard any mussels that do not close when tapped – they are dead – and after cooking throw out any that have not opened.

Most people know mussels in the form of moules marinière; opened with shallots, white wine, garlic and parsley in the pan. I like the lesser known mouclade, where the resulting liquor is thickened with a roux plus cream, egg yolks and a splash of an anise-based drink like Ricard. I also love the salad below, which is all the better for a firm, waxy variety of potato.

1½ lb (750 g) potatoes (a firm waxy variety)
2–3 lb (1–1.5 kg) fresh mussels
3 tbsp white wine
4 shallots, peeled and chopped
2 oz (60 g) fresh parsley
freshly ground black pepper
about 4 tbsp vinaigrette

Scrub the potatoes and boil them in their skins. When they are tender, peel them and slice them. Meanwhile, put the mussels in a large pan with the wine, shallots, a couple of sprigs of parsley and a generous amount of pepper. Set on a high heat, cover and after a few minutes shake the pan. The mussels will open in the boiling liquid and the resulting steam. When all are opened, excluding the duff ones, remove them and strain the mussel liquor through the finest possible sieve over the potatoes. A counsel of perfection would be to line your sieve with muslin or a tea-towel wrung out in hot water. Remove the mussels from the shells. When the potatoes are cool drain them and mix with the mussels. Dress with vinaigrette and sprinkle with chopped parsley. I like this salad served still lukewarm.

OYSTER STEW SERVES 2-4

This recipe was sent to me in a letter from a 49-year-old American architect who added as a p.s.: 'This is a very high cholesterol dish not suitable for overweight men in their fifties.' Perhaps the legendary restorative powers of oysters will counteract the butter, cream and milk. Anyway I have tried this dish and it is delicious, quick, satisfying enough for a main course, easy to keep ready in a double boiler or bain-marie and relatively inexpensive to make using frozen Japanese oysters obtainable in oriental supermarkets. These oysters have good flavour and obviate struggling to prise open shells and probably stabbing yourself with an oyster knife. Savoury crackers, like cream crackers or Saltines, are the correct accompaniment.

4 shallots, trimmed and finely chopped
3 oz (90 g) butter
12 fl oz (375 ml) milk
4 fl oz (120 ml) double cream
16–20 frozen oysters
½ tsp salt
white pepper or paprika
chopped fresh parsley

FOR A BISQUE:
2 egg yolks

Use a heavy-bottomed pot that later you can surround with water in a larger pot, i.e. a double boiler or a bain-marie. Sauté the shallots in the butter gently until they are softened. Bring the water for the double boiler arrangement to a simmer. Into your sauté pan put the milk, cream, oysters, salt and pepper. Cook slowly over, or surrounded by, water until the oysters float, where-upon the stew is ready. Check the seasoning, sprinkle with parsley and serve.

To make this into an even more wickedly rich dish, turn it into a bisque. Beat two egg yolks in a bowl and slowly add a few spoonfuls of the oyster stew liquid. Whisk until foamy. Return this to the stew, mix gently, and heat through without boiling until slightly thickened.

SCALLOPS WITH LEEKS
SERVES 2-4

One of the more palpable benefits of *nouvelle cuisine* is that whereas once the mention of scallops would conjure up a picture of fish in white sauce banked in by mashed potato, now it is as likely to bring to mind visions of pearly discs lightly steamed, garnished with threads of vegetables and perhaps some fresh root ginger. Scallops are a gift to chefs; delicate in flavour, quick to cook and well suited to portion control. The result of this seems to be that they are more easily available. The plastic boxes of scallops that some supermarkets sell are enough for a lightning, luxury meal for two. Because I love leeks, and they are in their prime at the moment, I have adapted a recipe of Roger Vergé that combines the two.

4 thin or 2 fat leeks
1 oz (30 g) butter
4 tbsp water
6–8 scallops
5 tbsp of the white wine you have chosen to drink with the meal
squeeze of lemon juice
3 tbsp double cream
salt and pepper
fresh parsley

Trim the leeks and clean them really thoroughly, sacrificing outer layers until you are sure that no grit lurks. The root and most of the green part must be taken off. Cut them in half lengthways and then into narrow strips, about $1\frac{1}{2} \times \frac{1}{4}$ in (or 4 by 0.6 cm). Melt half the butter in 4 tbsp water in a small saucepan and cook the leek strips until tender – about 15 minutes. Set on one side, but keep warm. Cut each scallop in two horizontally but leave the corals whole. Remove the thin, dark intestine and the little muscle which would toughen. Melt the remaining butter. Sauté the scallops for a few seconds and then add the wine. Bring to the boil and simmer for 2 minutes. Remove the scallops and keep warm with the leeks. Reduce the scallop liquor by boiling it vigorously. Add the cooking juices from the leeks, plus a squeeze of lemon juice. Boil again until you are left with about 4 tbsp of liquid. Add the cream, boil briefly, season. Arrange the leeks and scallops prettily on a warmed plate. Pour over the sauce and scatter with chopped parsley.

STUFFED SQUID SERVES 4

'A perfectly adequate primitive form of contraception,' remarked
a friend of mine, watching me clean some squid. I saw his point,
but don't let such observations or any atavistic fear of creatures
with tentacles put you off buying these cephalopods which many
enterprising fishmongers now sell. They must be cooked either
briskly or at length.

It is sometimes possible to buy them ready to cook, but once
you have got the hang of their constitution, it is a matter of
moments to prepare them yourself. Immerse them in water. Pull
out the insides and the bone which looks like a plastic quill.
Squeeze them like a tube of paint to remove any other matter. Cut
the tentacles away from the rest of the insides at a point where
they will hold together, making sure you discard the little beaky
mouth. Pick off the purply membrane that sometimes attaches
itself to the bodies and keep aside the triangular flaps which can
be chopped with the tentacles. Give the bodies a final rinse.

The stuffing below can be varied to taste, but the pine kernels
do add a nice flavour and texture.

2 lb (1 kg) small squid, cleaned as above
2 tbsp olive oil
1 onion
2 fat cloves of garlic, peeled and finely chopped
3 oz (90 g) ham, preferably raw ham like coppa or prosciutto
1 tbsp pine kernels (optional)
8 oz (250 g) cooked rice, preferably basmati
salt and freshly ground black pepper
a little chopped fresh parsley (optional)
splash of white wine

Pre-heat the oven to 180°C/350°F/gas mark 4. Clean the squid.
Chop the tentacles and flaps finely. Heat 1 tbsp of olive oil in a
frying pan. Add the onion and cook to soften. Add the tentacles,
flaps and garlic. Cook until they lose their translucency. Add the
ham and pine kernels and turn until the kernels are golden. Add
the rice, salt and pepper and some chopped fresh parsley if you
have it. Remove from the heat and, when cool, stuff the prepared
squid sacs loosely. Close them with a toothpick or cocktail stick.
Using some of the remaining oil, grease a shallow ovenproof dish
and lay the squid in one layer. Pour on some wine, the last of the
oil and sprinkle with more salt and pepper. Bake for about 15
minutes. Serve with a salad rather than a cooked vegetable.

POULTRY AND GAME

There is, mercifully, these days a movement that campaigns to restore proper flavour to food; to instil sunniness into tomatoes, to preserve noticeable variety in potatoes and apples, to put back the earthiness in carrots, and the cheesiness in cheese and so on. Perhaps the most flagrant success of this caucus is the improvement over the last few years in the taste of poultry, putting back a grain-fed flavour, or similar, into chickens. It does not take particularly shrewd buying nowadays to avoid getting chickens seemingly fed on fish food.

An improvement to the already improved flavour can be effected by seasoning the chicken (or turkey) under the skin. Butter, fromage blanc, vegetable purées, strips of bacon or anything reasonably unctuous can be slid under the skin of a bird once it has been worked free from the few membranes that keep it attached to the flesh. It makes such logical sense – basting the flesh rather than the skin – that once you have mastered this simple process you will invariably utilise it.

When you require roast chicken in a hurry it is worth remembering that a chicken, particularly a small chicken or spring chicken (poussin), can be cut along the backbone (that is along the bottom), flattened out and grilled, first on one side and then on the other. It has an interestingly different effect from roasting, which is partly to do with things like charred wing tips.

Boiling, or poaching, is often overlooked as a cooking method for chicken, but it is palpably healthier, gives you a stock, and if you are preparing a subtle sauce or garnish makes a much more accommodating background. It is possible in some butchers, in particular kosher butchers, to buy boiling chickens whose long life of toil and trouble is reflected in a more mature taste. Roasting chickens when simmered should be watched carefully and pulled out before the flesh loses its grip.

Duck is not always easy to find and is often shunned because it seems bad value – only enough on it for two. Now that it is possible to buy 'magrets' of duck, essentially steaks taken from the breast, duck becomes more of an option for a fairly casual meal. Traditionally the richness of duck is cut with something tart such as Seville orange or Bramley apple and the fashion of using flavoured vinegars in the sauces seems to me one worth following.

As far as I am concerned, the redeeming feature of turkey is that it is seasonal, even though Easter now seems to get a look-in and butchers are fast latching on to Thanksgiving. I ignore the turkey rolls, menacing thighs, landlady breasts and so on that turkey producers would have us buy all year round. For this reason the recipes concerning turkey here are for dealing with leftovers, though Pulled and Devilled Turkey is almost a case for buying turkey on an everyday basis.

Game has acquired an élitist image because of the way in which it is shot. This seems a pity. Pigeon and pheasant are both relatively economical sources of first-class protein and they provide a much more emotive meal than does a chop or steak. Often *soi-disant* wholefooders and demi-veg gourmets will allow game in their diet because of the 'natural' life the birds or beasts are considered to enjoy. I just think one should tackle game because it is delicious and widens the scope of meals – and I include rabbit in the definition.

SERVES 4 INSULATED CHICKEN

The improvement in the quality of chickens is one of the more heartening aspects of life. Free-range and corn-fed chickens (the ones with a jaundiced look) are ousting the poor little bleak battery birds from the shelves of supermarkets and butcher's displays. Wheedling a layer of stuffing under the skin of any chicken improves it enormously, making a dull bird perky and a good one dramatically good. It is not difficult to separate the skin from the flesh; it's even oddly pleasurable. If you are in a hurry, you could use mashed-up Boursin cheese as stuffing.

1 chicken
1 tbsp vegetable oil
5 oz (150 g) fromage blanc or low fat cream cheese
2 oz (60 g) softened butter
fresh herbs, tarragon if possible, chopped
crushed garlic, optional
salt and freshly ground black pepper
watercress, to serve

Turn on the oven to 190°C/375°F/gas mark 5. First rub the chicken with the vegetable oil to make the skin more pliable. Starting with your fingertips at the edge of the breastbone at the top of the cavity, begin to work the skin loose from the chicken. Gradually creep your hand under and work towards the back and sideways over the thighs. After you have broken one or two toughish membranes it becomes easy to separate the whole top part of the skin from the flesh beneath. With a small fork, the tines held downwards, prick the flesh of the chicken in a few places, taking care not to puncture the skin. Mix together the cheese (some fromage blanc has 0 per cent fat and so is good for slimmers), softened butter and chopped herbs and, if you like, some crushed garlic. Season with salt and freshly ground black pepper. Push the cheese mixture under the skin and pat it around to distribute it evenly. Place any leftover mixture in the cavity of the bird. Season the skin with salt and pepper and roast as usual for about one hour. Serve with a large bunch of watercress and the accumulated pan juices. The chicken will be full of flavour from its ability to baste itself.

CHICKEN WITH TARRAGON   SERVES 4

Sometimes tried and true combinations are ignored in the scramble for originality in cooking. I was reminded of this recently when lunching with chef Simon Hopkinson. He had cooked two sensational first courses, one a Thai-influenced soup with coconut milk and lemon grass, the other a salad garnished with artichoke hearts and gizzards. This classic chicken dish followed on perfectly.

Tarragon has a peculiar affinity for chicken. The recipe below is taken from Elizabeth David's *French Provincial Cooking*. She got it from a restaurant in Paris called Mère Michel. Often the old ways are best. It is best made with fresh tarragon, but dried, or put up in brine, will suffice.

1 oz (30 g) butter
1 tbsp fresh tarragon or $\frac{1}{2}$ tbsp dried tarragon
$\frac{1}{2}$ clove of garlic, peeled and crushed
salt and freshly ground black pepper
1 chicken
1 tbsp olive oil
2 fl oz (60 ml) brandy
4 fl oz (120 ml) double cream

Turn on the oven to 190°C/375°F/gas mark 5. Knead the butter with the tarragon leaves, crushed garlic, salt and pepper. Either put it inside the bird or work the mixture under the skin of the chicken. Rub the chicken with the olive oil. Season. Lie the bird on its side on a grid in a roasting tin and cook for 25 minutes. Then turn the bird on the other side and cook for a further 25 minutes. When the bird is cooked, heat the brandy in a soup ladle or small pan, set light to it, and pour it flaming over the chicken.

Rotate the dish so that the flames spread and continue burning as long as possible. Return the bird to a low oven for 5 minutes, during which time the brandy sauce will mature and lose its raw flavour. Remove the chicken to a warmed serving plate. Stir the cream into the pan juices and, when well amalgamated, pour over the chicken. Spoon up some of the creamy tarragon sauce with each serving.

SERVES 4   CHICKEN À LA GRECQUE

My sister contrived to spend many long summers in Greece by cooking for villa parties of English people. The company that ran these villas wanted the food served to be faintly authentic, but not enough to disturb the usually unadventurous guests. Indeed, when once visiting my sister, I overheard one young lady say to her newly acquired husband, 'Eee Graham, what I wouldn't give for a laytely boiled egg.' However, this dish, typical of the sort of assembly Greek women might take to the bakers to have cooked in the oven, was always popular. The flavours of olive oil, lemon juice and Greek *rigani* (substitute ordinary oregano) are important. Greek chickens are rangier but tastier than ours, so be heavy-handed with the flavourings to be authentic. Try to get hold of a waxy variety of potato and cut them like very fat chips, that is each peeled potato cut in half lengthways and then into three.

1 medium chicken, preferably maize-fed, or 2 poussins
4 tbsp olive oil
3 cloves of garlic, peeled and crushed
salt and freshly ground black pepper
2½ lb (1.25 kg) potatoes, peeled and cut as above
juice of 1 lemon
1½ oz (45 g) butter
2 tsp dried oregano

Turn on the oven to 190°C/375°F/gas mark 5. Cut the chicken(s) along the backbone – in other words the underneath of the bird. Spread out and press down unrelentingly until you hear the breast-bone crack. Rub the chicken vigorously with some olive oil and the crushed garlic cloves. Sprinkle with salt and pepper. Put the remaining olive oil into a baking tin and turn the potatoes in it. Place the chicken on top, breast side up. Sprinkle the lemon juice on the chicken and rub it in – massage the bird. Dot it with pieces of the butter. Cut up the squeezed lemon halves and scatter the pieces among the potatoes. Sprinkle the chicken and potatoes with oregano and season with more salt and pepper on the potatoes. Cover with foil and bake for 40 minutes. Remove the foil, baste the chicken with the pan juice. Cook for another 20 minutes, or until the chicken is golden and the peaks of the potatoes tinged with brown.

SPATCHCOCKED CHICKEN   SERVES 4

What we call spatchcocked the French call *à la crapaudine* – like a toad. The first reference apparently dates from the sixteenth century and has some reference to the quickness of preparation. The French reference comes from the fact that a small chicken split down its backbone and then spread out bears some resemblance to a toad. Either way, it makes it possible to grill rather than roast a small bird and when you take trouble with the seasoning it is a perfect speedy supper. I would suggest a watercress salad as an accompaniment as I think watercress and chicken go well together, and I would dress the leaves simply by pouring on the hot juices from the grill pan.

4 poussins or 2 small (spring) chickens
juice of ½ lemon
2 fat cloves of garlic, peeled and crushed
salt and freshly ground black pepper
½ tsp cayenne pepper
1 tbsp olive oil
1 oz (30 g) butter
1 tbsp Dijon mustard
2 tbsp dried breadcrumbs (not orange packet crumbs)

Using poultry shears, cut the chickens along the backbone, the underside of the bird. Spread out and flatten completely by pressing down firmly on the backbone until you hear it crack. Be quite sadistic. Rub the top side of the chickens with lemon juice and then with the crushed garlic. Season with salt, black pepper and the cayenne pepper. Dribble some of the oil over the chickens and then dot with half the butter. Turn the grill to moderately high. Grill the prepared chickens, breast side up, for about 10 minutes. Turn over, season again, and anoint with the remaining oil and butter. Cook for another 10 minutes. Turn the chickens back, breast side up, and paint with the mustard. Sprinkle on the breadcrumbs and put back under the grill until the crumbs are crisp. Serve on hot plates with the salad described in the introduction above – or, whatever you fancy.

SERVES 4   # CHICKEN WINGS WITH CHICKPEAS

Of all the bits of chicken that are sold separately, I like the wings the best, but then I like skin and bones and joints and cartilage – and not too much meat. Marinated in garlic and lime juice and grilled until they crisp, they accompany well a drink or some green salad or both. Lebanese restaurants are adept at preparing spiced and grilled chicken wings. The recipe below produces a more substantial meal, one that I observe finds favour with children who like the licence to pick food up in their fingers. They can even be persuaded to see the point of chickpeas. I have suggested tinned chickpeas in the interests of speed. You could, of course, soak dried chickpeas overnight and then boil them for an hour or two, but chickpeas are so nobly resilient that the tinning process makes little impact.

3 tbsp vegetable oil
2 onions, peeled and finely sliced
2 cloves of garlic, peeled and crushed
1½ in (4 cm) piece of fresh ginger root, or ½ tsp powdered ginger (but that is less good)
1 tsp cumin seeds or powdered cumin
½ tsp cardamom seeds, taken from their husks
1 level tsp ground turmeric
1 tsp coriander seeds or ground coriander
12–15 chicken wings
about 1 pt (600 ml) light chicken stock
2 × 14 oz (430 g) tins chickpeas, well drained
salt and pepper
juice of ½ lime or lemon
plain yogurt, to serve (optional)

In a sauté pan or frying pan large enough to hold the wings more or less in one layer, heat the oil to a medium heat. Sauté the onions until they are softened. Add the garlic, ginger which you have rubbed through a grater and the spices. Stir around to cook, without catching, for about 3 minutes. Make sure the chicken wings are free of any stubble (cut off the wing tips if necessary). Add them to the spiced oil. Cook, turning and shifting them about until they are browned. Add the stock. Bubble up and then add the chickpeas. Simmer uncovered, but continually turning the wings until they are cooked and the sauce is reduced. Season. Sprinkle with lemon or lime juice and serve. Plain yogurt sits well alongside this.

CHICKEN KIEV SERVES 4

For some reason – an obvious reason I suppose – I like making the clichéd dishes of restaurants at home. Although chicken Kiev may strike you as a relic of the sixties' bistro boom, when it is made carefully, with a free-range chicken, fresh tarragon chopped into unsalted butter for the filling and fresh breadcrumbs for the coating, it can seem newly delicious. The garlic in the butter is optional, but do try to get some fresh herbs. Serve with a green salad and maybe some hot bread to mop up the buttery juices.

10 leaves fresh tarragon, finely chopped, or 1 tbsp parsley or chives, finely chopped
1 fat clove of garlic, peeled and crushed
juice of 2 lemons
rind of 1 lemon
salt and pepper
3 oz (90 g) unsalted butter
4 boned chicken breasts (suprêmes of chicken)
1 oz (30 g) plain flour
1 egg
1 tbsp vegetable oil
1 tbsp water
4 oz (120 g) fine white or brown breadcrumbs
vegetable oil, preferably sunflower oil, for deep frying

Beat the herbs, garlic, lemon juice and rind, and a good pinch of salt and pepper into the butter. Shape into a square on a piece of foil or greaseproof paper and set in the freezer or refrigerator to chill and firm up. With a sharp knife cut a deep slit in the thick edge of each chicken breast, making sure you don't come through the opposite side. Divide the chilled butter into four sticks and tuck one into the pocket in each chicken breast. Press the edges of the chicken flesh together so that no butter is peeping through. Season the flour and spread it in a shallow dish or plate. Beat the egg with the oil and water. Turn the chicken breasts in the flour then in the egg mixture. Coat each breast carefully with the breadcrumbs. Chill the chicken pieces for an hour or two – which will ensure the crisp coating – and then heat the oil and deep-fry until golden brown. Drain on kitchen paper and keep the first two breasts warm in the oven while frying the second batch. Be careful when you cut into them that the melted butter doesn't spurt on to your clothes.

SERVES 2   TEA-SMOKED POUSSIN

Loyal readers of my restaurant column will remember my week
of the ducks. I ate duck English style with apple sauce, French
style as a *ballotine*, Thai style in a curry and Chinese style tea-
smoked. I was determined to recreate this last, somewhat fugitive,
flavour at home and without filling the kitchen with acrid clouds.
A small biddable poussin, I thought, was a better subject than a
duck which might take too long in letting the flavour penetrate.
Also, since the smoking is almost a cosmetic process, rather than
a real means of cooking, I looked for complementary flavourings
to use when steaming the bird. Spring onions, ginger and soy
sauce seemed obvious, but the wily addition was orange peel; it
blended tremendously well with the tea. Tea-smoking is not the
greatest cooking mode on earth, but it is fun to do and is a good
variation for roast or boiled or fried or grilled chicken.

2 in (5 cm) lump of root ginger
1 poussin
soy sauce, as required
salt and pepper
3 spring onions, cleaned
a few strips of orange peel
1 tbsp rice
1 tbsp jasmine tea

Peel the ginger root, crush half of it and rub the poussin vigorously
with it (you could use powdered ginger but it is not so good). Now
rub in a little soy sauce, salt and pepper. Chop the spring onions
into 1 in (3 cm) lengths. Put some inside the bird, plus a strip or
two of orange peel. In a saucepan of a steamer which will take the
poussin, put water for steaming and add to it 1 tbs soy sauce, the
rest of the ginger, the rest of the spring onions and a strip of orange
peel. Steam the prepared chicken on the steaming tray for about
40 minutes or until it is cooked. Now line a heavy-bottomed
saucepan which has a tight-fitting lid with a double layer of foil.
Sprinkle on the rice and tea. Use a grid or fix up some other
contraption to hold the chicken above the rice/tea. Put the saucepan on a high heat. When the smoke starts, place the chicken on
your grid, cover the pan and smoke for 10–15 minutes. If you have
the right sort of pan you could put the whole contraption into a
high oven. Serve with noodles.

WATERZOOI

Whilst not being particularly fond of soups, which I find tend to drown my appetite, I rather like soupy main courses – dishes that have to be served in a bowl and eaten with a spoon, knife and fork. Bouillabaisse and bourride are examples, as is this Belgian dish which originated in Ghent. It can be made with a mixture of fish or with chicken. The stock is thickened with egg yolks and cream or, if you are feeling a little health and weight conscious, just egg yolks. The beauty of a dish such as this is that you can dispense with a first course and just serve either buttered French bread or plain boiled potatoes as the accompaniment. With the various vegetables that are part of the assembly, even a salad seems super-flous. If you prefer to use fish in place of the chicken detailed below, curtail the cooking time and use more white wine mixed with water or fish stock.

2 oz (60 g) butter
3 leeks, cleaned and roughly chopped
3 carrots, peeled and chopped
2 onions, peeled and chopped
3 stalks of celery, cleaned and chopped
3 tbsp chopped fresh parsley
1 chicken, cut up into 8 pieces
1 pt (600 ml) hot chicken stock
salt and pepper
1 bay leaf
splash of white wine
2 egg yolks
3 tbsp double cream (optional)
juice of $\frac{1}{2}$ a lemon

Melt the butter in a large heavy casserole and gently sauté the vegetables plus 1 tbsp of the parsley for about 5 minutes. Place the chicken pieces on top and pour in enough hot stock to come level with the meat. Season with salt and pepper and add the bay leaf and a splash of white wine. Cover the casserole and simmer, either on top of the stove or in a moderate oven, for just over an hour. When the chicken is tender, remove it and cut it into smaller pieces or, if you prefer, bone them and cut the meat into squares. Keep warm. Beat the egg yolks, cream (if you are using it) and the lemon juice in a small bowl. Add a couple of tablespoons of the hot stock and beat again. Keeping the stock just below simmering, stir in the egg yolk mixture and cook very gently until the sauce is slightly thickened. Divide the chicken between individual heated soup dishes. Pour over the sauce, making sure each serving has some of all the vegetables. Sprinkle on the remaining parsley and serve.

SERVES 4

POACHED CHICKEN WITH ALMOND SAUCE

Thickening a sauce with ground almonds is something that may, or may not, have occurred to you. The result is creamy but not over rich, with a texture that is interestingly knubbly. Once you have tasted the effect, you will doubtless include it among your cooking techniques. The recipe below is my own version of Circassian Chicken, a popular Middle Eastern dish. The flavoured red oil which you trickle on to the beige sauce covering the golden chicken makes a design that could remind you, not irrelevantly, of Persian carpets. A boiling chicken invariably has better flavour than a roaster, but takes much longer to cook.

1 boiling or roasting chicken, preferably free-range
4 tbsp vegetable oil
2 cloves of garlic, peeled and slivered
pinch of ground cinnamon
pinch of turmeric
pinch of ground ginger
2 tsp cayenne pepper or paprika
6 oz (175 g) ground almonds

FOR THE STOCK:
1 onion
1 carrot
1 stick of celery
few sprigs of fresh parsley
1 bay leaf
salt and pepper

If you are using a boiling chicken, remove any stubble and the fat in the body cavity. In a pot large enough to hold the chicken, heat 2 tbsp of the oil and gently fry the garlic. Stir in the cinnamon, turmeric and ginger and cook for a minute or two. Turn the chicken in the spiced oil until it is golden all over. Remove the chicken and wash the pan. Return the bird to the clean pan, add water just to cover and the stock flavourings. Simmer gently until tender. A medium to large roasting chicken will take about an hour, a boiler between two and three hours, depending on how hectic a life it has led. Ten minutes before the chicken is due to be done, mix the cayenne (if you like it hot) or the paprika into the remaining 2 tbsp oil. Remove $\frac{3}{4}$ pt (450 ml) stock from the pan and pour into a smaller saucepan. Dribble in the ground almonds and boil gently until you have a sauce with the consistency of double cream. Adjust the seasoning. Place the chicken on the warm serving dish. Coat with almond sauce and use the red oil to make a mystical pattern. Strain the stock and keep it in the refrigerator.

GARLIC CHICKEN   SERVES 4

The basis for this idea came from one of my favourite books, *Simple French Food* by Richard Olney. The author is an American living in the South of France and his taste, where food is concerned, is well nigh faultless. The title of the book is something of a misnomer; although the ingredients are fairly straightforward some of the processes are almost tortuous, as in boning and stuffing an oxtail. However, the only technique required here, apart from the leap of faith that forty cloves of garlic when cooked are deliciously mild and nutty, is sealing your cooking pot with a snake of dough. It is easy and it looks wonderful when you bring it to the table and proceed to smash the seal. It is becoming easier (and cheaper) to buy garlic by weight in this country.

1 chicken, cut up into 8 pieces, or use chicken pieces, the breasts halved, the thighs and drumsticks separated
4 heads of garlic weighing about 6 oz (175 g), broken into cloves, left unpeeled but cleaned of loose papery bits
4 tbsp olive oil
1 tsp crumbled dried thyme
salt and pepper
a bouquet garni (tie together a celery stalk, parsley sprigs, bay leaf and leek greens)
plain flour for dough

Set the oven to 180°C/350°F/gas mark 4. In an earthenware casserole with a lid, or similar ovenproof dish, put the chicken pieces, garlic, oil, thyme, salt and pepper. Using your hands turn everything around until liberally coated with oil and seasoning. Push the bouquet into the centre, pack the chicken around and fill cracks and crevices with the garlic cloves. Make a dough with flour, water and a dribble of oil. Roll it into a long sausage. Moisten the rim of your cooking pot with water, press on the snake of dough and then the lid on to that, sealing it hermetically. Cook for $1\frac{1}{2}$ hours.

Break the seal at the table. The garlic can be squeezed out from
its skin and the purée spread on toasted rough brown bread.

SERVES 4　# CHICKEN TAGINE

Seeing a tagine on sale among the wok sets and tandoori kits the
other day, I was reminded of this North African stew. Rather like
a casserole, the name of the dish is synonymous with the actual
cooking pot. Although the high pointed lid of the earthenware
dish helps condense the steam and keep the meat moist, this recipe
can, of course, be cooked in an ordinary pan with a cover. Indeed,
since a tagine itself cannot be assumed to be a part of everyone's
batterie de cuisine, I shall only assume that you have a suitably
rustic serving dish. The combination of meat with fruit is typical
of North African and Middle Eastern cookery and is a taste easily
acquired.

2 tbsp oil
2 onions, peeled and finely chopped
2 tsp ground ginger
a few strands of saffron or a pinch of turmeric
3 lb (1.5 kg) chicken, jointed
4 oz (120 g) stoned prunes or raisins
1 tsp ground cinnamon
2 tbsp clear honey
a few slices of fresh or preserved lemon (see page 285)
salt and freshly ground black pepper
4 oz (120 g) almonds, blanched and fried in butter till golden
1 tbsp sesame seeds, roasted in a dry iron frying pan

Heat the oil in a saucepan large enough to hold the chicken pieces
and gently fry the onions without letting them brown. Stir in the
ginger and saffron or turmeric, and then add the chicken pieces,
turning them in the flavoured oil until coloured. Add water to
come level with the chicken pieces (don't swamp them) and bring
to a simmer with the lid half on. Cook until the chicken is tender –
about 50 minutes – and then remove the chicken pieces with a
slotted spoon. Set aside, keeping them warm. Add the prunes or
raisins to the pan juices and stir in the cinnamon, honey and a
slice or two of lemon. Simmer until the sauce is thick and syrupy.
Season. Return the chicken pieces and cook until heated through.
Place the chicken on a warm dish (or the tagine), pour on the sauce
and garnish with the almonds and sesame seeds. You can, if you
wish, dribble on a little more oil.

KOREAN MARINADE FOR GRILLED MEAT SERVES 4

This recipe was given to me by David Queensberry, who is a dab hand in the kitchen. Although the preparation needs to be done a couple of hours before you want to eat, it takes only minutes to cook and is a very effective means of jollying what you suspect might be a dreary chicken. I have left the recipe that follows in David's words and I would only add that meat treated this way is well accompanied by rice or noodles and a green salad, perhaps with a few toasted sesame seeds scattered over the top.

'This recipe was given to me many years ago by a Korean friend and it has stood me in good stead. I use it mainly for cooking outside on a barbecue, but it can be used inside if you have good extraction and a very hot grill or cast-iron steak griddle. Do not try to fry. The meat that responds best to this treatment is beef, chicken and pork. It is a mistake to leave the marinade too long. I have sometimes used meat that has been marinating, let's say, overnight and the marination takes over.'

The meat needs to be cut into portions that can be cooked quite quickly – not too thick. A chicken for example, I cut into eight pieces. Basically the marinade needs to cover the meat, therefore the quantity can be adjusted accordingly. For a 2½–3 lb (1.24–1.5 kg) chicken, I would suggest:

4 fl oz (120 ml) soy sauce (I think Japanese is best; Chinese-Hong Kong is also OK; Amoy is always readily available)
4 fl oz (120 ml) dry white wine (any rubbish will do as long as it has not turned to vinegar)
1 slightly heaped dsp sugar
lots of coarsely ground black pepper
1 heaped tsp grated fresh ginger (not essential)
2 fat cloves of garlic, crushed

Mix all the ingredients for the marinade in a bowl. Place meat in a ceramic or glass dish and cover with the marinade. Put in the fridge or cool place for two to four hours. It is a good idea to turn the meat once to make sure it gets properly steeped in the marinade. The meat is now ready to grill.

TURKEY STUFFINGS

That turkey meat is dull seems to me indisputable. All the more important, then, that the stuffing(s) should be delicious so that you can ooh and aah over the look of the golden-brown bird and concentrate on tasting what is in effect a sort of pâté made more flavoursome by being cooked inside a meat container.

The recipes below are how I remember making my own stuffings, designed, I must admit, to appeal to the grown-ups more than the children, who, given the choice, would rather have a pork sausage. Ingredients like dried Chinese mushrooms are dispensable but they give an interesting dark colour as well as flavour.

TO STUFF THE FRONT (NECK) PART:

4 shallots or 1 small onion
1 tbsp butter
the turkey liver
12 oz (375 g) brown breadcrumbs or steamed bulghur (cracked wheat)
2 tbsp pine kernels
2 tbsp chopped fresh parsley
2 prunes, stoned and chopped
grated rind of 1 small lemon
salt and pepper
2 eggs

Chop and fry the shallots or onion in the butter. Chop the turkey liver and sauté very briefly with the onions. Let this mixture cool. Add it to all the other ingredients except for the eggs. Beat the eggs and stir them in. Fill the neck cavity loosely with the stuffing and sew up the skin or pin well with small skewers.

TO STUFF THE BODY CAVITY:

2 onions, peeled and chopped
1 oz (30 g) butter
2 lb (1 kg) belly of pork, minced
3 stalks of celery, finely chopped
6 dried Chinese mushrooms (or other dried mushrooms), soaked and chopped
1 dsp chopped fresh ginger root
2 cloves of garlic, finely chopped
2 tbsp chopped fresh parsley or coriander
2 tbsp soy sauce
freshly ground black pepper
1 egg

Fry the onions until soft in the butter. Add the pork and stir until lightly cooked. Add all the other ingredients except for the egg. Stir-fry for a minute. Let the mixture cool. Mix in the egg and stuff the body cavity of the bird.

PULLED AND DEVILLED TURKEY   SERVES 4

As Jane Grigson, who features this recipe in her book *English Food*, says, it is one of the most delicious dishes of eighteenth-century cooking; indeed one of the best of all English dishes. It is certainly the best thing to do with leftover turkey and a reason next time for buying an even bigger turkey than the one you think you need. The same principle – devilling the dark meat and bathing the white meat in a creamy sauce – can be applied to chicken or pheasant and these make good dinner party dishes that can be prepared ahead of time. Devilling is more satanic if you can leave the dark meat spread with the sauce for a few hours to give the flavours a chance to penetrate.

Leftover turkey, both white and dark meat

FOR THE DEVIL SAUCE:
1 tbsp Dijon mustard
1 tbsp mango or peach chutney
1 tbsp Worcestershire Sauce
¼ tsp cayenne pepper
salt
vegetable oil

FOR THE PULLED SAUCE:
3 oz (30 g) butter
6 oz (175 ml) double cream
lemon juice
salt and pepper
chopped parsley

Pull the breast meat apart into thin pieces about 1½ in (4 cm) long, following the grain of the meat. Take the brown meat off the bones and divide into quite large pieces. Slash each one two or three times. Mix the devil sauce ingredients together, chopping up any large pieces of fruit in the chutney. Coat the brown meat with it, pushing it into the slashes as best you can. Arrange the pieces in a single layer on the rack of a foil-lined grill pan, and grill under a high heat until the pieces develop an appetising brown crust. Keep them warm. For the pulled sauce, melt the butter in a wide frying pan and stir in the cream. Let it boil, stirring all the time until you have a thick sauce. Put in the breast meat and any scraps of meat jelly. Stir about until it is all very hot. Season with lemon juice, salt and pepper. Put the pulled meat in the centre of a serving dish, sprinkle on the parsley and surround it with the devilled pieces. Serve with good bread or toast.

TACCHINO TONNATO

The fact that in some Italian dishes turkey and veal are inter-changeable only says something, one might think, about the inherent passivity – or tastelessness – of the meats. But in the case of this quite inspired combination of cold meat with a tuna fish sauce, the blandness of the main ingredient sets off the creaminess of a sauce that is made a little spiky with anchovies. You can, of course, use poached veal for this recipe, but turkey is quicker and cheaper. If you find turkey sold in pieces, as many supermarkets will do these days, this is a good way of jollying it. It makes a perfect supper on a warm evening, should there be such a thing. To give it true Italian *brio* start with a dish of hot pasta.

2 turkey breasts, weighing about 2 lb (1 kg)
1 carrot, peeled
1 stalk of celery
1 onion, peeled
parsley stalks
1 bay leaf
a few peppercorns
7 oz (160 g) tin of tuna
3 anchovy fillets, drained of oil or brine and rinsed
1 tbsp lemon juice, or less to taste
freshly ground black pepper
capers, to taste

FOR THE MAYONNAISE:
2 egg yolks
½ pt (300 ml) olive oil
salt
squeeze of lemon juice

Find a pan not much bigger than the turkey breasts. Put the turkey in it, add water just to cover. Now, and this is important, remove the turkey. Chop the vegetables roughly and add them with the herbs and peppercorns to the water, which will be just the right amount. Bring to a simmer. Replace the turkey, poach for 30 minutes, turn off the heat and let the meat cool in the liquid. Make your mayonnaise; I would urge you to do it by hand with bowl and wooden spoon (see page 6), rather than in a blender or food processor. Use one of those gadgets to whizz the drained tuna fish to a purée, incorporating the anchovy fillets and the lemon juice to taste. Gradually fold, by hand, the tuna purée into the mayonnaise. Taste for seasoning. Grind on some black pepper. Slice the cooled turkey breast. Arrange on a pretty plate. Coat the meat thinly with the sauce and scatter the dish with capers. If you wish to make the dish in advance, it only improves with keeping (within reason). It can be covered with clingfilm and refrigerated for 24 hours.

DUCK BREASTS WITH APPLES SERVES 2

Although *magret de canard*, the style in which duck breasts so often appears on menus, no longer tempts me in restaurants, it makes an ideal quick and luxurious meal at home. Sauces that contain white wine, brandy and cream strike me as almost unpleasantly rich accompaniments to duck and I would go for something fruity to cut the fattiness of the meat. The idea below is adapted from a recipe of Anton Mosimann. You could also make use of fruit tinned without syrup, such as blackcurrants, blueberries or blackberries, to make a sauce that you pep up with red wine, freshly ground black pepper and any meat juices from cooking the duck, and thicken with $1\frac{1}{2}$ tsp arrowroot first mixed into a little of the liquid, then returned to the sauce.

2 duck breasts
salt and pepper
a little ground ginger
1 oz (30 g) butter
1 dessert apple, peeled, cored and cut into crescents
4 tbsp apple juice
1 tbsp green peppercorns in brine, drained well (optional)

Vigorously season the duck breasts on both sides with salt, pepper and ginger. Make your grill and grill pan red hot and place on it the duck, skin side down in order to brand the skin. Lower the heat to medium and turn the meat over. Cook 5–6 minutes, turn again and cook until the meat *just* loses its pink; in all about 10–12 minutes. While this is going on, melt the butter in a small pan. Add the apple slices and cook gently. After they are glazed, pour in the apple juice, add the peppercorns if you are using them and bubble the juice until slightly reduced. Serve the duck breasts, either as they are or sliced across the grain and fanned out, with the apples and the sauce poured around.

LETTUCE-WRAPPED DUCK

You may have noticed in Thai and Chinese restaurants that wrapping things in lettuce is all the go. It does lend a pleasant, if somewhat bogus, air of healthiness and also contributes a contrasting texture to the meat, poultry, diced seafood or whatever makes up the contents of the package. This crib on Peking Duck makes the bird go further – meaning that one duck can serve four as a main course – and has a good *involving* quality for your family or friends. Ideally, a duck roasted in this fashion should be hung to dry for at least 12 hours, but we will cheat with a hair dryer. Hoisin sauce, also sometimes called barbecue sauce, can be got at oriental supermarkets, as can plum sauce.

1 fresh duck
2 tbsp honey
1 large cos or Webb's lettuce, or similarly crisp variety
½ cucumber, cut into matchsticks
1 bunch of spring onions, trimmed and sliced lengthways into strips
3 tbsp plum sauce or Hoisin sauce

Wash the duck and place it in a large sieve or colander. Bring a kettle full of water to the boil and, when boiling, pour it over the duck, turning the bird once or twice so that it is well and truly scalded. Pat dry and place in a large bowl. Melt the honey in a jug with ½ pt (300 ml) of hot water. Pour it over the duck, then drain it off back into the cup and repeat. Turn the duck over and repeat again. You can even use a pastry brush to brush the sweet solution into parts of the duck you thought you might never reach. Contrive some way of hanging the duck up (you can use a butcher's hook or wire coat hanger, for instance) and train a warm (not hot) hair dryer on it until dry. You can, of course, just leave it in an airy place overnight. Heat the oven to 200°C/400°F/gas mark 6. Roast the duck on a wire grid, breast side up, for 20 minutes. Turn over (without puncturing the skin) and roast for a further 25 minutes. Turn over again and roast 20 minutes more. The skin should now be crisp and golden. Prepare the lettuce leaves, washing and drying only if strictly necessary. Arrange the cucumber and spring onions in small dishes. Put the plum or Hoisin sauce in a pretty bowl. Carve the duck, both the skin and the meat, into bite-size pieces and place on a warm serving dish. To eat, spoon a little sauce into a lettuce leaf, add a few strands of onion and cucumber, some duck, and then make a neat parcel and pop into your mouth.

QUAILS WITH INTERESTING RICE SERVES 4

Quails are often sold in packets of six. You will need at least two quails per person. Even then what you get is not a massive amount of protein, which makes the sausage meat in the rice a welcome addition.

This is a very pretty assembly. I have served it with success at parties and it has the added advantage of being quick to cook. If you do not happen to have the spices mentioned in the recipe, don't fret. Use what is to hand but remember that quails need a bit of gingering up, quite literally, as they are farmed birds without the benefit of an interesting or even hazardous life. Sometimes I use the pan juices plus cream to make a small amount of sauce to dribble over the birds.

8 quails
½ a lemon
spices: ground coriander or cumin, cardamom, ginger, black
pepper
8 oz (250 g) basmati rice
2 oz (60 g) butter
½ pt (300 ml) light stock, or water
1 tbsp vegetable oil
4 oz (120 g) sausage meat
1 small round lettuce, trimmed and cut across into thin ribbons
4 fl oz (120 ml) cream (if you want to make a sauce)

Rub the quails with the lemon and then with a mixture of the ground spices. Let them sit absorbing these flavours while you prepare the rice. Wash it well to remove any clinging starch and then either sauté it first in 1 oz (30 g) of melted butter and add enough light stock to cook, or cook in water, according to preference. About 15 minutes before the rice is ready, heat the oil and the rest of the butter and sauté the spiced quails, first turning them until evenly browned and then cooking them over a gentle heat until all traces of pink in the flesh are gone. In a separate pan fry the sausage meat, breaking it up with a fork until it resembles crumbs. Mix the cooked rice with the sausage meat and the lettuce, folding it in sensitively. Arrange the quails on top. If you want to make a sauce, add cream to the pan juices and bubble the mixture. It should have a nice deep gold colour.

SERVES 2-3   # NORMANDY PHEASANT

When the pheasant season is at its end, there are sometimes bargains around. Even if not, pheasant prices compare quite well with those for corn-fed chickens and it does have a more glamorous image. If necessary, use a frozen pheasant, carefully and slowly defrosted.

I remember doing this recipe early on in my cooking experience and being surprised how such a simple method turned out such a silky, luxurious dish. Casseroling the bird keeps it from going dry and the sauce assembles itself in the cooking process. Puréed Jerusalem artichokes would be a lovely accompaniment.

2 oz (60 g) butter
1 tbsp vegetable oil
1 plump pheasant
2 dessert apples, peeled, cored and sliced
2 tbsp Calvados or ½ pt (300 ml) cider, reduced by vigorous boiling to 2 tbsp
1½ pt (300 ml) double cream, or 5 fl oz (150 ml) double cream and 1 Petit Suisse or some fromage blanc
salt and freshly ground black pepper

Turn on the oven to 190°C/375°F/gas mark 5. In half the butter and the oil, sauté the trussed pheasant (without its pork back fat if any) until golden on all sides. Remove from the pan and in the remaining butter and other pan juices gently fry the apples slices. Find an earthenware casserole, or similar ovenproof dish with a lid, which will hold the pheasant quite snugly. Place the apples in the bottom, the pheasant on them. Add the Calvados or cider to the pan juices, bubble them for a minute or two and then pour them on the pheasant. Cover and cook in the oven for about 30 minutes. Remove the casserole from the oven, add the cream. If you are wanting to use less cream for health reasons, do as the French do and put one Petit Suisse cheese inside the birds and pour in the smaller amount of cream. Season with salt and freshly ground black pepper. Take the opportunity to turn the pheasant over so that it is breast side down. Return the casserole to the oven for another 15 minutes. Serve the bird on a warm dish. Stir the sauce until well amalgamated, reducing if necessary by boiling for added thickness. Pour it around the pheasant.

PHEASANT STUFFED WITH CRACKED WHEAT

SERVES 2-4

A pheasant will feed two greedy people, or three more restrained eaters, or even four disciplined ones. The stuffing detailed below will fluff it out considerably. The basis of the stuffing is cracked wheat or bulghur, available in health food shops or the health sections of supermarkets. Couscous could be substituted. The other ingredients can be varied according to taste, but a slightly sweet element, as in the raisins or carrots, is a good idea.

1 pheasant, preferably larded with pork fat or bacon
salt and pepper
8 oz (250 g) bulghur or couscous
4 fl oz (120 ml) warm water
1 largish onion, peeled and chopped
2 oz (60 g) butter
2 tbsp roasted or unroasted cashew nuts
1 tbsp pine kernels (optional)
1 large carrot, peeled and finely grated, or 3 strips of orange peel, cut into threads
1 tbsp raisins
3 juniper berries, crushed, or 1 tsp coriander seeds
1 tsp finely chopped fresh parsley
1 dsp plain flour

Turn on the oven to 220°C/425°F/gas mark 7. Wipe the pheasant inside and out and season with salt and pepper. If it is not larded with fat, drape a few rashers of bacon on top. Make the stuffing by first putting the bulghur into a bowl and pouring on about half a cup of warm water. Leave for 10 minutes for the grain to swell and check to see if it will absorb some more. Sauté the onion in the butter until softened. Stir in the nuts and pine kernels (if you are using them) and let them brown lightly. Add the carrot or orange peel, raisins, juniper berries or coriander seeds and lastly the soaked bulghur. Toss the mixture in the pan until all is well amalgamated. Check for seasoning and stir in the parsley. Stuff the pheasant with the mixture. Any excess mixture can be cooked in a small ovenproof dish, on a lower shelf of the oven. Place the bird in a roasting pan and place in the oven for 45–50 minutes. Ten minutes before the end of cooking time, remove the bacon or fat, dredge with flour and return the bird to the oven.

PIGEON BREASTS WITH GARLIC

The received idea about English wood pigeons is that they are
tough little birds and must have tenderness stewed into them with
hours of casseroling. I find that such an approach renders them
stringy and sour. A far better method is to remove the breasts in
one graceful movement and grill them briefly. They will be tender
and rosy pink. I have adapted an idea of Dr Jack Gillon, who was
a winner of the Mouton Cadet Dinner Party Menu competition
and went on to publish a book called *Le Menu Gastronomique*. The
sauce is slightly simplified in the interests of those who have had
a hard day at the office and the meat is marinated in case you are
fearful of the notion of briskly cooked pigeon. Serve with mashed
potatoes or a puréed root vegetable to paddle in the sauce and
meat juices.

1 pigeon per person
a little olive oil
a little lemon juice or wine
salt and pepper
1 carrot, peeled
1 onion, peeled and stuck with a clove
1 celery stalk
1 bay leaf
a few whole peppercorns
4 trimmed but unpeeled cloves of garlic per person
1 tsp arrowroot
a little port or red wine
a little ground ginger

Using a sharp, cunning little knife, take off the pigeon breasts
by working the knife between the flesh and breast bone. They
practically slide off. Trim any gristle or skin that overhangs the
'suprême'. Mix together some olive oil, a little lemon juice or wine,
salt and pepper. Turn the breasts in this and leave to marinate.
Use the carcasses and vegetables to make stock, adding the bay
leaf, some peppercorns and the garlic cloves. Simmer for up to $1\frac{1}{2}$
hours, as long as time allows. Strain the stock and put aside the
garlic cloves. Continue to boil the stock until it is well reduced.
You want only a couple of tablespoons per person. Mix the arrowroot with a little port or red wine. Stir into the stock to make it
glossy. Remove the pigeon from the marinade. Sprinkle with a
little ground ginger and some black pepper. Grill the breasts under
a moderate heat for a few minutes on each side, then switch off

the grill and let the meat rest under it for another 10 minutes. To serve prettily, slice the breasts across and fan out the slices on a warmed plate. Surround with sauce. If you like garlic (by now it will be mild and nutty), sauté the cloves briskly in a little butter and serve alongside.

RABBIT AS I REMEMBER IT IN ITALY   SERVES 4

The Italians and the French approach rabbit with considerably more enthusiasm than do the British, who seem lastingly haunted by the spectre of myxomatosis. Those dire days now long gone, it is time to appreciate the mildly gamy, lean flavour of rabbit, invariably more interesting than chicken. Soho butchers often have rabbits, tame and wild, hanging in their shop windows and they will skin them for you. If you buy a wild rabbit, get a small young one. Enterprising supermarkets sell frozen rabbit, much of it coming from China. Do not give it to the cat; follow the recipe below, which is as close as I can come to emulating a dish of rabbit I ate in a country inn in Italy. The sauce had an almost jammy consistency and the scent of olive oil and wild thyme beckoned. Indeed, if you are sure you have a tender rabbit, the creature is also excellent simply roasted in the oven with those two flavourings plus garlic. A particularly robust chicken could be substituted for rabbit in this dish.

4 tbsp olive oil
6 oz (175 g) belly pork or bacon, cubed
1 onion or 3 shallots, peeled and chopped
1 young rabbit, jointed, or 2 lb (1 kg) frozen rabbit, defrosted
2–3 cloves of garlic, peeled and slivered
7 fl oz (200 ml) red wine
1 × 14 oz (400 g) tin of peeled tomatoes or carton of sieved tomatoes
2 tbsp tomato paste
juice of 1 small lemon
1 scant dsp dried oregano or thyme
good pinch of brown sugar
salt and pepper
tiny pinch of chilli powder or red pepper flakes

FOR THE GARNISH:
chopped fresh parsley
slices of French bread rubbed with garlic and toasted in the oven

In 2 tbsp olive oil sauté the salt pork or bacon until the fat begins to run. Add the onion and stir until softened. Add the rabbit and the garlic and sauté, turning, until the meat is lightly browned. Add the wine, bubble up and reduce it a little. Add the tomatoes, tomato paste, lemon juice, another 2 tbsp olive oil and herbs and seasonings. Simmer, uncovered, until the meat is tender; up to an hour depending on the youth of the rabbit. When tender, remove to a warm serving dish. Reduce the sauce until it is thick and shiny and only enough to coat the meat meanly. Taste for seasoning and adjust if necessary. Pour the sauce on the rabbit. Sprinkle with parsley and serve with the toasted bread.

SERVES 4 VENISON STEAKS WITH FARTHINGHOE SAUCE

Some years ago, Nicola Cox won a Cook of Britain competition and now she and her husband, Simon, run the Farthinghoe Cookery School and wine business in their house near Banbury. *Nicola Cox's Good Food from Farthinghoe* is the paperback edition of her first cookery book. Her recipes are well suited to entertaining at home and the book is divided by the different kinds of occasions, such as informal lunch parties, buffet parties, spontaneous entertaining and so on.

Mrs Cox apparently demonstrates at an annual game fair, and this is her recipe for venison steaks. The sauce is also good with other game.

2 tbsp olive oil
4 venison steaks
salt and pepper
3–4 tbsp port
bunch of good watercress

FOR THE SAUCE:
rind and juice of $\frac{1}{2}$ lemon
5 generous tbsp redcurrant jelly
2 tbsp port
$\frac{1}{2}$ stick of cinnamon
2 oz (60 g) butter

Heat the pan until very hot, add a little oil and cook the venison steaks very fast for about $1\frac{1}{2}$–2 minutes on each side. Season with salt and dish up on a heated dish. Add the port to the pan, swirl round to remove the tasty juices and pour over the steaks. Garnish with watercress and serve at once, the Farthinghoe sauce handed separately.

To make the Farthinghoe sauce, take julienne strips from half the lemon, place in plenty of cold water in a saucepan, bring to the boil and blanch for 5–10 minutes until no longer bitter; drain and refresh under the cold tap to set the colour. Gently melt and heat the jelly, port, cinnamon, julienne strips and a long strip of thinly pared lemon rind. Simmer for 5–10 minutes, then add the juice of $\frac{1}{2}$ lemon, remove the long lemon strip and cinnamon stick, and whisk in the butter in little bits. Turn into a sauceboat and keep warm.

BEST BREAD SAUCE

When game is in season, my thoughts turn not to the perfect partridge but to bread sauce. I love it and want to promote it. Thickening a sauce with bread is an idea that dates from the Middle Ages, when sauces had to have a consistency that prevented them from trickling off the trencher. It was presumably not over-looked, even then, that bread also added its nutty flavour and an interesting and soothing texture (think of that childhood dish of bread and milk). It is rare in restaurants to encounter a really well made bread sauce and it is worth taking the time at home to steep the onions and flavouring in the milk for quite some time and to cook the finished sauce in a double boiler to allow it to develop. Use a good, not white sliced, loaf. Roast chicken is, of course, a good excuse for bread sauce, but it accompanies equally well any other bird and even sausages.

$\frac{3}{4}$ pt (450 ml) full cream milk
1 onion, peeled and stuck with 3 cloves
2 bay leaves
4 oz (120 g) bread, with the crusts removed
salt and pepper
a little nutmeg
1 oz (30 g) salted butter
2 tbsp double cream

Put the milk in a heavy-bottomed saucepan and add the onion stuck with cloves and the bay leaves. Bring to just below the boil and steep at this shuddering heat for as long as possible, up to 45 minutes. The more flavoursome your milk, the better the sauce. Tear up the bread into small pieces and place in another pan, non-stick if you have one. Pour the milk through a sieve, pressing the onion against the sieve so as to add its juices. Stir well to break up the bread and season with salt, pepper and a scraping of nutmeg.

Stir in the butter and cream and cook extremely gently, preferably in a double boiler arrangement, for at least another 15 minutes. If the sauce seems too thick, add a little more milk. Many people prefer more bread sauce than meat. Fried breadcrumbs may be thought to be gilding the gingerbread, but they are a wonderful side-kick.

DEVILMENT

With the easy availability of tropical spices, the plethora of Indian cookery books on the market and the various ready-prepared mixtures, like Tandoori and Madras mixes, the British mode of devilling food tends to get forgotten. The difference between currying and devilling is not only in the ingredients used, but in the method. A devil mixture is often used to coat cold cooked meat, for example chicken or game, and the meat is then grilled. The ingredients in a devil mixture might use a proprietary sauce like Worcestershire, also mustard, anchovies, vinegar, black pepper, cayenne, and cream or butter. Applied to uncooked meat or fish, the devil process is a quick way to liven up what might seem the arid prospect of a supper of chop or chicken leg. The following recipe comes from *Food for the Greedy* by Nancy Shaw, which was published in 1936.

Oven cooking and the inclusion of cream averts the problem of dryness which is inherent in grilling cooked food. The devil butter is good for steaks or chops – or indeed anything that can successfully be grilled.

WHITE DEVIL SAUCE

1 tsp French mustard, and more, as required
1 tsp anchovy sauce
1 tsp wine vinegar
1 tsp salt
1 tsp sugar
1 tsp Worcestershire Sauce
¼ pt (150 ml) double cream

Mix together all the ingredients except the cream. Whip the cream until quite stiff and stir in the seasonings. Using more mustard, spread chicken pieces with a thin layer. Place them in an ovenproof dish and spread the sauce on top. Cook in a hot oven, until heated through if you are using cooked chicken or until cooked.

DEVIL BUTTER

salt and freshly ground black pepper
cayenne pepper
4 oz (120 g) butter
4 anchovy fillets, drained of oil or brine, rinsed and chopped
1–2 cloves of garlic, peeled and chopped
1 tbsp made English mustard
good dash of Tabasco sauce

Rub the meat with plenty of freshly ground pepper, some cayenne pepper and salt. Mix the remaining ingredients for the devil butter together (easy if the butter is room temperature). Coat the meat and grill. Serve with a pat of leftover devil butter.

MEAT

The preponderance of recipes in this book for minced meat of one kind or another is not just because mince is quick to cook. Not being keen about eating great slabs of meat, I like the way mince is biddable; accepting other ingredients and a range of herbs and spices and in no disturbing way resembling the beast from where it comes. I like good sausages for the same reasons. You must trust a butcher or supplier where minced meat is concerned. If in doubt, make your own. A food processor is invaluable here as it chops the meat rather than squeezing the essence out of it.

Expensive cuts of meat have their place but I feel they should be an occasional treat, both for reasons of finance and health. The Chinese understand well the role of meat as supporting actor rather than star of the meal and it is no coincidence that most of the pork recipes in this section are Chinese-inspired.

The fact that there is one veal recipe – Blanquette de Veau – conveys my worry that veal is still sometimes reared in an unacceptable manner. The situation is improving, but it is by no means ideal.

Stew is a dismal word but replace it with vocabulary like 'daube', 'carbonnade', 'tagine' and 'hot-pot' and you begin to get the point about slow-cooked meat. In an odd way, lengthy cooking – when something is prepared in the morning for the evening, or the day before for the following day – can become another interpretation of 'fast food'. It is also consoling.

On the whole, offal can be, and should be, cooked quickly and, in my view, quite often.

CARPACCIO SERVES 4

There are certain dishes which by their very nature would seem to belong in restaurants. Carpaccio, thin, thin slices of raw beef, would seem to be one of them, just as sashimi, raw fish, would seem to be another. It would seem odd that we should entrust restaurateurs rather than ourselves to procure the good enough ingredient. The thinness of carpaccio, achieved by slicing with a razor-sharp knife and some judicious beating out, in an odd way removes the terror of the raw and produces a subtle flavour, 'cleaner' than, say, steak tartare. Serving fillet steak in this manner also makes a little go a long way and conveys the notion of luxury and even perhaps sophistication. That there are few calories is also worth a mention. Italian restaurants often serve this with a mustardy mayonnaise which you achieve by mixing Dijon mustard into mayonnaise, home-made or bought. You could, however, make the sauce below, a kind of sauce ravigote, which is sharper

and, it has to be said, slightly healthier. Serve your carpaccio as a
first course with some rye bread and a nice little salad or some
crudités.

8 oz (250 g) fillet of beef, trimmed of fat and membranes

FOR THE SAUCE:
1 oz (30 g) fresh parsley, finely chopped
1 oz (30 g) watercress or chives, finely chopped
4 anchovy fillets, drained of oil or brine, rinsed and chopped
1 tbsp chopped shallots
1 dsp chopped capers
2–3 gherkins, finely chopped
2–3 tsp wine vinegar
4 tbsp oil, preferably olive oil
1 heaped tsp Dijon mustard

Chill the beef briefly in the freezer, which will make it easier to
slice. Slice it as neatly and thinly as you can. Beat out the slices
between clingfilm until they are paper thin. Arrange on plates. To
make the sauce you can use a liquidiser, or do it by hand. Mix the
first seven ingredients. Slowly stir in or blend in the oil. When
thickened, add the mustard to taste. Use your judgement over salt
or pepper. Trickle the sauce meanly over the meat and serve the
rest alongside.

SERVES 2–3 # COLD SPICED STEAK

Collected recipes from well-known people, sold in aid of charity,
are frequently rum affairs. However, despite its sexist overtones I
like *Men's Menus*, compiled in aid of the Cornwall Historic
Churches Trust. I know the Earl of Gowrie to be a good cook.
Nowadays, he apparently only cooks at weekends in Wales. He
claims to have invented the cold spiced steak given below, and it
strikes me that it would be a very nice commodity to have in the
fridge to come home to.

3–4 tbsp black peppercorns
3–4 tbsp juniper berries
*rump steak, sliced 1½ in (4 cm) thick, weighing about 1 lb (500 g) and
long enough just to fit in a large cast-iron frying pan*
Dijon mustard
1 tbsp olive oil
scant 1 tbsp butter

Grind, but not too finely, the black peppercorns and juniper

berries, then thickly smear the steak, trimmed of fat, with plain
Dijon mustard. Scatter the spices all over it so that they stick to
the mustard. Get the cast-iron frying pan very hot and put a
tablespoon of olive oil in and then a bit less of butter. When the
foam dies down, fry the steak on one side for 7–8 minutes. Wearing
oven gloves and making use of a spatula, pour out the fat. Place a
plate over the frying pan and turn the steak. Repeat the process,
making sure you get the pan hot enough again. Let the steak cool
on the plate, then refrigerate for 4–5 hours. Slice lengthways, fairly
thinly. The meat should be very rare but cool and appetising, and
its redness counter-balanced by the spicy black crust.

BEEF ON A STRING WITH ICED HORSERADISH

SERVES 4

Partly because you encounter it too rarely in restaurants, partly
because it is healthier, I like boiled meat. The flavours that result
are often more subtle than with other modes of cooking and sauces
can play a suitably important role. Roasting a small piece of beef
usually has disappointing results and, since few of us can afford a
huge joint (making roast beef from the trolley a sensible choice in
a restaurant), it is worth considering this method of dangling the
meat in boiling water. You need good quality beef, preferably top
rib, and you should ask your butcher to tie it in a neat, square
shape. For the horseradish ice-cream, try to get bottled grated
horseradish rather than horseradish sauce which has a nasty acidic
quality. The contrast of hot, rosy beef and cold stinging sauce is
rather thrilling.

¼ pt (150 ml) double cream
1 tbsp grated horseradish
squeeze of lemon juice
1 tbsp sea salt, and more to serve
2 lb (1 kg) good quality beef
bunch of watercress

Whip the double cream until quite stiff. Fold in 1 tbsp grated
horseradish, or horseradish sauce if unavailable, adding more or
less, depending on how pungent a taste you like. Stir in a squeeze
of lemon juice. Freeze in a small container. Half an hour before
you want to eat bring a large saucepan of water to the boil. Add a
good 1 tbsp sea salt. Attach a long piece of string to your parcel of
beef. Tie one end to the saucepan handle in such a way that the
beef will hang in the pan without touching the base. You could

also fool around hanging it from a wooden spoon laid across the pan. Replace the pan lid. After the water resumes boiling simmer the meat for 30 minutes, which will give you nicely rare results. For larger or smaller quantities of meat allow exactly 15 minutes per lb (450 g). Serve the beef sliced, with generous quantities of watercress, a bowl of sea salt and the iced horseradish, and perhaps some potatoes boiled in their skins.

SERVES 2   # BISTECCA ALLA FIORENTINA

The idea for including this recipe came from a visit to Tuscany. Meat grilled over the fire, preferably one of chestnut wood, is a speciality of Florence and the key to success is a well-hung piece of steak, a hot fire and little interference otherwise. Since a fragrant wood fire is hard for most of us to arrange, I am instead going to quote from some notes of an American friend of mine on the cooking of a perfect steak which requires instead a heavy-based, preferably cast-iron, frying pan. It is in the spirit of Bistecca alla Fiorentina.

He makes the point quite emphatically that there is no sense in following these instructions if you do not like the taste of beef. 'To achieve the best from the meat, one tries to cook in such a manner that it is charred almost black on the outside and remains red (or just barely turning to pink) in the centre. All well-grilled or roasted beef ideally should have this range from black to red in each mouthful. If you say you don't care for it that way, you actually don't care to get the best from the taste of beef, so why bother to pay the extravagant price?'

2 steaks, such as T-bone, rump or sirloin, cut at least 1 in (2.5 cm) thick
a little olive oil
salt and freshly ground black pepper
lemon wedges

Put the frying pan, which should not be a flimsy affair, on the hob and turn on the gas or electricity to maximum. Leave the pan on for about five minutes until it seems almost red hot. Now drop in the steaks without butter, oil or seasoning (seasoning before cooking toughens the meat). Turn the meat after two minutes, using a spatula or tongs or wooden spoons: you want to avoid piercing it. Rub the cooked side with a little olive oil. Cook the other side until it, too, has a dark crust. Season after cooking and serve on heated plates (otherwise the surface temperature of the steak will fall fast). Garnish with lemon wedges. If you like the flavour of garlic rub the surface of the meat with a cut clove before grilling.

BOEUF EN DAUBE   SERVES 4-6

Virginia Woolf's *To The Lighthouse* was required reading when I was doing English 'A' levels. Although, sadly, there was no question requiring a recipe, I can remember today the tantalising description of this Provençal casserole. It was perhaps not a perfect recipe to give in an evening newspaper, as a good daube requires that the meat be marinated, but I find that assembling a dish in two stages gives the illusion of halving the work. When I made this dish recently in France, in a feckless holiday manner, I let the meat sit in the wine, oil and seasonings for two days and I am sure it was all the better for it. Buttery mashed potatoes was the accompaniment we chose, and very good they were too, but noodles or white haricot beans would go equally well.

$2\frac{1}{2}$ lb (1.25 kg) good quality stewing beef, e.g. topside, silverside, brisket
4 tbsp good olive oil
$\frac{3}{4}$ bottle of plonky red wine
2 large onions, peeled and quite thickly sliced
3 cloves of garlic, peeled and finely chopped
2 sprigs of fresh thyme or oregano, or 1 tsp dried herbs
2 slices of fresh orange
salt and freshly ground black pepper
6 oz (175 g) unsmoked streaky bacon in a piece
3 carrots, peeled and cut into chunks
a few dried mushrooms, soaked for 20 minutes in warm water, or fresh
sliced mushrooms
2 bay leaves
handful of black olives

Trim the meat of fat and cut into large cubes. Turn it in a dish in 2 tbsp of the olive oil. Pour on the wine and mix in the onion, 1 chopped garlic clove, the herbs, the bay leaves, orange slices and a good pinch of salt and pepper. Mix around once more and marinate the meat like this for at least 12 hours, preferably longer. When you are ready to cook the daube, turn on the oven to 160°C/325°F/gas mark 3. Drain the meat from the marinade, reserving it. In the other 2 tbsp of olive oil sauté the meat in an ovenproof casserole until lightly browned. Remove the rind from the bacon (and reserve), cut the chunk of bacon into cubes and sauté that with the beef. Into the casserole put the carrots, the mushrooms, the remaining garlic, the olives, the bacon rind and the marinade. Bring to a simmer on the top of the stove. Using aluminium foil if necessary to ensure a tight fit, cover the casserole and cook in the pre-heated oven for about 3 hours. Letting it go to 4 hours shouldn't hurt. Taste for seasoning and serve.

SERVES 4-5 # CARBONNADE OF BEEF

If you are a woman reading this recipe and you are having difficulty persuading a man to make a meal for you, try this notion on him as, in my experience, men think that cooking with beer is a very proper and suitably macho thing to do and have unshakeable faith that the outcome will be nourishing and good. Carbonnade, originally a Flemish dish, can be made with stout or brown ale. This might be the moment to try a 'real' beer, buying, of course, enough to have a swig or three while slicing the onions and chopping the meat. The mustard-spread bread is an idea that can be usefully adapted to other beef stews for at one simple stroke it adds flavour, a contrast of texture and some carbohydrate.

2 lb (1 kg) stewing steak e.g. chuck
2 oz (60 g) butter
2 tbsp olive oil or vegetable oil
3 onions, peeled and thinly sliced
3 fat cloves of garlic, peeled and slivered
salt and freshly ground black pepper
2 tbsp plain flour
1 tbsp soft brown sugar
½ pt (300 ml) beef stock
1 tbsp red wine vinegar
¾ pt (450 ml) beer (see above)
2 bay leaves
3 slices of brown bread, toasted or dried out in the oven
2–3 tbsp Dijon mustard

Turn on the oven to 160°C/325°F/gas mark 3. Cut the beef into slices about ½ in (1.5 cm) thick. Brown them quickly in a mixture of the butter and oil in a large sauté pan. Remove the meat from the pan, set aside and on a more gentle heat fry the onions until they are golden. Towards the end of the cooking time for the onions, stir in the garlic and cook until softened. Put a layer of onions in a deep casserole, followed by a layer of beef and continue in this manner, finishing with a layer of meat. Season each layer with a little salt and freshly ground black pepper. Heat the pan juices that remain from frying the meat and onions and stir in the flour and sugar. Cook for a few minutes. Add a little stock and stir until smooth. Bring to the boil, add the rest of the stock, the vinegar and the beer. Simmer for a few minutes. Add the bay leaves and pour the liquid into the casserole, enough just to cover the meat. Cover the casserole and cook in the pre-heated oven for 2½ hours. At the end of this time, spread the toasted bread with mustard and lay it, mustard side up, on top of the stew, which you have uncovered. Cook for another 30 minutes, uncovered, at a slightly higher temperature. Serve with salad or a green vegetable.

BOEUF MIROTON   SERVES 4

The method for this is one that the French might use in order to deal with leftover roasted or boiled beef, but the finished product is so pleasant and suppery, it is worth buying slices of rare roast beef from the butcher or delicatessen to make it, for in my experience leftover roast beef is a figment of a more lavish past. If you do happen to have boiled some beef, use the beef stock in the sauce. Otherwise you must resort to a stock cube. It is important that after adding the beef you do no more than warm it through; otherwise it may become leathery. Boeuf Miroton is good served with plainly boiled, or baked, potatoes and a green salad.

2 oz (60 g) butter or beef dripping
1½ lb (750 g) large onions, peeled and finely sliced
1–2 bay leaves
1 tbsp plain flour
¾ pt (450 ml) beef stock
2 tsp red wine vinegar
1 dsp French mustard
salt and pepper
about 1 lb (500 g) sliced cooked beef
chopped fresh parsley

Melt the butter in a heavy-bottomed pan and gently cook the sliced onions with the bay leaf or leaves. Let them stew for at least 15 minutes until they are softened and turning gold. The longer you cook them, the better, within reason. Add the flour and stir well. Add the stock and vinegar and blend until you have a cohesive sauce. Cook for another 20 minutes or so. Add the mustard, stir and taste for seasoning. Lay the slices of meat on top of the onion mixture. Cover the pan and cook very gently just until the meat is heated through. Sprinkle with the chopped parsley and serve.

CHILLI CON CARNE

Elizabeth Taylor ordered gallons of it to be air-freighted to the set of *Cleopatra*. President Johnson stipulated that it should be served without red kidney beans. Many people are earnest about chilli, but so often what you find here in pubs and wine bars and American-style restaurants is hotted-up mince with a tin of beans stirred in. How chilli should be composed is, however, a matter of heated debate, with devotees usually hinting at a secret recipe that they will not divulge but which is the only authentic chilli. 'No living man', an Illinois writer once said, 'can put together a pot of chili as ambrosial ... as the chili I make ... That is the way of us chili men. Each of us knows that his chili is light years beyond all other chili in quality and singularity.' The fact that this man did not come from Texas would offend some devotees, for starters. The recipe below, adapted from one given in *A Taste of American Cooking* by Clare Walker with Keryn Christiansen, is my idea of how chilli should be, one personal detail being the omission of tomatoes. Tinned kidney beans have been used for speed but you could, of course, soak dried beans overnight (using half the quantity) and cook them.

2 lb (1 kg) good quality stewing beef
1–2 tbsp chilli powder
hefty pinch each of ground cumin, dried oregano and ground coriander
1 tsp ground turmeric (optional but enriching)
1 onion, peeled and chopped
2 fat cloves of garlic, peeled and chopped
stock or water, to cover
1 × 14 oz (400 g) tin of red kidney beans, drained
salt and freshly ground black pepper

Cube the beef (I am from the non-mincing camp) and roll it in the spices, adding a little flour if you want a thicker sauce. Fry the onion in the oil until softened. Add the beef and fry until lightly browned and the spices form a sediment. Add the garlic and fry a couple of minutes more. Cover the meat with stock or water and simmer until it is tender (timing will depend on the quality of the meat). When it is nearly ready, heat the beans according to the instructions on the tin and stir in gently. Leave the dish to simmer

and meld. Add salt and pepper. Plain white rice is a good
accompaniment, as are tortillas or even poppadums.

STIR-FRIED BEEF WITH VEGETABLES   SERVES 2-3

One of the cookery books among my large collection with which
I feel most in tune is *Particular Delights* by Nathalie Hambro. The
recipes are original and delicate and exactly the sort of food you
might hope someone would prepare for you if you were going
round to supper. Recently she has had published a second book,
Visual Delights, with colour photographs that convincingly display
her empathetic and artistic approach to ingredients. The division
of the book is by seasons. This recipe is chosen from spring
although its lightness and the yogurt and courgette sauce suggested
as an accompaniment would also suit warmer weather. Here is a
moment to employ a wok should you have one. Otherwise just use
a sauté pan.

8 oz (250g) lean beef
1 tbsp soy sauce
2 garlic cloves, peeled and finely chopped
1 tsp sherry
1 broccoli spear (a fat branchy one)
1 large carrot
1 generous tbsp olive oil
salt
1 in (2.5 cm) piece fresh ginger root, peeled and finely shredded
6 water chestnuts, quartered
6 whole baby sweetcorn cobs

FOR THE SAUCE:
8 oz (250g) courgettes
2 tsp olive oil
10 fl oz (300 ml) yogurt
¼ pt (150 ml) soured cream
1 tbsp thyme, fresh if possible
salt and freshly ground black pepper

Cut the beef into thin, finger-long strips. Toss in the soy sauce,
garlic and sherry. Chop the broccoli into small pieces, keeping the
florets intact. Peel the carrot and, still using a vegetable peeler,
take off long thin strips. Make the sauce. Trim the courgettes,
rinse and pat dry. Chop into small cubes. Sauté in the 2 tsp oil,
moving them with a wooden spoon and tossing for about 2 minutes.
Beat together the yogurt and soured cream. Add the thyme, crush-

ing it a little. Season to taste and stir in the courgettes. Heat half the tbsp of oil for stir-frying. When it is sizzling add a little salt and swirl round. Add the beef and stir-fry until it begins to brown. Remove and keep warm. Heat the remaining oil. Add the ginger and all the vegetables, cutting the corn lengthwise if it is on the large side. Stir-fry for a minute or two. Add a pinch of salt and mix with the beef.

STEAK TARTARE
SERVES 2

There are various schools of thought about steak tartare, not even counting the one that thinks that eating raw meat is a fiendish thing to do. There is the school that has for its headmistress Prue Leith, who says firmly that if you do want to eat raw meat then you should like the taste of it and not mask it with anchovies and capers and the like. There is the unit, mostly staffed by waiters, who see steak tartare as an opportunity to show off and ingratiate themselves with restaurant customers and who want to mix in everything under the sun. There are those, like my mother-in-law, who see it as a natural spread for open sandwiches and then there are people like me, who feel that raw food is somehow actively slimming and every now and then resolve to be like Leslie Kenton and make raw food the basis of a diet. Finally there are those people who just like steak tartare. Here is a recipe to see if you do. It does have the advantage of speed of making.

8 oz (250 g) lean steak, minced by your butcher or by yourself
1 tbsp olive oil
2 egg yolks
1 onion, peeled and finely chopped
1 dsp capers, chopped
2–4 anchovy fillets, chopped
salt and pepper
cayenne pepper, to taste
mustard, to taste
Worcestershire Sauce, to taste

Rather than risk suspect mince, buy a piece of steak and chop it in a food processor or put it through a mincer. If you then want to be straightforward and you think you know how you and your companion like it flavoured, mix in the oil, egg yolks, and other seasonings to taste, form the meat into two patties, rather like ebullient hamburgers, and serve. Alternatively, you could mix the meat with the oil, salt and pepper, adding some cayenne, mustard and Worcestershire Sauce if you like it hot, form the meat into patties, nestle the egg yolk in a half egg-shell, one on top of each patty, and tastefully arrange the other ingredients in little heaps around. Let the diner mix them in to taste. It almost goes without saying that you discard the egg shell. Hot potatoes are surprisingly nice with steak tartare. Pommes allumettes, matchstick chips, are best of all and cheerfully they scupper the slimming theory.

CHAPPLI KEBAB   SERVES 3-4

Helen Saberi is an Englishwoman who lived in Afghanistan for ten years until, in March 1980, the Soviet invasion and resulting turmoil obliged her to leave. She had married into an Afghan family and her interest in, and affection for, the country and its people included research into Afghan cooking and the customs of hospitality and celebration. She has written *Noshe Djan, Afghan Food and Cookery*. As the author says, an exodus of refugees can mean a consequent dispersal and destruction of a culture and the book is her attempt to keep a record. Royalties from its sales will go to charitable organisations sending humanitarian aid to Afghanistan. Apart from that fact, the book is worth buying if Middle Eastern, Indian or Far Eastern food interests you for, ironically, the geographical situation of the country at a crossroads of cultures is as beneficial for its cuisines as it is dangerous for its politics. It is difficult to find a taste of Afghan food in restaurants, but if you can reach London's West End try Caravan Serai in Paddington Street. 'Chappli' in the recipe below means sandal and refers to the shape of the patties, ideally cooked over charcoal.

1 lb (500 g) minced beef or lamb
12 oz (375 g) spring onions, trimmed and finely chopped
4 oz (120 g) plain white flour
½ green or red sweet pepper, finely chopped
½ fresh green chilli pepper, finely chopped
3–4 tbsp fresh coriander, finely chopped
2 tsp ground coriander seed
salt
oil, for frying

TO SERVE: *tomato and onion salad*
soft Indian bread, such as nan, or pitta bread
lemon quarters
fresh coriander

Mix together the meat, onion, flour, peppers and corianders, adding salt to taste. Shape the mixture into flat oblongs about $\frac{1}{4}$ in (6 mm) thick, measuring about 6×4 in (15×10 cm). Heat enough vegetable oil in a frying pan nearly to cover the kebabs. Fry over a medium to high heat until they are brown on both sides and cooked through – about 10 minutes. Serve with the tomato and onion salad and Indian bread or pitta bread. Supply lemon quarters for squeezing and sprinkle some more chopped fresh coriander over the dish.

SERVES 4   # MEXICAN WORLD CUP TV DINNER

I have to admit – confess strikes me as an inappropriate word – to never having watched a match in any World Cup. Restaurateurs tell me that business always goes down because potential customers are glued to the television. Restaurateurs can always be counted on for a theory. During the last World Cup in 1986, the company which markets the Old El Paso range of Mexican foodstuffs came up with all sorts of jolly ideas for snacks while viewing; as the copywriters put it, 'how to score in the food stakes ... is yet another challenge facing Mums (sic) throughout June ...' Not especially wanting to pass on recipes for World Cup Tostada Butties, Hat Trick Toasts and Goalies' Dunk Pot, I thought I would suggest to readers some items that they could combine with taco shells.

I don't suppose many people want to start adding slaked lime to corn meal and patting out their own tortillas when it is easy to buy them. Taco shells come a dozen to a pack and require heating in a moderate oven for 2–3 minutes. They are then crisp and ready to be filled and garnished. You can simply open a tin of taco filling, but I would suggest the following which means you will miss out on the odd emulsifier and additive.

1 large onion, peeled and finely chopped
2 cloves of garlic, peeled and finely chopped
a little vegetable oil
1 lb (500 g) minced beef
1 tsp ground cumin or cumin seeds
1 tsp oregano
pinch of chilli powder or 1 fresh chopped chilli or 1 tsp chilli sauce
dash of soy sauce
salt and pepper
pinch of sugar

FOR THE SAUCE (SALSA CRUDA):
4 tomatoes
2 tsp wine vinegar
½ onion, peeled and finely chopped
2–3 tinned jalapeños peppers, chopped
pinch of oregano
salt

Fry the onion and garlic in a little vegetable oil. Add the beef mince and stir until browned. Season with cumin, oregano, chilli and a dash of soy sauce. Season with salt, pepper and a pinch of sugar. To make the salsa cruda, grill the tomatoes until the skins blister and can be removed, then blend the flesh with the wine vinegar, chopped onion and peppers, oregano and salt. Put out the heated taco shells, a bowl of the spiced beef and another of the sauce alongside bowls of shredded lettuce; grated cheese; avocado mashed with a peeled, seeded and diced tomato, lemon juice and chilli sauce; yogurt or soured cream. Viewers assemble their own tacos with the constituent parts. Shredded cooked chicken, or fried crumbled chorizo or Toulouse sausages, are additional notions.

STUFFED CABBAGE LEAVES SERVES 4-6

It might come as a surprise to some to hear that cabbage is the unquestionably chic vegetable of the eighties. I am sure it will come as a surprise to all cabbages. It is ousting those little bundles of matchstick beans and the three-mangetouts garnish fancy chefs send out with their creations. I am very pleased for cabbage that it has attained this stature as it has always seemed to me an underrated vegetable, most probably for the good reason that it is usually badly cooked. Stuffed cabbage has long been a popular dish in France and throughout Eastern Europe, but even traditional recipes can be improved, I think, by quicker cooking. The following is a basic recipe: you can vary seasonings and to some extent the ingredients to suit your taste. You may also prefer to substitute a tomato sauce for the soured cream.

4 oz (120 g) fresh breadcrumbs or cooked rice
a little milk or water
4 rashers of bacon, chopped
1 onion, peeled and finely chopped, or 1 bunch of spring onions,
trimmed and chopped
1 clove of garlic, peeled and slivered
¾ lb (375 g) minced beef, pork or veal, or a mixture
1 egg
¾ tsp grated nutmeg or 1 tsp dill or caraway seeds (all optional)
pinch of dried oregano
salt and freshly ground black pepper
1 crisp Dutch or Savoy cabbage
2 oz (60 g) butter, and a little more to grease the dish
1–2 tbsp water or white wine
1 tsp plain flour
½ pt (300 ml) soured cream or Greek yogurt

Turn on the oven to 180°C/350°F/gas mark 4. Soak the bread-crumbs in a little milk or water and then squeeze them out. Gently fry the chopped bacon and in its fat sauté the onion and garlic until softened. Mix together the minced meat, crumbs or rice, bacon mixture, egg and your choice of seasoning. Using clean hands is the best method. Trim the cabbage of any discoloured leaves. Bring a large pot of salted water to the boil and simmer the whole cabbage for a few minutes. Drain and separate the large leaves, cutting out any very hard stalk. Shred the rest of the leaves to cook swiftly in a little butter as an accompaniment. Spread out the leaves on a work surface, place a spoonful of stuffing in the centre of each one and roll up to make a parcel, turning the sides in over the stuffing first. Butter a shallow casserole that will hold the bundles in a single layer and pack them in. Dot with the rest of the butter and trickle on the water or white wine. Cover and cook for 40 minutes. Ten minutes before the end of the cooking time, whisk the flour into the soured cream or yogurt and pour it on to the cabbage rolls. Cook uncovered from then on.

SERVES 6 ## MEAT LOAF

If you think of meat loaf as a species of pâté – which it is – then it immediately seems much less humdrum. Carefully made, that is, not used as a receptacle for little dishes of leftovers, it can be delicious either hot with a spicy tomato sauce or cold with pickle or Cumberland sauce. Meat loaf can be made with minced beef alone, but it does improve if you use pork and veal as well and runs less risk of being dry and crumbly. Most supermarkets sell minced pork and veal as well as beef. The vegetables in the recipe happen to be ones I like to include; the aubergine adds a nice texture. But if you like, say, chopped green pepper, well, why not use that?

½ aubergine, cut into small cubes (optional)
1 lb (500 g) minced beef,
8 oz (250 g) minced veal and
8 oz (250 g) minced pork, or
2 lb (1 kg) minced beef alone
2 eggs
4 oz (120 g) fresh brown or white breadcrumbs
2 carrots, peeled and grated
2 oz (60 g) mushrooms, cleaned and chopped
2 onions, peeled and finely chopped
2 cloves of garlic, peeled and chopped
dash of soy or Tabasco sauce
salt and freshly ground black pepper

Turn on the oven to 180°C/350°F/gas mark 4. If you are using aubergine, salt the cubes and let them sweat until wilted. Pat dry. Mix all the ingredients – use your hands for the best result – and then press the mixture into a loaf tin or a casserole of suitable size. Smooth the top into a slightly rounded shape. An alternative method is to sauté the vegetables until soft before you mix them with the meats. If you are using aubergine, it is a good idea. Bake in the oven for 1–1½ hours. Pour off any accumulated fat and serve. If you prefer to serve it cold, wrap it in foil, weight it with a couple of tins until quite cool and refrigerate.

AN ACE SALT-GRILLED HAMBURGER SERVES 2

An American friend taught me this hamburger. Perhaps since, in the interests of their blood pressure, Americans no longer eat salt, they feel that flinging it in the pan doesn't count. What it achieves is a nice crust on the meat and a virtuous, salt-free centre. A good hamburger is something not to be despised. Because you can flavour it in fairly ingenious ways it strikes me as more interesting to eat than a steak and is, of course, considerably cheaper. If you want to serve a hamburger grandly and as more of a meal you can make a quick 'pan gravy', as the Americans call it, for which I give directions below. However, in that case abandon the salt-grilling method as it would make the sauce unpalatable.

8 oz (250 g) minced beef (not too lean as some fat is desirable)
1 small onion, finely chopped
1 egg yolk
1 clove of garlic, squeezed through a garlic crusher
1 tsp soy sauce
freshly ground black pepper
handful of sea salt

FOR THE SAUCE:
½ oz (15 g) butter
1 tsp olive oil
1 dsp flour
milk, as required
1 tbsp cream (optional)

Using your hands, mix the beef with the onion, egg yolk, garlic, soy sauce and some pepper. Form into two hamburgers. Scatter the sea salt in a heavy-bottomed frying pan. Place on the stove and when hot cook the hamburgers (with no fat) until brown and crusty on the outside but a little pink inside. To make the hamburgers with the sauce, add a little salt to the mixture and fry the burgers in a mixture of butter and olive oil. When cooked, remove the burgers and keep them warm. Stir the flour into the fat and meat juices in the pan until well amalgamated and lightly brown. Slowly stir in milk, until you have a sauce the consistency of double cream and free of lumps (sieve if necessary). Taste for seasoning and if you are using cream, stir it in. Serve the burgers with this 'pan gravy'.

SERVES 4   # CORNED BEEF HASH

This recipe may seem, how shall we say, artless, but it is a good short-order dish, possible often to assemble from what you have in your stores. The important factors about corned beef hash are a crisp crust on the bottom, an enlivening ingredient such as a splash of Tabasco, Worcestershire Sauce or chilli sauce and, arguably, one fried egg for each person perched on top. It is an ideal vehicle for leftover boiled potatoes, but if you are cooking them just for this dish bring them to the point of being slightly underdone. Since learning that corned beef hash was, and maybe still is, a favourite dish at that chic nightclub Annabel's in Berkeley

Square, I have stopped feeling apologetic about serving it.

1½ lb (750 g) boiled potatoes
1 lb (450 g) tin of corned beef
1 large onion, peeled and finely chopped
freshly ground black pepper
Worcestershire Sauce, Tabasco or chilli sauce, to taste
1 oz (30 g) butter
2–3 tbsp vegetable oil
1 egg per person (optional)

Cube the cooked potatoes. Open the tin of corned beef carefully (apparently horrible accidents are caused every year by fumble-fingers with the corned beef tin). Break up the meat and in a bowl mix it with the potatoes and onion. If you prefer, you can fry the onion first until it is limp and beginning to brown. Season the mixture with pepper and a hot sauce. Melt the butter in a frying pan with 2–3 tbsp vegetable oil. When hot add the hash mixture and press down quite firmly. When a crust begins to form on the bottom, turn the mixture to bring some crust to the top and to allow a new one to form. Cook slowly until you are satisfied there is enough crust. Turn out on to a hot plate and serve with a fried egg on top if you fancy that.

BLANQUETTE DE VEAU   SERVES 4

When I was about eighteen I had a friend called Mary Moore who once astounded me by embarking on and cooking, fairly quickly and very successfully, a blanquette de veau. It seemed to me then such a 'grown-up' dish, the sort of thing only mothers could produce. You rarely see blanquette de veau on restaurant menus. which is one reason I cook it. Another is its wonderful soothing quality. It is quite the best thing to do with the pie veal sold in butcher's shops and supermarkets.

1½ lb (750 g) pie veal
1 onion, peeled and stuck with a clove
2 carrots, peeled
6 peppercorns
grated zest and some juice of 1 small lemon
1 oz (30 g) butter
1 oz (30 g) flour
2 egg yolks
3 tbsp cream
salt and more pepper, if required

Tidy the veal and cut it into cubes if this has not already been done. Put it in a saucepan and cover with cold water. Bring to the simmer and skim off any grey froth that appears. Add the onion, carrots, peppercorns and the grated zest of the lemon. Simmer for about one hour, making sure the cooking liquid only shudders. Drain off about ½ pt (300 ml) of the liquid through a sieve leaving the meat to continue gently cooking in the rest. In another pan melt the butter, stir in the flour and use the hot stock to make a thin sauce, as if you were making white sauce. Beat together the egg yolks, cream and a dessertspoon of lemon juice, add a couple of tbsp of hot stock and add the mixture to the sauce. (If you prefer to avoid butter and flour, the stock from simmering the meat can be reduced by boiling in a separate pan and then thickened with the egg, cream, and lemon mixture, but this is a slightly more tricky procedure.) Cook without boiling until the sauce is slightly thickened. Add the meat, removed from its stock, and heat through, making sure the sauce never reaches boiling point. Taste for seasoning and serve, perhaps with rice.

SERVES 6   LAMB WHICH CRIES ON TO POTATOES

I got the idea of slashing the lamb in the manner described below from the recipe of a winner of a meat-cooking competition run in the *Sunday Times*. Sophie Tanner, the author, has a felicitous background, being the daughter of a French mother and the wife of a butcher's wholesaler. When spring lamb is in the shops it is a good moment to try this method, using a whole small leg. The point of the recipe, which is one that can be adapted for other purposes, is that the meat is roasted alone on an oven rack and its juices 'weep' on to a roasting tin of sliced potatoes sitting below. This causes the potatoes to be delicious and the meat to be crisply cooked since it hasn't been sitting in a pool of fat. Use lots of garlic. It enhances lamb so well.

1 leg of English lamb
6–8 cloves of garlic, peeled and chopped
herbs e.g. rosemary and mint
salt and pepper
a little olive oil
3 lb (1.5 kg) firm, waxy potatoes, peeled and thinly sliced
1 oz (30 g) butter

Turn on the oven to 200°C/400°F/gas mark 6. Make deep diagonal slashes in the lamb, rather as if you were criss-crossing on a baked ham. Push three-quarters of the chopped garlic into the cuts and sprinkle with herbs. Season with salt and pepper and dribble olive oil over the whole leg. Layer the potatoes in a roasting tin, interspersing the layers with salt, pepper, dots of butter and the remaining garlic. Set the tin on the bottom rack in the pre-heated oven and the meat on a rack above. Roast for about 1½ hours if you like the meat pink; if you like it quite well done for another ½ hour at a lower temperature. Slice the meat and serve on the juice-impregnated potatoes. If you have slashed the meat enthusiastically it will have opened out into a new look for roast lamb, so you might prefer to bring it to the table whole. Letting a large joint 'rest' in a warm place for 15 minutes is always a good idea. During that time you can brown and crisp the potatoes on a high shelf in the oven.

LAMB CUTLETS IN PASTRY

This dish is made on the same principle as Boeuf en Croûte or Beef Wellington, but works rather better, I think, as it is easier to get the timings right so the pastry is puffed and golden, the meat cooked but rosy pink in the centre. It is important to have small, neat cutlets, well trimmed of fat and with a long thin bone protruding. Tell the butcher that you want best end cutlets prepared in the French style. Crimp the pastry, rather like a three-cornered hat, around the meat and glaze with an egg wash. That way you will have a dish flattering to your family or stylish enough for any kind of entertaining.

1 oz (30 g) butter or 1 tbsp vegetable oil
1 large onion, peeled and finely chopped
4 oz (120 g) mushrooms, cleaned and finely chopped
1 clove of garlic, peeled and finely chopped
1 tbsp chopped fresh parsley
1 lb (500 g) frozen puff pastry, defrosted
8 best end lamb cutlets, trimmed of fat
salt and freshly ground black pepper
1 egg, beaten with pinch of salt (egg wash)

Turn on the oven to 220°C/425°F/gas mark 7. In the butter or oil sauté the onion until softened. Add the mushrooms and sauté until cooked. Stir in the garlic and cook for a minute. Add the parsley and season the mixture. Roll out the pastry very thinly and cut into eight triangles, each one just large enough to wrap around the meat. In the cleaned-out sauté pan, quickly brown both sides of

the chops in a little more oil or butter to seal them. Remove and
let drain. Season the meat. Pour off any liquid from the onion and
mushroom mixture. Put a heaped teaspoon of the mixture into the
centre of each pastry triangle. Place a cutlet on the stuffing and
pinch the pastry around it, making a firm seal. Trim away any
excess pastry and if you are feeling creative make little leaves to
stick on top of the parcels. Brush on the egg wash. Place the parcels
on a wet baking sheet and cook in the pre-heated oven for 15–20
minutes or until the pastry is flaky and golden. Serve with redcurrant jelly.

SERVES 4-5   ## LANCASHIRE HOT-POT

When too many fancy meals have come your way it is good to
have something homely like a hot-pot. It is a dish that makes no
demands on your punctuality for meal-times, which is another
point in its favour. I am becoming more and more refined, or you
could say simplistic, about food. Though you could add oysters
or field mushrooms or bacon or carrots to this assembly, I like
the straightforwardness of lamb, onions and potatoes with some
lamb's kidneys to add richness to the gravy. The traditional pot
for a hot-pot is a tall, round-bellied earthenware one. The *raison
d'être* of the dish, to my mind anyway, is the layer of potatoes on
top that become rich with the fat from the meat and crusty-brown
from the heat of the oven.

2 lb (1 kg) middle neck or best end lamb chops
seasoned flour, as required
2–3 lamb's kidneys
4 onions, peeled and sliced
1½ lb (750 g) potatoes, peeled and sliced
1 bay leaf
salt and freshly ground black pepper
¾ pt (450 ml) water

Heat the oven to 150°C/300°F/gas mark 2. Trim obvious fat from
the chops and melt it in a frying pan. Flour the chops and brown
them gently in the fat. This step improves the colour and the
texture of the gravy. Put the chops into the pot, either standing
up or lying down, depending on the shape of your pot. Trim the
kidneys of any fat or skin and chop them into pieces. Layer the
kidneys, onions and potatoes, adding a bay leaf and seasoning as
you go along, and finish with a layer of overlapping potato slices.
Add ¾ pt (450 ml) of water. Brush the top surface of the potatoes

with melted butter or dripping, sprinkle with salt and pepper and put in the oven with a lid on the pot. After 1½ hours, remove the lid, turn up the oven a little and cook for a further hour.

LAMB TAGINE WITH APRICOTS   SERVES 4-6

In miserable winter weather apricots, even dried ones, glow with the promise of sunshine. Apricots have a particular affinity with lamb. The sweetness somehow ameliorates the richness of the meat. Tagine refers to the earthenware dish in which the meat is cooked. If you have a heat-diffusing mat it is possible to use most earthenware dishes on top of the stove and it does have a more satisfactory effect and a more authentic Middle Eastern feel than cooking in a saucepan. Fresh apricots have great charm but dried ones have more intensity of flavour. Best of all, buy Hunza apricots, which are dried without sulphur, from health food shops. They have stones whose weight should be allowed for.

6 oz (175 g) dried apricots
2 tbsp vegetable oil
1 large onion, peeled and grated or finely chopped
1½–2 lb (750 g–1 kg) lamb, trimmed of fat and cut into chunks (I like taking it from a shoulder of lamb)
1 tsp ground allspice, or ground coriander, cumin, cinnamon and ginger mixed together
salt and freshly ground black pepper
1 tbsp ground almonds
1 tbsp sesame seeds
12 oz (375 g) basmati rice (optional)

If you have no time to soak the apricots, cover them with boiling water and let them simmer while you get on with trimming the meat. Heat the oil, preferably in an earthenware pot on a heat-diffusing mat. Add the onion and cook until soft and golden. Add the meat and the spices with salt and pepper to taste. Fry it, gently stirring and browning for about 5 minutes. Add the fruit and the ground almonds moistened with the apricot cooking or soaking water. Add the rest of the apricot water and enough extra to just cover the meat. Simmer, covered, for about an hour or until the meat is tender. Roast the sesame seeds in a dry frying pan until golden. Use to sprinkle over the meat at the moment of serving. Another, delicious way of presenting the meat is to half cook the basmati rice and to layer it with the meat and fruit, ending with a layer of rice. Cover closely, using a tea-towel under the lid, and steam for about 20 minutes until the rice is tender and some of the sauce is absorbed. This is called Lamb Polo.

SERVES 6

MY SISTER'S SHEPHERD'S PIE

This pie, which is regularly served at Green's Champagne Bar and Restaurant where my sister is now chef, is a good example of the small but definite influence that spending many summers in Greece has had on her cooking. Even the Green's customers, suspicious of anything 'foreign' and much consoled by nursery memories, have taken to it, and this despite the fact that nursery cooks most certainly do not put cinnamon and mint into their shepherd's pies. Nor did they probably use fresh minced lamb, but it gives a better result than beef and it seems unlikely these days that anyone would have 2 lb (1 kg) of leftover meat from a joint.

4 oz (120 g) finely chopped bacon
1 tbsp olive oil
2 onions
3 carrots
4 celery stalks
1 clove of garlic, finely chopped
2 lb (1 kg) minced raw lamb
3 fl oz (90 ml) milk
14 oz (400 g) tin of tomatoes
1 dsp dried oregano
1 tsp ground cinnamon
1 tbsp Worcestershire Sauce
1 tbsp chopped fresh mint
2 lb (1 kg) potatoes, cooked and mashed with hot milk and butter
2 oz (60 g) grated Cheddar or Gruyère cheese

Either cook the lamb and then turn on the oven to 200°C/400°F/gas mark 6 to heat the pie through, or turn immediately to 150°C/300°F/gas mark 2 if you intend to simmer the lamb in the oven. Fry the bacon until the fat runs. Add the olive oil. Clean and finely chop the vegetables or, preferably, put all three through the grating blade of a food processor. Sauté them with garlic until softened. Stir in the meat and brown it carefully. Add the milk and let it bubble away, which lends a desirable sweetness. Whizz the contents of the tin of tomatoes in a liquidiser or food processor and add to the meat with the seasonings. Simmer gently on top of the stove or in the oven for at least an hour, but longer is all to the good. Turn into a pie dish. Cover with the mashed potatoes. Sprinkle with grated cheese and heat through in the oven, or if the meat and potatoes are hot, under the grill.

BOBOTIE SERVES 4-6

On the grounds, which I would adhere to, that exploring other cuisines should override political boycotts, here is a South African recipe. This riposte to shepherd's pie perhaps was evolved when, before the advent of refrigeration, meat sometimes had to be jollied, chivvied – disguised – with the help of spices and strong flavouring. Looking at the contents, you might predict a result rather like the sort of curries we made in the days Before We Knew Better, but the addition of the soaked bread and the custard lends an interesting texture and, so long as your curry powder has not lived for years on your shelf, the flavour is gutsy and good. I first tried Bobotie at a party – it suits being made in large quantity.

2 onions, peeled and chopped
2 dessert apples, peeled and chopped
2 cloves of garlic, peeled and crushed
3 tbsp butter
2 tbsp fresh (i.e. not stale) curry powder
2 lb (1 kg) minced lamb or beef
2 oz (60 g) flaked almonds
3 oz (90 g) raisins
1 tsp mixed dried herbs
1 tbsp chutney
juice of ½ a lemon
1 tbsp wine vinegar
salt and freshly ground black pepper
3 slices of white bread
1 pt (600 ml) milk
3 eggs

Set the oven to 180°C/350°F/gas mark 4. Fry the onion, apples and garlic gently in the butter. Add the curry powder and cook for a minute or two to dispel the 'raw' taste. Put the minced meat in a bowl, add the contents of the frying pan, plus the almonds,

raisins, herbs, chutney, lemon juice, vinegar and salt and pepper.
Mix well (use your hands). Soak the white bread in the milk and
then squeeze it out, conserving the milk. Mix the bread and one
egg into the meat mixture and spread it all in a well buttered pie
dish. Beat the remaining milk with the two remaining eggs. Pour
over the meat. Bake for one hour, when the mixture should be set
and the top lightly browned.

SERVES 4   # ROAST STUFFED FILLET OF PORK

A helpful letter from a butcher pointed out to me that customers –
and butchers – are often confused by the various terms for meat.
They can mean different things to different people. By fillet of
pork I mean the long, lean, cylindrical cut usually sold in one
piece. Sometimes it is called tenderloin. This is one of the quickest
ways I know of having 'a roast'. The Italian sausage provides
instant stuffing and if you have a splash of red wine to put in the
roasting pan, you will get a thin but potent gravy.

1 pork fillet
1 long, thin, spicy fresh sausage
2 rashers of bacon
3–4 bay leaves
salt and pepper
red wine, as required

Turn on the oven to 190°C/375°F/gas mark 5. With a sharp knife,
score the fillet twice lengthways, spacing the cuts evenly and
making sure you don't cut right through the meat – just about
halfway down. You can now flatten it out into an oblong shape by
banging with a mallet or other suitable blunt instrument. Trim
the sausage to the length of the meat and lay it down the middle.
Wrap the meat round the sausage. Lay the bacon pieces along the
join and tie in several places to make a neat parcel. Tuck some bay
leaves under the string. Season with a little salt and a lot of freshly
ground black pepper. Place the meat in a roasting pan, surround
it with cheap red wine and cook for about 45 minutes, checking
from time to time that the wine has not completely evaporated and
adding more wine, stock or water as necessary. You should finish
with about a cupful of sauce. When sliced, the meat looks pretty
with its kernel of stuffing, the nitrite from which might have lent
the pork fillet a rosy glow. Mashed potato (see page 228) is a fine
accompaniment.

STUFFED BELLY OF PORK   SERVES 4

Belly of pork, particularly the thicker, meatier end, is a favourite
cut of mine for roasting. The crackling tends to crackle more
vociferously and the skeins of fat in the meat stop it drying out
and becoming boring. Also, belly of pork is considerably cheaper
than most other cuts. This recipe was the cosmopolitan creation
of a friend of a friend – a Swedish woman living in Ibiza. The
cinnamon-dusted apples are a particularly nice accompaniment;
small Cox's Orange Pippins are perfect for it.

2 lb (1 kg) piece of belly of pork
1 onion
1 tbsp vegetable oil
2 oz (60 g) chopped mushrooms
1 tsp curry powder
2 oz (60 g) rice, cooked
1 tbsp currants
1 oz (30 g) pine kernels (optional)
1 tbsp snipped fresh coriander (optional)
salt and pepper
4 dessert apples such as Cox's, peeled and cored
ground cinnamon, as required
a splash of red wine, if you have it

Turn on the oven to 200°C/400°F/gas mark 6. Score the fat if the
butcher has neglected to do so. Using a small sharp knife, cut a
horizontal pocket in the meat, approaching from one of the long
sides. Do not cut right through. Peel and finely chop the onion
and fry in the vegetable oil. Add the chopped mushrooms, soften.
Add the curry powder and cook for a few minutes to obviate any
raw taste. Add the rice, currants, pine kernels and coriander, if
you are using them. Mix well and season with salt and pepper.
Fill the pocket in the meat with the stuffing. Using a large darning
needle or similar, sew up the pouch with thick cotton and large
stitches – this is no moment for embroidery. Place the meat in a
roasting pan. Put the apples around it and sprinkle them quite
colourfully with ground cinnamon. If you have some wine open,
put a splash into the pan; it makes the foundation for a thin sauce.
Roast the meat and apples for one hour. If the crackling is not
brilliant by the end of the cooking time, put just the meat under
the grill and watch carefully so the fat blisters and burnishes but
does not burn.

SERVES 4   # LACQUERED SPARE RIBS

When I did an in-depth investigation of spare rib restaurants in the restaurant column, I mentioned I would pass on my own approach. The sauce, which I feel should be practically *enamelled* on to the ribs – not served separately – has a key ingredient, which is condensed consommé. Whatever the magic ingredient – caramel, gelatine, colouring or so on in this soup – when reduced down, it produces the shiny dark brown glaze that is the effect, I would say, to aim for. You must be prepared to give the ribs long enough in a hot oven to evaporate the sauce completely, but if you want to hurry things, you could grill the ribs after a spell in the oven, basting them frequently.

2 sheets of pork spare ribs (make sure the butcher understands it is the 'American' cut of ribs you want)
3 tbsp vegetable oil
3 medium onions
12 oz (340 g) tin condensed consommé
2 cloves of garlic, peeled and finely chopped
2 tbsp tomato ketchup
1 tbsp honey
1½ tbsp soy sauce
1 dsp chilli sauce
1 dsp wine vinegar or lemon juice
2 shakes of Worcestershire Sauce
brown sugar
salt and pepper
pinch of mustard powder

Turn on the oven to 200°C/400°F/gas mark 6. Chop the meat into single bones if the butcher has neglected to do so. Trim off any obvious fat. Arrange the ribs in a large roasting tin, aiming for one layer. Cover with foil and put in the oven while you prepare the sauce (more fat is driven off this way). Heat the oil and fry the finely chopped onions, stirring conscientiously until the pieces are well browned. They, too, add their colour and caramelised quality to the sauce. Away from the heat and standing at arm's length, add the consommé then all the other ingredients, using your judgement about the brown sugar. The quantity depends on how emphatic you like the sweetness in sweet and sour; I use a dessertspoon. Back at the stove simmer the sauce for 5–10 minutes. At this stage it should taste unpalatably strong. Remove the tin from

the oven, discard the foil, pour, away any fat or meat juices. Tip
on the sauce, swirling it about the tin. Turn up the oven a little
and replace the ribs. Cook for one hour, basting and jiggling the
ribs frequently and gradually turning the oven up to cook away
the sauce. Pile on to a heated plate and serve.

SWEET AND SOUR PORK   SERVES 4

The contrast between the popularity of sweet and sour pork and
the usual disagreeable dish served up in its name is either fascinating or depressing – or both. From time to time in Chinese
restaurants, particularly when I have my children in tow, I order
sweet and sour pork to see if it can be good, but invariably receive
lumps of batter in orange glaze. Wanting to disguise some pork
cutlets the other evening for children who think grilled meat is
boring, I chopped them up and made them according to the recipe
below. The cubes of meat were excellent, crisp outside and moist
and flavourful inside, and the sauce, rather to my astonishment,
received great acclaim from the children as being almost identical
to that you get in restaurants. Never has a supper been more
popular.

3 pork cutlets or 12 oz (375 g) pork fillet
1 dsp soy sauce
1 fat clove of garlic, crushed
1 egg, beaten
vegetable oil for deep-frying
2 tbsp cornflour
1 onion, peeled and finely chopped

FOR SAUCE:
2 tbsp potato flour
4 tbsp water
4 tbsp pineapple or apple juice
2 tbsp wine vinegar
3 tbsp sugar
2 tsp soy sauce
2 tbsp tomato ketchup
2 tsp Worcestershire Sauce

Chop the meat into 1 in (3 cm) cubes. Put in a bowl with the soy
sauce and garlic and turn with your hands to coat well. Meanwhile,
mix together the sauce ingredients, stirring the liquids and then
the sugar and sauces into the potato flour. Add the beaten egg to

the meat and stir again. Heat the oil in a wok or deep-fryer to a depth that will cover the meat (a bit of swirling about means you can use less oil). Roll each meat cube in cornflour and assemble them on a plate. When the oil is chip-frying hot, add the meat and cook until the outside is crisp and lightly browned. Drain the meat on kitchen paper. Fry the onion in a little fresh oil in a smaller pan. Add the sauce mixture and bring to a simmer. It will thicken and shine. Repeat the meat frying for a minute or two only. Add a little more oil to the sauce, which will obviate any glueyness. Serve the meat on boiled rice with some sauce trickled over and the rest served separately for real enthusiasts.

SERVES 4 # PORK IN LETTUCE WRAP

Wrapping things in lettuce leaves is all the go in Chinese restaurants these days. Quite often the menu will claim that the substance to be wrapped is minced quail or squab (young pigeon), but in reality it is most likely to be pork, as below. One of the advantages of this mode of eating, alongside the illusion of healthiness, is the *involving* quality of the activity, which therefore makes it a good dinner party dish if you are a bit short on conversation. This is a somewhat simplified version of a Chinese recipe, but once you have got the hang of it you will think of your own mixtures.

2 tbsp vegetable oil or lard, according to preference
12 oz (450 g) minced pork
pinch of salt
1 tsp of sugar
1 tbsp chopped onion
1 tsp grated fresh ginger root
4 celery stalks, de-stringed and diced
1 tbsp soy sauce
2 tbsp dry sherry
3 tbsp chicken stock (from a cube will suffice), and 2 tbsp more for cornflour
½ cucumber, diced
½ tbsp cornflour, whisked into 2 tbsp stock
2 tsp sesame oil or other vegetable oil (optional)
1 iceberg or Webb's lettuce, the leaves separated, washed and dried

Heat the oil or lard (the latter gives a more unctuous effect) in a large frying pan or wok. When hot, add the pork. Sprinkle with a good pinch of salt and a teaspoon of sugar and stir-fry for 2 or 3 minutes, or until there is no trace of pink in the meat. Add the onion and ginger. Stir-fry for 2 minutes. Add the celery, soy sauce, sherry and stock. Fry for a minute, then add the cucumber and cook until it is heated through but still crunchy. Give the cornflour mixture a stir to create a cloudy liquid and pour on to the meat. Stir-fry for a minute. Finally, glaze the meat by dribbling on the sesame oil or a little vegetable oil if that is all you have to hand. Serve on a heated dish with the lettuce leaves stacked on a separate plate. Each person takes a leaf, spoons in the pork mixture, makes a parcel and eats.

SZECHUAN BEAN CURD   SERVES 4

Although I know, as no doubt do you, that bean curd is the most sane form of protein, I have been nervous of cooking it. I was surprised and impressed, therefore, when lunching with a friend, to see her turning cubes of bean curd in wholemeal flour and frying them to a reasonably crispy consistency to add to some stir-fried vegetables. It made a good and virtuous-feeling meal. Thus emboldened, I have found a more ambitious process for bean curd. If you want a non-meat meal, the minced pork or beef could be omitted. The first four ingredients and bean curd can be bought in any oriental supermarket.

3 tbsp Chinese dried shrimps
4 medium dried mushrooms
1½ tbsp salted black beans
2 dried chillis or 1 fresh chilli
4 tbsp of vegetable oil
1 onion, peeled and sliced
2 cloves of garlic, peeled and slivered
pinch of salt
8 oz (250 g) minced pork or beef
splash of soy sauce
2 tsp cornflour mixed with 8 tbsp stock
3 cakes of bean curd
a few spring onions, trimmed and finely chopped

Soak the shrimps and mushrooms in warm water for 30 minutes. Drain and chop, pushing aside the mushroom stems. Soak the black beans in water for a few minutes. Drain. Finely chop the chillis, discarding the seeds. You might want less chilli if you dislike fiery food. Heat the oil in a frying pan or wok. Add the onion, garlic and a pinch of salt and stir-fry for a couple of minutes.

Add the chillis, shrimps and mushrooms and stir-fry for 2 minutes. Add the mince and black beans and cook until the meat is browned. Add a splash of soy sauce. Simmer the mixture for 5 minutes. Pour in the blended cornflour and bring to the boil again, stirring until the mixture thickens slightly and shines. Add the bean curd. Heat it through carefully to avoid it breaking. Serve in a bowl with the spring onion sprinkled on top and some boiled rice as an accompaniment.

SATAY

SERVES 4

Satay (or saté or sateh) has become the most familiar dish of Malaysian and Indonesian cooking. In restaurants serving this style of food, satay has become popular in the way spare ribs did in Chinese establishments. Like many restaurant dishes that are cooked to order, these little kebabs make ideal fast food at home. Marinating the meat improves the flavour, but it is a step that can be forfeited if speed really is of the essence. The peanutty sauce is an essential accompaniment but you might prefer to serve plain boiled rice in place of the traditional pressed rice cakes and a cucumber salad (especially good made with rice vinegar available from oriental grocers) in place of just chunks of cucumber. Beef, pork or chicken all respond well to this treatment and an assortment makes a more diverting meal than a choice of one.

1 lb (500 g) lean meat (lamb, beef, pork, chicken or a mixture)

FOR THE MARINADE:
1 onion, finely chopped
tbsp dark brown sugar
2 tbsp soy sauce
1 tbsp lemon juice
1 tbsp oil
2 cloves of garlic, peeled and crushed
1 dried red chilli or 1 tsp chilli sauce

FOR THE SAUCE:
1 onion, peeled and finely chopped
1 tbsp oil
chillis or chilli sauce, to taste
6 oz (175 g) crunchy peanut butter
about 6 fl oz (175 ml) water
1 tsp sugar
juice of ½ lemon
1 tbsp soy sauce

Chop the meat into small cubes or strips. Combine the marinade ingredients and turn the meat in this mixture. Leave for about 1 hour.

To make the sauce, fry the onion in the oil until golden. Add just one chilli or ½ tsp chilli sauce, unless you like hot-hot food, the peanut butter, water and the sugar. Stir well and simmer the mixture until you have a thick, cohesive sauce. Add the lemon juice and soy sauce. Taste for further seasoning. Thread the skewers with the chunks of meat and grill, turning frequently, until the meat is browned, basting with the remaining marinade.

PLUM SAUCE

Similar to the Chinese plum sauce, this can be used as they would use it or served with roast meat, like duck or pork; or used as a coating for spare ribs. It will keep well in covered jars in the refrigerator.

1 cooking apple
4 tbsp water
8 oz (250 g) dark red plums
8 oz (250 g) apricots
5 oz (150 g) granulated or light brown sugar
4 oz (120 g) white wine vinegar
1 chopped fresh chilli or 2 dried chillis or pinch of chilli powder

Peel, core and cut up the apple. Cook with 4 tablespoons of water in a covered pan until soft. Add the rest of the ingredients. Cover and simmer for about one hour. Sieve to remove stones. Taste; it may need more sugar. Can be used hot or cold.

HAM IN A PIQUANT SAUCE SERVES 4

This is a recipe based on one of Elizabeth David's in *French Provincial Cooking*. One Sunday I served this dish for lunch. Too idle and feckless to shop on Saturday when the butcher was open, I had to rely on the delicatessen for cooked ham. Even in this somewhat simplified form, it was a considerably finer dish than ham in white sauce. I did make a lovely dish of fresh peas stewed with spring onions and lettuce to go with it. The recipe for that is on page 218.

4 shallots or 1 onion
2 juniper berries
4 tbsp wine vinegar
2 oz (60 g) butter
2 tbsp flour
8 fl oz (250 ml) stock or ½ stock cube and 8 fl oz (250 ml) water
splash of white wine (optional)
5 fl oz (150 ml) double cream
salt and pepper
3–4 thick slices of ham (from a whole cooked ham, not out of a packet)

Turn on the oven to 180°C/350°F/gas mark 4. Peel and finely chop the shallots or, failing shallots, an onion. Put the shallots, the juniper berries and wine vinegar into a small saucepan. Bring to the boil and reduce until there is practically no vinegar left. In a larger saucepan melt the butter, stir in the flour and continue stirring watchfully until the mixture is smooth and a pale coffee colour. Make up the stock cube with water or heat the same amount of stock should you have some. Add to the flour and butter mixture gradually, stirring until the mixture thickens. Add a splash of white wine if it is around and the shallot mixture. Cook gently until there is no taste of flour (about 20 minutes). Stir in the cream, taste for seasoning and thin if necessary; you want a fairly liquid sauce. Arrange the ham in a single layer in a shallow ovenproof dish. Strain the sauce over the ham and heat through in the oven.

SERVES 4   BACON AND CABBAGE

Talk to Irish people about food and it is almost certain that, sooner or later, they will start to reminisce mistily about bacon and cabbage. When I visited Galway, I took the opportunity of asking various people the secret of this blessed combination. The answers revealed little more than a recipe whereby you boiled the bacon and, after a while, added the cabbage to the cooking water. Parsley sauce was often mentioned as an indispensable accompaniment. There is no doubt that the three constituents meld well, but I looked further to see if there could be more to this dish than childhood memories. The recipe below, which has some twists and turns, comes from *Irish Traditional Food* by Theodora Fitz-Gibbon. Some brown Irish soda bread (page 276) would not come amiss here.

1 large Savoy cabbage
8 thick rashers of streaky bacon
salt and pepper
4 cloves
4 allspice berries
about ½ pt (300 ml) bacon or chicken stock

Trim the cabbage of any duff leaves. Cut it in half and boil for 15 minutes in salted water. Drain, soak in cold water for one minute, then drain well and slice. Line the bottom of a casserole with half the bacon rashers, then put the cabbage on top and add the seasonings. Add enough stock, barely to cover, then put the remaining rashers on top. Cover and simmer for one hour until most of the liquid is absorbed.

TOAD IN THE CLOUDS

My mother, who cut out this recipe from a newspaper in 1971, said, as she handed it to me, 'No one will remember it, darling.' She has had great success with it and it is a much more interesting dish than toad in the hole where the batter often tends to be saggy in parts. Choose sausages with a high meat content and a mustard that has zing. It is a good-looking dish, like a brown, shiny soufflé.

1 lb (500 g) pork sausages
8½ fl oz (260 ml) milk
2 oz (60 g) butter and more to grease dish
5 oz (150 g) sifted self-raising flour
4 eggs
2 large tomatoes, skinned and each one cut into 8 crescents
salt and pepper
mustard, as required
a little top of the milk or thin cream
2 oz (60 g) diced cheddar cheese

Turn on the oven to 220°C/425°F/gas mark 7. Skin the sausages and divide each one lengthways into two. Make the batter, which is a gougère batter, rather than a Yorkshire pudding one, as follows. Put the milk into a large heavy saucepan. Cut the butter into it in flakes. Set on the heat, allowing the butter to melt by the time the milk has reached boiling point. At this stage tip in the sifted flour. Let the milk seethe up over it. Remove from the heat and beat vigorously until smooth. Beat in the eggs one at a time. Butter a 10 in (25 cm) diameter soufflé dish. Cover the base with some of the batter. Arrange the sausages on the top, with the tomatoes tucked in between. Season with salt and pepper and spread the sausages lightly with mustard. Cover with the remaining batter, smoothing the surface with a knife dipped in cold water and making sure the sausages and tomatoes are completely covered. Brush the surface with milk or cream and sprinkle with the cheese. Bake near the top of the oven for about 40–45 minutes until richly brown and well risen.

BRATWURST WITH HOT POTATO SALAD

SERVES 4

The range of sausages in most supermarkets and delicatessens gets better all the time, which means that the standby of sausages for supper need no longer just be bangers and mash, though that is an estimable dish. Bratwurst is a German sausage, pale in colour, made from finely minced pork or veal. It would seem to be less fatty than other types of sausage and lends itself well to either frying or grilling. I cook Bratwurst on a ridged cast-iron pan to give them that 'branded' look. Try to get a waxy variety of potato for the salad, though I know that in this country it is easier said than done. New potatoes will suffice. The trick about this dish is to dress the potatoes while they are hot and to serve them still pretty warm. Prepared this way, they will absorb a good quantity of the dressing and thus have a vibrant flavour.

1½ lb (750 g) potatoes
5 tbsp good olive oil
2 tbsp red wine vinegar
1 tsp German mustard
salt and freshly ground black pepper
1 heaped tbsp finely chopped parsley
2 shallots or a bundle of chives
8 Bratwurst sausages

Peel the potatoes and cook them in boiling salted water. They will cook in 10–15 minutes, depending on their size. Mix together the oil, vinegar, mustard and seasonings for the dressing and then stir in the parsley and finely sliced shallots or chopped chives. Put the sausages to cook, either under the grill, in a pan with a little oil, or as described above. When the potatoes are tender, drain and let them sit for a few minutes to let off steam. Slice them and put them into a bowl. Pour on the dressing and mix in carefully. Serve with the sausages and some German mustard.

SAUCISSES DE MONTAGNE WITH TOMATO SAUCE
SERVES 3

I am always on the lookout for new products. Once I found these Saucisses de Montagne, 100 per cent cured pork sausages cooked in duck fat, in Marks and Spencer's. You can eat them cold or boil them in a bag, which is what I did. The richness of the duck fat makes a dish of lentils or a purée of split peas an ideal accompaniment. A couple of crisp dessert apples, peeled, sliced and sautéed in butter with a little cider or Calvados added towards the end of cooking time, is also an apt partnership. With these or any other noble sausages, you could serve the spicy tomato sauce described below.

1 oz (2 tbsp) olive oil
1 oz (30 g) butter
8 oz (250 g) onions, peeled and sliced
3 cloves of garlic, peeled and finely slivered
1 lb (500 g) tomatoes, peeled and sliced
1 tsp brown sugar
splash of Worcestershire Sauce
2 tsp soy sauce
salt and pepper
1 tbsp tomato ketchup
chopped fresh parsley or basil for garnishing
French bread, to serve

Heat the oil and butter together and add the onions and half the prepared garlic. Cook gently, but keep going until the onions start to brown at the edges. Add the tomatoes and the seasonings. If you like hot food you could also add a teaspoon of chilli sauce or chilli powder. Stir in the tomato ketchup. Simmer together until the sauce thickens and the tomatoes break down. Boil the sausages in their bag, or grill, depending on your sausage source. Just before serving the meal, taste the sauce for seasoning. Add a few grinds of the pepper mill, the rest of the garlic and stir. Sprinkle with parsley or basil. Put into a hot dish with the sausages on top and have French bread on hand to mop up the sauce.

SAUTÉED KIDNEYS
SERVES 4

I remember reading a recipe for kidneys which mentioned their 'goût très prononcé d'urine si désagréable', which you might get the gist of even if you don't read French and which might reinforce any prejudice you have about offal. The recipe below neatly side-steps this problem and has the advantage of speed and deliciousness. It should convert non-believers and will work equally well with lamb's or veal kidney and even ox and pig's kidney. If you are not counting calories, serve the kidneys in their sauce with plain boiled rice, but also with triangles of fried bread on to which you sprinkle a little finely chopped garlic mixed with chopped parsley.

1 lb (500 g) lamb's kidneys
½ pt (300 ml) milk
2 tbsp vegetable oil
2 tbsp butter
2 tbsp brandy
5 oz (150 ml) double cream
salt and pepper

FOR SERVING: *boiled long grain rice (preferably basmati)*
triangles of fried bread, sprinkled with chopped garlic and parsley

Remove the hard core of white fat from each kidney and slice into pieces at least ¼ in (6 mm) thick. Soak the kidney slices in milk for 30 minutes. This removes any strong flavours and also tenderises the meat. Put the rice on to cook. Heat the vegetable oil until fairly hot. Drain the kidneys from the milk and pat dry with a clean tea-towel or kitchen paper. Fry the kidneys in the oil quickly, turning with a spatula, and when browned but still with a pink centre tip into a sieve or colander to drain. Clean the pan and melt the butter in it. Return the kidneys to the hot butter and sauté quickly for a second time. Warm the brandy. Add to the pan and flame. When the flames have subsided, stir in the cream. Swirl it around until you have a cohesive sauce. Season with pepper and just a scrap of salt. Pack some of the cooked rice into a small cup, turn out on to a warmed plate and put a quarter of the kidneys and their sauce beside it. Repeat three more times. Garnish with the fried bread.

FEUILLETÉ OF KIDNEYS

Feuilleté is a popular expression on restaurant menus these days. It means puff pastry and a receptacle fashioned of that can enable a restaurateur to 'stretch' a relatively small amount of whatever ingredient becomes the filling, be it seafood or meat. My children like food presented this way and refer to it as *vole*-au-vent. They might equate kidneys with that very rodent – what they like is chicken in white sauce – but for adults this is a very satisfying dish providing nice contrasts in texture and about as much kidney as any rational person usually wants to eat. The mustardy sauce is rich and delicious. Try to buy fresh lamb's kidneys. If you have a tame butcher he might be persuaded to rip them from the sheep carcasses. Better still you can use calf's kidney.

1 lb (500 g) lamb's or calf's kidney
8 oz (250 g) frozen puff pastry or 1 large vol-au-vent case
2 oz (60 g) butter
2–3 shallots, or 1 onion peeled and finely chopped
1 clove of garlic, peeled and finely slivered
1 tbsp sherry vinegar or wine vinegar
splash of madeira or port (optional)
¼ pt (150 ml) veal or chicken stock
1 egg yolk
2 tbsp double cream
1 generous dsp Dijon mustard
salt and freshly ground black pepper

Turn on oven according to pastry instructions on the packet. Trim the kidneys of any gristle or membrane and winkle out the fatty core. Leave lamb kidneys whole. Slice the veal kidney into ¼–½ in (6–12 mm) slices. While you cook your puff pastry in the shape you fancy, round or oblong, and according to packet instructions, start on the kidneys and sauce. Melt the butter and gently sauté the kidneys for about 5 minutes. You want them to stay a little pink at their heart. Remove them and keep warm. Sauté the onion or shallots and garlic until softened. When the shallot is golden add the vinegar and bubble fiercely (a splash of madeira or port would only improve matters). Add the stock and simmer for about 15 minutes. Beat the egg yolk and cream in a small bowl. Add 2 tbsp of the stock to the egg mixture. Return this, well mixed, to the sauce and cook over a low heat until it is thickened. Stir in the mustard and season. Heat through. Slice the kidneys if they are whole and warm them through in the sauce. Sandwich between the pastry or spoon into the vol-au-vent case.

LIVER 'VENEZIANA' SERVES 4

In common with practically all dishes there are two ways of approaching this one: the first will give you delectable, sweet fegato alla Veneziana, the other will result in liver and onions, that hard, sour dish often encountered in caffs. It is important, of course, to start with good calf's liver and to find a butcher who will slice it evenly and thinly. You want the slices about $\frac{1}{4}$ in (6 mm) thick. Prepared this way, it should fry in less time than it takes to read the recipe. The onions may be cooked ahead of time, but it is important that they, too, should be carefully cooked – browned but not scorched. Italian mashed potatoes, puréed and beaten with hot milk, butter or olive oil and grated Parmesan cheese, is a fine accompaniment.

$1\frac{1}{2}$ lb (750 g) calf's liver, sliced $\frac{1}{4}$ in (6 mm) thick
3 tbsp vegetable oil
6 medium onions, peeled and thinly sliced
salt and freshly ground pepper

Pick over the liver and cut away any skin, gristle or tubes. Cut the liver into pieces about the size of a visiting card. Heat the oil in a large frying pan large enough to hold the liver slices in one layer, and sauté the sliced onion over a gentle heat for about 15 minutes or until soft and golden brown. Remove the onion with a slotted spoon, leaving the oil behind. Keep the onions warm. Turn the heat right up and when the oil is very hot, add the liver. As soon as the liver loses its raw colour, turn it. Add salt and freshly ground pepper and, a few seconds later, the onions. Give everything one more turn and serve immediately on a warm dish. If cut in the right way, the liver should cook in less than a minute and be as tender as butter.

SERVES 4
CALF'S LIVER WITH SESAME SEED AND MUSTARD CRUST

Children have been known to observe that the things you do not want to eat are invariably those that are good for you. Some grown-ups have that point of view about liver and this recipe should convert those who heretofore have been deaf to the tales of liver's fantastic Vitamin B quality.

I took the recipe from *The Café des Artistes Cookbook* by George Lang. The Café des Artistes is an historic restaurant in New York and George Lang is a legendary figure in the restaurant trade in America. He is also the author of *The Cuisine of Hungary*, a book I greatly admire.

1 lb (500 g) best calf's liver, thinly sliced
freshly ground black pepper
about 5 tbsp yellow mustard seeds (available in health food shops and
oriental groceries)
about 5 tbsp sesame seeds (untoasted)
3 tbsp Dijon mustard
2 oz (60 g) butter
2 tbsp vegetable oil

Season the liver slices with pepper. If the slices are large, cut them
to weigh about 1½–2 oz (45–60 g) each. Mix together the mustard
and sesame seeds. With a pastry brush, paint the liver on both
sides with mustard, (or do your best using a knife) and dredge on
both sides in the mixture of seeds, pressing them on firmly to
make a coating. Heat the butter and oil in a large sauté pan or
frying pan and when it is hot slip in the liver slices and cook for
2 minutes on each side. The seeds should be golden, not burned.
Since the crust is apt to break up and break away, fish out any
stray bits from the oil, drain, and scatter on to the meat. Drain the
liver on kitchen paper and serve on warmed plates.

OXTAIL STEW SERVES 4

This is a dish that benefits from being made one day and finished
off the next, a kind of cooking that sounds laborious but is in
reality very practical. I have decided that the secret of good oxtail
is to roast the bones before the second cooking. It makes an
appreciable difference to the texture and the flavour of the finished
dish. This is perfect cold-weather food and, incidentally, children,
who all seem to like to gnaw on bones, do not take exception to
oxtail. You will notice there are no tomatoes, nor tomato paste in
this recipe. To my mind they echo tinned soup in this and are the
ruination of oxtail.

3 lb (1.5 kg) oxtail pieces
1 tbsp flour
1 dsp Bisto
1 large onion, peeled and sliced
3 carrots, peeled and chopped into large pieces
1 tbsp olive oil or other vegetable oil
½ bottle rough red wine
½ tsp ground cumin
1 tsp dry English mustard
1 tsp ground ginger
½ tsp ground coriander
½ tsp freshly ground black pepper
salt
soy sauce

The first day or in the morning for the evening: trim the oxtail pieces of any large lumps of fat. Dust them in the mixture of flour and Bisto (you might clear your throat here, but it actually is a positive contribution). Fry the onion and carrot briefly in the oil, add the oxtail pieces and sauté them until they are browned all over. Pour in the red wine and then enough water to reach the top of the meat. Simmer on top of the stove or in the oven for 3 hours. When the meat is tender, remove it to a bowl and pour the sauce into another bowl. Refrigerate both. Next day, or the evening of the same day, arrange the bones in a baking tray. Scatter half the mustard and ginger, some cumin and coriander and black pepper on them and roast them in a hot oven for about 6 minutes. Turn them over, season, and roast for a further 6 minutes. Take the fat off the stock. Heat the stock, add the oxtail and simmer until well heated through. Taste for seasoning and adjust salt with soy sauce. If the sauce tastes flimsy, remove the meat and reduce by fast boiling. Serve in an earthenware casserole. Mashed potatoes are lovely with it.

VEGETABLES

Vegetables could be the subject of the sort of Hollywood movie where someone from the chorus line becomes the star. A star overnight would not quite be the case, but the truth is that few people nowadays will look askance if offered a main course that revolves around the virtue of some vegetable, be it parsnip or cabbage, that humble green that at the moment of writing has assumed great chic among star-studded chefs. Devotees of *haute cuisine* speak reverentially of the salsifis of Robuchon, and the mashed potatoes of Girardet where once only foie gras or langoustines would get a mention. Health consciousness plays a part in this phenomenon but, quite apart from that, vegetables have always had the potential for beauty and admiration, like Doris Day in the first reel.

Although what strikes me as an excessive emphasis on imports provides us with practically all vegetables all year round, seasonality should play an important role in vegetable preparation. It is worth waiting for English asparagus in May and June, Jersey potatoes at much the same time, garden peas and broad beans a month or so later, sprouts shaped up by the first frost, red cabbage for its warming glow in winter. I am generally in favour of planning meals around shopping expeditions, but particularly so where vegetables are concerned. It is also true that if you have potatoes in the house you are never going to lack a meal, and packets or tins, such as bacon or anchovies, can be pressed into service to give vigour and bite.

For most of us salad has come to mean much more than a bowl of lettuce, tomato, cucumber and spring onion – the English salad – but its worth, whatever combination you conjure, will always lie in the dressing; good quality olive oil and vinegar, fresh herbs when possible. Most of the recipes in this section would make a creditable main course and it is fertile ground for vegetarians or spasmodic vegetarians.

AÏOLI SERVES 4-6

Sometimes given the name 'the butter of Provence', this golden pungent sauce is a great accompaniment to cold meats or vegetables, or can form the centrepiece of '*un grand aïoli*' when a bowlful is surrounded by salt cod or fresh cod, hard-boiled eggs, boiled potatoes, sweet peppers, artichokes, green beans and the like. Aïoli is also good served with spring chicken simply grilled after spending a little time bathing in lemon juice, olive oil and herbs. As a guideline to the amount of garlic to use, try two fat

cloves per person – the sauce should almost sting your palate –
but adjust it according to your preference. I use half olive oil, half
vegetable oil if the olive is strong, but do not use just vegetable oil
or you will mislay the South of France quality. Also, do make this
sauce by hand with a bowl and a wooden spoon, not in a blender
or food processor. The texture of a hand-made mayonnaise is quite
different. The finished product should be as stiff as an ointment.

*6–8 cloves of garlic, peeled and any trace of green in the centre
removed*
pinch of sea salt
2 egg yolks
½–¾ pt (300–450 ml) olive oil and vegetable oil
squeeze of lemon juice
freshly ground black pepper

Crush the peeled garlic, either through a garlic crusher or using a
pestle and mortar. Put it in the bottom of a mixing bowl. Add a
pinch of sea salt. Add the egg yolks and mix until well amalgamated. Start to add the olive oil drop by drop while mixing with
a wooden spoon. Keep at it until the mixture begins to thicken,
which will take a little longer than with ordinary mayonnaise as
the garlic thins the yolks to some extent. When you have a cohesive
mass, you can begin to add the oil more recklessly. Two egg yolks
should absorb the full ¾ pt (450 ml) of oil, but stop when you feel
you have enough sauce for your purposes. Taste for seasoning and
add a little lemon juice. Should your mixture separate through
adding the oil injudiciously, put another egg yolk in a clean bowl
and slowly stir your separated mixture into that. All should be
well.

SERVES 4-6   # HOME-MADE BAKED BEANS WITH PORK

One week, along with the bills, a can of nutritionally improved
baked beans with 25 per cent less salt and 50 per cent less added
sugar arrived in the post. According to the newsheet attached,
each 15 ounce can of baked beans contains more protein than a
pint of milk, but, ounce for ounce, fewer calories and fat than eggs,
meat or cottage cheese. I suspect that the latter is a slightly weasely
statistic because you are unlikely to eat only 2 ounces of baked
beans, but you might well stop after one egg. However, it made
me think about doing a recipe for home-made baked beans, which

can be delicious and, no doubt, more wholesome than the tinned variety since the amount of salt, fat and sugar is within your control. The advantage of the high fibre content is also there, and pork and beans is an easy dish to assemble to feed numbers of people. If you are trying to coax people like children into accepting a home-made version of something they like to see in tins, you could colour and flavour your stock with tomato purée, but I have not put it into the recipe.

1 lb (500g) dried white haricot beans
8oz (250g) salt pork or, failing that, belly of pork or a piece of streaky bacon
1 tbsp dry English mustard or Dijon mustard
2 tbsp treacle or molasses
1 tbsp dark brown sugar
1 large onion, peeled and sliced
salt and freshly ground black pepper

Soak the beans overnight or all day for the evening if that is feasible. If neither is practical, bring the beans to the boil, cook for a few minutes, remove from the heat and let stand for an hour. Cook the beans in their soaking water for one hour. Drain them, keeping the liquid. Cut the pork into thick slices, putting one slice into the bottom of an earthenware casserole or other suitable folksy-looking pot. Add the beans and the rest of the pork, reserving one slice for the top of the pot. Heat the bean water and mix in the flavourings, including the onion. (Frying it before you add it makes it more interesting.) Pour on to the beans. Cut notches in the rind of the remaining piece of pork. Place on top of the beans. Cover and cook in a moderate oven, 180°C/350°F/gas mark 4, for at least an hour. Remove the cover for the last 20 minutes so the top piece of pork browns and crisps.

CHICKPEAS WITH SPINACH AND FRIED BREADCRUMBS

SERVES 4

An item that emerges from a tin fairly unscathed is chickpeas. I dare say their quality of seemingly never becoming overcooked, even when you soak dried ones and boil them for hours, is a contributory factor. You can make quite satisfactory instant hummus with tinned chickpeas whizzed in a food processor with olive oil, lemon juice, and tahini (sesame paste) – better and

cheaper than the little pots of the stuff. Or you can try the recipe
below, which has ingredients that are possible to buy at the last
minute and which turns out, I trust you will agree, to be considerably better than a sum of its parts. If you think I am obsessed
with fried breadcrumbs, it is because I think they are so delicious –
and why should pricey grouse and partridge have them all to
themselves?

2 medium onions
olive oil, as required
1 lb 2 oz (500 g) frozen leaf spinach
2 × 14 oz (400 g) tins of chickpeas
1 dried red chilli
2 slices of white or brown bread
1 clove of garlic
salt and freshly ground black pepper

Peel the onions and slice from tip to base in thin crescents. Fry
them until golden in 1 tbsp olive oil. Add the leaf spinach and
cook according to the packet instructions until softened. Drain
away any excess water. Drain the tinned chickpeas and stir into
the spinach with a dribble more of olive oil and the crumbled chilli
pepper. Cover the pan and allow to simmer. Season. Meanwhile,
fry the bread in olive oil into which you have put a finely chopped
large clove of garlic. When the bread is golden, drain on kitchen
paper and then crumble it roughly on to the spinach and chickpeas.
You could, if you wish, fry another slice of bread, cut it into
triangles and tuck into the corners of the finished dish. Eat before
the crumbs have lost their crunch.

SERVES 4   # LEEK AND BACON PUDDING

I tried this rather unlikely sounding idea as a way of using up
some large leeks that were languishing in the larder. Although it
takes two hours to steam, it is quick to assemble and there is
something consoling about having your supper bubbling away
while you get on with other things; it makes you feel organised,
on top of things. The butter added to the filling combines with
the water and the juice of the leeks to make a nice little sauce, on
the same kind of principle as Sussex Pond Pudding, but you could
melt a little more butter, or make a beurre blanc, further to enhance
the dish.

8 oz (250 g) self-raising flour
4 oz (120 g) shredded suet
1 tbsp chopped fresh parsley
salt and freshly ground black pepper
6 rashers of bacon
5–6 leeks, trimmed and carefully washed
2 oz (60 g) butter

Sift the flour, add the suet and chopped parsley and plenty of salt and pepper. Stir in enough water to make a firm dough. Roll it out and use two-thirds to line a pudding basin, reserving the other piece for the lid. Fry the bacon until crisp and drain on kitchen paper. Chop the leeks into thick slices, checking that all grit or sand has been washed away. Chop the bacon. Put leeks and bacon into the suet-lined basin. Add the butter and 1 tbsp water and a little salt and pepper. Cover with a suet lid. Tie foil on to the basin and steam in a large pan of boiling water that comes halfway up the side of the bowl for 2 hours or more. Turn the pudding out on to a heated plate.

PAN BAGNA SERVES 2-3

While I wait for someone in London to open a charcuterie or delicatessen to rival the *traiteur* of an average French village, thereby making the speedy preparation of meals at home as easy for us as it is for any French person, I am glad to be able to report on a wonderful new group of bread shops with produce so good all you need for a meal would be butter, some ham or cheese and perhaps a bunch of radishes.

The branch of the Italian bakery, La Fornaia, that I visited is at 66 Notting Hill Gate, W11. There is another branch in Richmond and one in the Fulham Road, and I trust there will be more to follow. There is an astonishing range of bread and sweet baked goods including petits fours. After much deliberation I bought an olive bread, studded with green olives and something they called a 'slipper', the description referring to the shape. The texture was slightly chewy, the taste flirting with sour. I hadn't tasted bread like it since being on holiday.

The recipe below for Pan Bagna, which is traditionally eaten while playing *boules*, is just one way of using such a bread. A round, flat, soft bread or a French baguette would work equally well.

1 'slipper' loaf or round flat soft bread or French baguette
¼ pt (150 ml) virgin olive oil
1–2 fl oz (30–60 ml) wine vinegar, to taste
salt and pepper
1 clove of garlic, peeled and crushed
2 large 'Mediterranean' tomatoes
1 large Spanish onion
1 green or red pepper, de-seeded and thinly sliced
1 small tin of anchovy fillets, drained of oil or brine and rinsed
2 oz (60 g) black olives, stoned

Slice the loaf in half horizontally. Make up a vinaigrette with the oil, wine vinegar to taste, salt, pepper and garlic. Sprinkle the cut sides of the bread liberally with the vinaigrette. Arrange sliced tomatoes, onion and peppers on the bottom half of the bread. Garnish with the anchovy fillets and olives. Place the top half of the bread on the sandwich, wrap it tightly in aluminium foil and leave for an hour or two with weights on top for the flavours to meld and the sandwich to form a solid mass easy to slice and serve.

SERVES 4–6   # PISSALADIÈRE

If you think, from looking at my recipes, that I am fond of onions, then you are right. That they are good for you and, some say, break down cholesterol in the blood, is only a plus. I like the way they can be crisp and stinging, or melting and sweet. I like spring onions, shallots, leeks, English onions, red onions and Spanish onions, and I am particularly fond of this pie, which is the Niçois version of a pizza. Like pizza, it should be made with a bread base, but I think it works just as well with pastry, which, if crisp, provides a nice contrast to the softness of the onions. If you were feeling really idle you could use thick slices of bread, cut lengthways from a loaf fried on one side in olive oil. The key to a good pissaladière is cooking the onions long and slow – allow at least 40 minutes for the process. Also use a good olive oil to achieve the correct sunny, South of France flavour.

2½ lb (1.25 kg) onions, peeled and quite thinly sliced
5 fl oz (150 ml) olive oil
2 cloves of garlic, peeled and crushed or chopped
8 or more anchovy fillets, drained of oil or brine and rinsed
9 or more black olives

FOR THE PASTRY:

6 oz (150 g) plain flour
2 generous tsp powdered English mustard
2 oz (60 g) butter
1 oz (30 g) lard
pinch of salt
about 1½ tbsp cold water

Make up the shortcrust pastry, using the quantities above (or your own recipe, in which case take on board the inclusion of the mustard which goes well with the onions). Roll out thinly and line a large pie dish. Bake in an oven set at 190°C/375°F/gas mark 5, with foil over the base of the pastry and some dried beans dotted about on top, for 15 minutes. This 'baking blind' gives a crisper result. Cook the sliced onions gently in 4 fl oz (120 ml) of the oil, stirring occasionally. After about 20 minutes, add the garlic. At the end of the cooking time, the onions should be almost a purée. Spread the onion mixture on the pastry. Arrange anchovy fillets in a lattice pattern and place olives in some of the diamond shaped spaces. Dribble on the remaining oil and bake in the oven (temperatures as before) for 30 minutes. Eat hot, or even nicer, warm.

GREEK SPINACH PIE SERVES 4-6

Filo pastry is the point of this pie. If you have not discovered this commodity yet, you will thank me once you do because it is the starting point for all manner of impressive dishes.

In the past when I have served this, or a variation of it, and been congratulated on my extraordinary skills as a pâtissier, I have cast my eyes modestly downwards. Now the secret is out. All you need is an enterprising supermarket, delicatessen or bakery that sells the raw dough in packets. I use Cypriot bakeries in Kentish Town and Camden Town in North London.

Once you have understood the technique of filo, which consists of separating the paper-thin sheets of dough with oil or melted butter, you will start to improvise with fillings. Chicken in béchamel or mushrooms and chopped hard-boiled egg in a parsley sauce are two possibilities, but the recipe below is more authentically Greek and merits being called spanakopitta.

1 lb (500 g) fresh spinach or ½ lb (250 g) packet frozen leaf spinach
¾ lb (375 g) ricotta or other fresh curd cheese
¼ lb (120 g) feta cheese or, if unobtainable, grated Parmesan or
coarsely grated Gruyère
2 eggs, beaten well
salt and pepper, to taste
pinch of grated nutmeg or mace
2–3 oz (60–90 g) butter or vegetable oil

Turn on the oven to 190°C/375°F/gas mark 5. Wash the fresh spinach, cook it in the water that clings to it, drain and chop; or cook the frozen spinach according to the packet instructions and chop. Mix together the cheeses. Add the spinach, the beaten eggs, freshly ground pepper and a pinch of nutmeg or mace. Be judicious about the salt; if you have used feta cheese you may not need any. Melt the butter in a small pan. Oil will work if you prefer to use it for considerations of health though it will deplete the flavour slightly. Using a pastry brush, paint the bottom of a roasting tin, roughly the size of the sheets of filo with the butter or oil. Lay in a sheet of dough. Brush with butter or oil and continue this way for five or six sheets. Spread on the spinach and cheese mixture and then lay on four or five more sheets of dough, each separated with butter or oil. With a small sharp knife score the pastry in a large diamond pattern.

Bake in the pre-heated oven for 45 minutes. Increase the heat and bake for another 5–10 minutes, watching carefully until the top is golden brown and curling at the edges crisply. Serve hot or lukewarm.

SERVES 4 SPINACH SOUFFLÉ WITH ANCHOVY SAUCE

This soufflé is inspired by one of the more famous first courses served by Richard Shepherd at Langan's Brasserie. However, this is not his recipe.

Most of the work can be done well before the meal. When you serve the dish, stab the soufflé dramatically with a spoon and pour the sauce into the middle.

Friends will applaud your insouciance in the face of a culinary marvel and any dryness or monotony in the soufflé will be obviated by the tingling, hot, creamy anchovy.

1 lb (500 g) fresh spinach
2 oz (60 g) butter
3 tbsp flour
½ pt (300 ml) milk
4 oz (120 g) cream cheese
1 oz (30 g) grated Parmesan cheese (optional)
salt and freshly ground black pepper
4 eggs
1 × 2 oz (50 g) tin of anchovies, drained of oil or brine
1 oz (30 g) butter
¼ pt (150 ml) double cream

Turn on the oven to 190°C/375°F/gas mark 5. Wash the spinach leaves, trim off any hard stalks and cook the leaves in the water that clings to them until it is tender. Drain in a colander and, when it is cool enough, squeeze it with your hands to get it as dry as possible. Chop it finely. Melt the 2 oz (60 g) butter, stir in the flour to make a roux. Slowly add the milk until you have a thick, smooth sauce and then beat in the cream cheese, bit by bit. Add the Parmesan if you are using it. Stir in the spinach and season quite vigorously. Let cool a little and beat in the egg yolks one by one. All this can be done ahead of time. When you are ready to cook, whip the egg whites until stiff. Fold about a quarter of them into the soufflé mixture to lighten it, then fold in the rest with an even gentler hand. Pour into a buttered soufflé dish and bake for 25–30 minutes. To make the sauce, soak 5–6 anchovy fillets in warm water briefly, pat them dry. Melt the 1 oz (30 g) butter, add the fillets, stir around until they break up and then pour in the cream. Bring to the boil, give a quick bubble and serve.

STACKED SPINACH PANCAKES SERVES 4

I am sure some people are discouraged from cooking by the myths that surround the activity; soufflés are temperamental, eggs will curdle as soon as look at you, pancake batter must be left to stand before it can be cooked. There is a basis, in fact, for most of these beliefs, but they should not be allowed to act as constraints. They can sometimes be successfully ignored. Running late with the children's supper one evening, I made pancakes without letting the batter sit for even a minute and the pancakes were fine – perhaps not the best ever, but absolutely fine. These described below look prettiest if stacked into a layer cake with your choice of filling or sauce. I have suggested ham, tomato sauce and cheese, but equally you could make, an excellent vegetarian supper with fillings such as mushrooms in cream or a purée of sweetcorn alternating with tomato sauce.

1 lb (500 g) tomatoes or 1 × 14 oz (400 g) tin of tomatoes
1 oz (30 g) olive oil
2 cloves of garlic, peeled and chopped
pinch of sugar
salt and freshly ground black pepper

FOR THE FILLINGS:
4 oz (120 g) thinly sliced cooked ham
2 oz (60 g) grated Cheddar or Gruyère cheese

FOR THE BATTER:
½ lb (250 g) raw spinach, or ¼ lb (120 g) frozen chopped spinach
4 oz (120 g) plain flour
pinch of salt
1 egg
½ pt (300 ml) skimmed milk or whole milk mixed with water
1 dsp vegetable oil

Make the pancake batter. Cook the spinach, chop to a fine purée and drain thoroughly. Sift the flour and salt into a basin. Make a well and drop in the egg. Start to mix with a wooden spoon, slowly incorporating the flour and gradually adding the milk or milk and water until you have a smooth batter the consistency of double cream. Mix in the puréed spinach and the vegetable oil. Let sit if you have the chance. During that time make a thick tomato sauce by heating the peeled chopped tomatoes in olive oil, adding the garlic and seasonings and simmering to reduce. Make the pancakes in the usual manner, aiming for six to eight. Keep them warm. In a suitable ovenproof dish layer the pancakes in one stack, like a layer cake, alternating the sliced ham and the tomato sauce as fillings and finishing with the cheese on top. Heat through in a hot oven until the cheese has melted and is golden. Serve cut into wedges.

SERVES 2
STIR-FRIED VEGETABLES WITH CURRIED OMELETTE

Any mixture of vegetables can be stir-fried, but sometimes the simpler the combination the better. This dish, which I quite often make when I'm in for supper by myself, works perfectly well just with onions and carrots, but if you want a lighter, greener look, try an assembly along the lines of mangetouts, broccoli florets, spring onions and courgettes. When making the curried omelettes, do one at a time to keep the oil hot enough to puff them up dramatically. Otherwise they droop rather discouragingly. The notion of omelette as a garnish can be extended to other dishes. Strips of omelette, for example, are good in consommé. I have given a guideline to a choice of vegetables; use your imagination but not, I think, the cabbage family.

2 tbsp vegetable oil
2 oz (60 g) shallots or spring onions, peeled and sliced
1 large carrot, peeled and thinly sliced
4 oz (120 g) mangetout peas, trimmed
2 oz (60 g) thin green beans, chopped into 1 in (3 cm) lengths
2 courgettes, cut into matchsticks or thin ribbons with a vegetable peeler
4 oz (120 g) broccoli florets
1 fat clove of garlic, peeled and cut into slivers
salt and pepper
2 eggs
2 tsp water
2 tsp curry powder or garam masala

Here is the moment your wok, should you have one, can come into its own. In that, or a frying pan, heat about 1 tbsp vegetable oil. Add the prepared shallots or spring onions, carrots, mangetouts and beans and stir-fry. A few minutes later add the courgettes and broccoli and garlic and stir-fry for a few more minutes, until the vegetables are hot and cooked but still crunchy. Sprinkle with salt. Keep warm on a low heat while you make the omelettes. Beat one egg with 1 tsp water in a bowl. In a small frying pan make extremely hot 1 dsp vegetable oil. Quickly add 1 tsp of curry powder to remove the raw taste and pour in the egg. It should puff up. When it does, flip it over and it will rise to even greater heights. Serve the omelette immediately on top of the vegetables and, halfway through the meal, make another omelette the same way.

TIAN   SERVES 4

After I returned from a holiday in Provence, the spirit of that area – expressed in culinary terms as olive oil, garlic, basil and a wide range of vegetables – infused my cooking for quite some time. Tian, a characteristic peasant dish to be enjoyed hot, warm or cold, can be made with various mixtures of vegetables or, in an austere fashion, with chard alone. Optional embellishments are salt cod or anchovies and a refinement is a topping of breadcrumbs and cheese, as detailed below.

Elizabeth David recounts a story in *A Book of Mediterranean Food* about six gourmets who met for a picnic each having agreed to contribute a dish. Six monumental tians were brought and all were devoured with patriotic enthusiasm: 'Not one of the guests had been able to imagine that there was a better dish in the world.'

1 lb (500 g) courgettes, trimmed and grated
salt
12 oz (375 g) fresh spinach
1 large onion, peeled and chopped
3 tbsp good olive oil
3 cloves of garlic, peeled and slivered
2 oz (60 g) rice, cooked, or 1 cup drained tinned chickpeas
freshly ground black pepper
3 eggs
3 oz (90 g) grated hard cheese, e.g. Cheddar, Gruyère, Parmesan, or a mixture
2 oz (60 g) fresh breadcrumbs

Turn on the oven to 180°C/350°F/gas mark 4. Put the grated courgettes in a sieve, salt them lightly and leave to 'perspire'. Trim the spinach of any hard stalks, wash it well and cook in plenty of boiling salted water until it is limp. Refresh with cold water, squeeze out the moisture with your hands and chop quite finely. Either wring the salted courgettes in a clean tea-towel or squeeze with your hands to extract their moisture. Sauté the chopped onion in the olive oil and when it starts to brown add the garlic. Stir round. Add the courgettes and cook for a few minutes, then stir in the spinach and cook for a few minutes more. Add the rice, stir round and season vigorously with pepper and more salt if it is needed. Remove to a bowl. Beat the eggs in another bowl, stir them into the vegetable mixture. Oil a shallow gratin dish (earthenware is traditional). Spread the mixture in the dish. Mix together the grated cheese and breadcrumbs and sprinkle over the top. Bake for about 35 minutes.

ASPARAGUS WITH THREE SAUCES OR RED PEPPER PURÉE

Though asparagus is frequently used as a garnish to signal luxury or fancy cooking, in my view it should only be contemplated as a course in its own right, its healthy low-calorie appeal confounded with a buttery sauce or supported by a piquant vinaigrette. When you buy asparagus try to find stems of equal size. Trim them and cook, tied into bundles, in boiling salted water, testing after 10 minutes as you want them tender but not waterlogged. Drain on a tea-towel.

To go one further than melted butter as an accompaniment, you could offer three dipping sauces: browned butter in a small pot (just cook the butter gently until it turns a nutty colour), a softly boiled 3-minute egg, and a little heap of salt and freshly ground black pepper. Dip your asparagus spears by turn into the browned butter and the egg yolk. I also like a mixture of freshly ground Parmesan tossed gently with hard-boiled egg yolk that has been rubbed through a sieve. These golden grains, which you sprinkle on the asparagus after you have dipped it in melted butter, add a nice texture, and lively flavour.

Finally, if you have rejected these ideas as well as the more usual vinaigrette, Hollandaise and beurre blanc, this very modern red pepper purée might appeal. The combination of green asparagus and scarlet sauce is appealing. You need some of the asparagus cooking water. This sauce should be made at the last minute as it tends to separate.

2 sweet red peppers
1 glove of garlic, peeled and chopped
1–2 anchovies, drained of olive oil or brine and rinsed (optional)
salt and pepper
pinch of sugar

The counsel of perfection would be to char the red peppers under the grill, put them in a polythene bag for 5 minutes to steam and then peel off the skin. This removes the possibility of bitterness and adds a smoky flavour. Remove all seeds and pith, chop into squares and boil with the garlic in enough of the asparagus water to cover, until tender. Alternatively you can just trim and de-seed the peppers, cut up and cook. When they are tender, liquidise with a little of the cooking liquid and the anchovies if you use them. Season with salt, pepper and sugar.

BROAD BEANS AND PEAS WITH SPRING ONIONS AND LETTUCE

I once spent a summer, starting in late April, in a seaside village on the mainland of Greece. There was no food market – the place was too small – and supplies to the shops were not so much erratic as here today, gone tomorrow. I learned my lesson over some kohlrabi. I saw it one morning and thought vaguely, as one does in hot places, about cooking it. I never saw it again. For a short, pleasant period, broad beans, peas, artichokes and dill were all in the vegetable shop at once. Actually, I might be fantasising about the artichokes. Anyway, I remember making several dishes along the lines of the one described below. They were all the more alluring for the built-in fleeting quality.

If you cannot find fresh dill, substitute parsley. I like the slithery texture of cooked lettuce – it acts almost as a sauce – but if you don't, you can leave it out and perhaps thicken the juices with a little cream or stock mixed with a teaspoon of cornflour or potato flour. I have made a successful version of this, when the need arose, using frozen peas.

1 tbsp vegetable oil
1 oz (30 g) butter
1 bunch of spring onions, cleaned and chopped
1 lb (500 g) fresh broad beans, podded
1 lb (500 g) fresh peas, podded
chicken stock, to cover
1 round lettuce, trimmed and cut across into shreds
salt and pepper
pinch of sugar
1 tsp chopped fresh dill
2 tbsp cream (optional)
1 tsp cornflour or potato flour (optional)

Heat the oil and butter in a heavy-bottomed pan. Cook the spring onions gently for a few minutes, then add the broad beans and cook for a few minutes. If the broad beans are tiny, they can be cooked with the peas. Add the peas, turn them to glaze with the buttery oil. Add enough stock to come just level with the vegetables, then the lettuce, a pinch of salt and sugar and the black pepper. Cover and simmer gently until the vegetables are tender – about 10–15 minutes. Check there is no scorching, but there should be no need for additional liquid. Add the dill and cream if you are using it. If you want a thicker sauce, mix 1 tsp cornflour or potato flour in a little more stock. Add and shake the pan to blend.

STIR-FRIED BRUSSELS SPROUTS SERVES 3-4

It was in quizzing fellow food writer Paul Levy about what he ate for Christmas lunch – it included a scallop and turkey terrine and charcoal-grilled pheasant breasts that had been marinated in pomegranate juice – that I got this recipe for stir-fry sprouts, an idea that Paul said originally came from Anton Mosimann, chef of The Dorchester Hotel. It does put this vegetable in a different light without going as far as some suggest and eating it raw in salads. There are two ways of handling the ginger and garlic flavours. One is to heat quite large pieces in the oil, then remove them, leaving a flavoured oil for stir-frying. The other way, which I prefer, is to cut them into tiny slivers and add them towards the end of the cooking time.

1 lb (500 g) Brussels sprouts trimmed to nice, tight heads
3 tbsp vegetable oil
salt
2 cloves of garlic, peeled and cut into slivers
½ in (1.5 cm) piece of fresh root ginger, peeled and cut into thin strands
freshly ground black pepper

With a sharp knife cut the Brussels sprouts into narrow shreds. A food processor slicing blade makes them too fine. Heat the oil, preferably in a wok, but a frying pan will do. When the oil is hot, add the sprouts and stir-fry. Cover the pan or wok for a minute so that the vegetable gets a chance to cook in the steam. Add salt, which helps to keep the sprouts green, then the garlic and ginger. Stir-fry some more until the sprouts are tender but still crunchy. Add pepper. Serve immediately.

PROFESSOR MONS'S BRUSSELS SPROUTS SERVES 3-4

Jane Grigson tells us in her *Vegetable Book* that Jean Baptiste Van Mons gave this recipe when addressing the Royal Horticultural Society in 1818 on the subject of Brussels sprouts, then a fairly new vegetable to his audience.

1 lb (500 g) Brussels sprouts, trimmed and washed
2 oz (60 g) butter
2 tbsp wine vinegar
fresh herbs (optional)

Cook the whole Brussels sprouts until tender in salted boiling water. Drain and keep warm. Heat up the butter until it turns nut-brown, not dark brown or black. Add the wine vinegar. Let the mixture sizzle and bubble. If you have some fresh herbs, chop them finely and add to this beurre noisette. Pour over the sprouts.

RED CABBAGE

SERVES 4-6

In cold weather I often find myself thinking lovingly of red cabbage, cooked long and slow with the sweetness of apples, the sharpness of vinegar and the glossiness of lard. It is worth making a quantity of this dish (and one large cabbage produces a lot) because it re-heats well and also freezes well. Smoked meats, either sausages or ham, are a good accompaniment. This is a moment to consider smoked chicken, cut in pieces and gently heated through on top of the cabbage. In other circumstances, smoked chicken seems to me a questionable item.

1 red cabbage
1 large Spanish onion
2 dessert apples
3 oz (90 g) lard or 3 fl oz (90 ml) vegetable oil
2 tbsp brown sugar
3 tbsp red wine vinegar
1 fat clove of garlic
1 strip of orange peel
pinch of mustard powder
pinch of mace or nutmeg
salt and pepper
5 crushed juniper berries or 1 tsp caraway seeds (optional)
½ pt (300 ml) cooking wine or water

Strip the outer leaves off the cabbage, trim the stalk, cut it into quarters and pare away the hard part of the central spine. Slice it finely, either with a knife or using a food processor. Peel and slice the onion. Core and chop the apples. Heat the lard in a large saucepan or flameproof casserole, add the cabbage, apple and onion, then flip and stir, until everything has a faint sheen. Add the other ingredients, including crushed juniper berries or caraway seeds if you like the idea. Add $\frac{1}{2}$ pt (300 ml) water or cooking wine if you have some handy (you will then need a dash more sugar). Bring to a simmer, cook on top of the stove gently or in a low oven for two hours. Taste for seasoning – you may need to juggle the sweet and sour – and serve. This is a dish that benefits from being made one day, re-heated and eaten the next.

CAULIFLOWER WITH MUSTARD SEEDS   SERVES 4

Cauliflower cheese has always struck me as a rather deadly meal, breaking all those rules you read in 'How to be a Hostess' articles about not making everything the same dull colour and texture. Cauliflower needs a bit of kick and crunch, which can be provided by dressing it with a vinaigrette whilst it is still warm then scattering chopped bacon and fried breadcrumbs and parsley on top, or by following this recipe, which has Indian snap and crackle. It is quick to make and rather healthy and stands up perfectly well to being a course on its own.

1 large cauliflower
2 tbsp vegetable oil or butter, or a mixture of the two
2 tsp yellow or black mustard seeds
1 in (3 cm) cube fresh ginger root, peeled and finely slivered, or $\frac{1}{2}$ tsp powdered ginger
2 fat cloves of garlic, peeled and finely chopped
2 tsp cumin seeds or fennel seeds
$\frac{1}{2}$ tsp paprika
salt and freshly ground black pepper

Trim the cauliflower of any dodgy bits. Remove the green leaves and the large stalks, and break the cauliflower up into really quite small florets. You want to end up with some pieces almost the size of large crumbs. Heat the butter or oil (or make a mixture of the two; the butter is really there for the flavour) and add the mustard seeds. When they begin to pop add the ginger (powdered ginger should be added with the cauliflower). Fry the ginger briefly. Add the garlic and stir around, but don't let it catch. Add the cauliflower pieces, stir-fry, and then add the cumin or fennel seeds, paprika, and a good few turns of the pepper mill. Keep stirring, season with salt and sprinkle on about a tablespoon of water. Cover the pan and turn the heat up high for one minute to build up steam. Turn the heat low and cook for about three minutes. Test for tenderness. Cook off any remaining moisture with the lid of the pan. Stir and serve. The cauliflower should be slightly crisp.

SERVES 4   # CORN FRITTERS

When corn on the cob is plentiful, you might want to do something more with it than boiling to serve with melted butter. If you scrape the kernels off the cobs with a sharp knife, after removing the outer leaves and 'silk' of course, you unleash a milkiness that lends itself well to a fritter batter. The effect can be enhanced by cutting down the centre of the rows of kernels before whisking them off.

Corn fritters are sometimes known as corn oysters in America. Whatever their name, they accompany well grilled meat, ham steaks, and, traditionally, Chicken Maryland.

4 cobs fresh sweetcorn
2 eggs
2½ fl oz (75 ml) milk
½ tbsp melted butter
3 tbsp flour
½ tsp baking powder
salt and freshly ground black pepper
sunflower oil or other vegetable oil, as required

Clean the cobs of leaves and strands of 'silk' and, holding the cobs vertical, slice off the kernels with a sharp knife. Put these into a bowl and, with the back of the knife, scrape the cobs to release the milky juices. Beat together the eggs, milk and melted butter. Into another bowl, sift the flour, baking powder and a pinch of salt. Using a wooden spoon, make a well in the flour and slowly and methodically beat the egg mixture into the flour until you achieve a smooth batter. Tip in the prepared corn and mix. Season with freshly ground black pepper. Pour a thin film of oil into a frying pan, heat and drop tablespoons of the batter on to it, each an inch or so apart. Flatten them slightly if necessary and cook until golden brown. Turn and cook the other side. Drain quickly on kitchen paper and serve with your choice of meat, or perhaps with bacon or sausages or grilled fish.

SERVES 2-3   # FENNEL BAKED WITH PARMESAN

I love the aniseedy flavour of fennel and find that, in restaurants anyway, it is not enough used, either in salads and vegetable dishes or as an ingredient in stock or sauces for fish or chicken. I remember long ago finding a recipe for fennel salad that required blanching, marinating in lemon juice and such processes that made you think it couldn't possibly be pleasant just raw. But it is. I often use fennel in 'hard' salads, such as those composed with apple, chicory, shredded cabbage or grated raw beetroot. Jane Grigson says in her excellent *Vegetable Book* that her favourite fennel dish is this one using butter and Parmesan cheese (it must be Parmesan and freshly grated too).

3 medium size bulbs of fennel
salt
1 oz (30 g) butter
freshly ground black pepper
2 tbsp grated Parmesan cheese

Trim the fennel of bruised leaves, stalk and leaves. Quarter it. Cook in salted water until tender. Take care you do not overcook it so that it becomes floppy. Drain well and arrange in a generously buttered gratin dish. Add pepper with a flourish. Sprinkle on the cheese. Put in the oven at 200°C/400°F/gas mark 6 until the cheese is golden brown and the buttery juices are bubbling energetically.

FENNEL FRITTERS SERVES 4–6

I like this Italian notion of making fennel into fritters. They make an interesting and quite luxurious accompaniment to plainly grilled fish or meat or poultry.

3–4 bulbs of fennel
4 oz (120 g) plain flour
1 tsp baking powder
1 egg
1 tbsp olive oil
¼ pt (150 ml) tepid water
salt and pepper

Trim the fennel bulbs, cut them in half and then in thin segments, each piece held together at the base. Put the flour and baking powder in a bowl. Make a well. Add the egg and olive oil. Start to beat. Slowly incorporate the tepid water. Season with salt and pepper. Dip the fennel pieces in the batter. Deep-fry in hot oil, preferably olive oil, until brown and crisp. Drain on kitchen paper. These are good served with lemon quarters.

'SEAWEED' SERVES 4

After you have tried this recipe you will not pay the almost invariably excessive prices asked for 'seaweed' as a first course on a Chinese restaurant menu. It is not a kind of algae, but good old spring greens sliced into threads and deep-fried in oil until they crackle like cellophane. When eating at home, use it as a vegetable rather than serving it as a first course since it could wander rather lonely around the plate without No. 6 and No. 11 on the menu to accompany it. It is excellent with simply cooked fish. People who crouch in cupboards at the sound of the word 'greens' will be won over by this way of treating them.

2 heads of bouncy looking spring greens, or you could use kale
vegetable oil for deep-frying
pinch of caster sugar
1 tbsp desiccated coconut (optional)
1 tbsp chopped dried prawns, available in oriental supermarkets (optional)

Trim away any discoloured leaves from the greens and, taking a few leaves at a time, roll them up into neat cylinders to facilitate making thin strips. Using a very sharp knife, cut across the cylinders in fine slices. Heat enough vegetable oil to deep-fry batches of your heap of threads. When it is nearly smoking hot drop in handfuls of the greens, avoiding crowding the pot, and cook briefly until they are translucent and crackly. Remove and drain on kitchen paper and, while very hot, sprinkle with just a pinch of caster sugar. It adds an intriguing crunch and sweetness. If you want to garnish the 'seaweed' you could toast some desiccated coconut until golden in a dry iron pan or finely chop some dried prawns, which would faintly resemble the shredded dried scallop used in Chinese restaurants. It occurs to me that crabmeat, preferably fresh, but defrosted or out of a tin, if that sounds more plausible, would be a good accompaniment.

SERVES 2 FRIED GREEN TOMATOES WITH MILK GRAVY

Walking round London you see people gardening everywhere – on balconies, window-sills, area steps, practically in cracks and crevices. I'm lucky enough to have a garden – and, some years, lots of green tomatoes. Since I imagine others might be in this predicament, here is a soul-food recipe for something other than making chutney that you might do with them. It comes from an American book called Princess Pamela's *Soul-Food Cookbook*. Princess Pamela ran a restaurant in Manhattan called The Little

Kitchen and was given to rather perspicacious homilies like, 'My uncle used to tell me, early to bed, early to rise, make a *man* healthy, wealthy and wise. I been followin' that routine all my life and I kin tellya that all it does for a woman is to make her tired, poor and not too bright.'

3 tbsp bacon fat
4 green tomatoes (or under-ripe tomatoes would do) sliced ½ in (1.5 cm) thick
1 egg, beaten
2 oz (60 g) dry home-made breadcrumbs
flour, as required
8 fl oz (250 ml) milk
salt and freshly ground black pepper

Heat the bacon fat (bacon gives the correct flavour) in a heavy frying-pan. Dip the sliced tomatoes in the beaten egg, then in the breadcrumbs. Slowly fry them in the bacon fat until golden brown on both sides. Remove them, drain them and keep them warm on a hot platter in a warm oven. Add plain flour to the fat in the pan to make a roux, using roughly the same volume of flour to the volume of fat. Blend well and slowly stir in the milk, cooking until you have a smooth, creamy sauce. Season to taste with salt and pepper. Pour on to the tomatoes and serve. This goes well with anything, fish or meat, plainly grilled.

SPICED PARSNIPS SERVES 4

I once contributed this recipe to a book called something like, *Darling, You Shouldn't Have Gone To So Much Trouble*, its premise being food that looked (and tasted) impressive but was deceptively quick to prepare. I'm not sure this really fitted in. My doubts were reinforced when I read the finished book. One of the recipes, called Potage Mauvaise Femme, was based on a tin of carrots and a packet of Smash.

The only trouble you may have to go to for this recipe, which is well worth the general benefit to your cooking, is to assemble various Indian spices in their whole form. The list may look daunting. You can vary the spices or omit some without the dish coming to harm, but cardamom and turmeric should not, I think, be left out. But if fenugreek, for example, is not at your local shop, don't abandon the recipe.

1 lb (500 g) parsnips
1 oz (30 g) butter
1 tbsp vegetable oil
1 tsp cumin seeds
1 tsp coriander seeds
½ tsp fenugreek
5 cardamom pods, seeds from
1 scant tsp black mustard seeds
1 dried red chilli (optional)
1 tsp ground turmeric
warm water
salt and pepper
squeeze of lemon juice
fresh coriander, parsley or watercress leaves

Peel the parsnips and cut them as if you were making chips – in half horizontally, then quartered vertically. Heat the mixture of butter and oil in a shallow pan or frying pan to which you can fit a lid. Add the cumin, coriander, fenugreek, cardamom, mustard seeds and chilli (if you like hotness), and fry until the seeds begin to pop, which they will do rapidly. Add the turmeric and stir some more until you have a loose paste. Add the parsnips and turn in the spicy mixture until they are covered and coloured. Add a couple of tablespoons of warm water and cook, covered, watching and adding more water in dribs and drabs until the vegetable is tender – 10–15 minutes. Season, add a squeeze of lemon juice, and garnish with fresh coriander, parsley or watercress. Because I like the odd vegetarian meal I would eat this just with basmati rice, poppadums and yogurt, but it also flatters grilled meat or fish.

SERVES 3-4   # RÖSTI

The reason that Swiss, or Swiss-trained, hoteliers are the best in the world is because the Swiss do everything correctly. Unimaginatively maybe, but correctly. It is important to make this dish correctly and put to the back of your non-Swiss mind ideas like throwing in some chopped ham or a handful of peas. Parboiled or steamed potatoes, butter and oil are all you need along with, preferably, a heavy non-stick frying pan. If plain grated potatoes sounds just too dull for words, it would not be cuckoo, I suppose, to mix in some grated Emmental cheese, but try it simply first. It makes a superb accompaniment to roast game and practically all children love it.

1½–2 lb (750 g–1 kg) large potatoes
1 oz (30 g) butter
1 tbsp olive oil or other vegetable oil
salt and pepper

The counsel of perfection is to peel then parboil the potatoes for 7 minutes, drain them and let them cool overnight in the refrigerator. This makes a difference to their texture, which in turn makes a difference to the finished dish, but if it's not possible just try to cook them somewhat ahead of time. Grate the potatoes using a coarse grater. Warm the butter and oil in a 9 in (23 cm) diameter heavy non-stick frying pan, or one more or less that size. Spread the grated potato evenly in the pan, sprinkle with salt and pepper. Put a plate of appropriate size upside down over the potatoes; the plate should fit in the pan, not sit on top of it. Cook gently for 10 minutes. Turn the rösti out of the pan by putting a wooden board, or similar, over plate and pan and turning the whole thing over. You should now have a circular potato cake sitting on the plate, ready to be cut into slices.

COLCANNON SERVES 4

I think potatoes are very underrated, or, perhaps more accurately, underused. They are not inherently fattening – it is the chip fat or butter lavished on them that loads them with calories – and they can be made so delicious that meat is hardly necessary. Understandably the Irish, more dependent on potatoes than the average nation, have evolved some good recipes.

2 lb (1 kg) potatoes (a large floury variety)
1 small cabbage or 1 lb (500 g) kale, which is traditional
¼–½ pt (150–300 ml) creamy milk
salt and freshly ground black pepper
4 oz (120 g) melted butter

My tip for mashed potatoes is to boil them mercilessly until they are waterlogged and falling apart and then not to drain them too carefully so that they remain wet which, surprisingly, ultimately makes them lighter. Tidy up, core and finely chop the cabbage or kale. Put it into a small quantity of boiling water and cook quickly, turning it occasionally until it is done. Mash the cooked drained potatoes. Heat the milk and beat enough of it into the potatoes to give a soft, but not sloppy consistency. Stir in the cabbage. Season to taste. Ensuring that the mixture is as hot as possible, pile it into a shallow dish. Make a well large enough to hold the melted butter in the centre and pour it in. If you serve the colcannon straight on to four heated plates, adding a quarter of the butter to each plate, you can eat it by taking forkfuls and dipping them into the butter, which is part of the joy of the dish.

CHAMP
SERVES 3-4

For those who do not like the flavour of cabbage there is a dish similar to Colcannon made with spring onions.

1 bunch of spring onions
¼ pt (150 ml) of creamy milk
1½ lb (750 g) potatoes, peeled, cooked and mashed
salt and freshly ground black pepper
2 oz (60 g) melted butter

Clean and chop the spring onions quite finely and cook in the milk in a small pan until they are soft. Put a sieve over a bowl and pour the milk through. Mix the onions that remain in the sieve with the mashed potato, then beat in the onion-flavoured milk until you have a smooth, soft purée. Season well and serve as above.

GIRARDET'S MASHED POTATOES
SERVES 4

These potatoes were the star of the show at a wonderful Sunday lunch cooked by Simon Hopkinson who was at that time chef of Hilaire in the Old Brompton Road. The Thai salad as a first course was jaunty, the pickled herrings and gravad lax were delectable, the veal in a tarragon-flavoured sauce you couldn't say a word against, but the potatoes, the mashed potatoes, were *incredibly* good. The recipe, it turned out, comes from Fredy Girardet, said by some to run the best restaurant in the world in Crissier in Switzerland. He suggests using new potatoes, but I think any potato suited to mashing works well. What is essential is really good olive oil.

2 lb (1 kg) potatoes
6 fl oz (175 ml) extra virgin olive oil
6 fl oz (175 ml) double cream
1 fat clove of garlic, peeled and crushed (optional)
salt
pinch of cayenne pepper

Scrub the potatoes, boil them in their skins and when they are very well cooked, drain. When they are cool enough to handle, peel off the skins. Either mash the potatoes or push them through a mouli-légumes, which is preferable. In another pan heat together the oil and the cream and, if you are using it, the garlic clove. Let it bubble and amalgamate. Beat this mixture in a thin stream into the potatoes, which should be on a low heat. Taste for seasoning and add salt and cayenne pepper. If you want to keep the potatoes warm in the oven, cover them with a piece of oiled paper. This is such a rich, fulfilling dish that it should be served with a plainly cooked piece of fish or meat.

GRATIN DAUPHINOIS SERVES 6

This is another dish which establishes the potato as a thing of beauty in its own right rather than just a sidekick. A creamy gratin, made according to the instructions below, makes a delicious first course to be followed by some simply grilled meat or fish or, with a well-dressed salad to accompany it, it can constitute a vegetarian supper. Use a floury variety of potato and don't rinse after slicing as you want the starch to make the potatoes adhere in a nice, comforting mass. The only trick with this recipe is to make sure that you cook the potatoes long enough. Although they are thinly sliced, they take their time in becoming tender.

$1\frac{1}{2}$ oz (45 g) butter and a little more to grease the dish
2 lb (1 kg) floury potatoes, peeled and thinly sliced
salt and freshly ground black pepper
pinch of grated nutmeg (freshly grated if possible)
2 cloves of garlic, peeled and halved
$\frac{1}{2}$ pt (300 ml) milk
4 fl oz (120 ml) cream, single or double
4 oz (120 g) grated Gruyère or Emmental cheese (optional, and I prefer not)

Turn on the oven to 180°C/350°F/gas mark 4. Lightly butter a shallow ovenproof dish, preferably an earthenware one. Put in the potato slices in overlapping layers, seasoning each layer with a little salt, pepper and nutmeg. Melt the $1\frac{1}{2}$ oz (45 g) butter in a pan, add the garlic pieces and fry until they are golden brown. Remove the garlic and pour the butter over the potatoes. Heat the milk and cream in another pan and pour it over the potatoes. Cover the dish with foil and cook in the oven for about 40 minutes. Remove the foil, sprinkle with the cheese if you are using it. Increase the oven temperature to 220°C/425°F/gas mark 7 and bake for another 20 minutes until the top is golden brown. Serve immediately.

SERVES 4 CELERIAC AND POTATO PURÉE

The root vegetable celeriac seems underrated in this country. Perhaps its appearance, that of a knobbly alien plant that has fallen to earth, deters people from approaching it and relishing its subtle flavour. It is much used in German cooking and in France nearly every *charcuterie* will have a salad of grated blanched celeriac mixed with a mustardy mayonnaise known as rémoulade (see page 27). Celeriac makes a good basis for a soup (try mixing in some soaked, dried mushrooms such as porcini) but, to my mind, it is best of all cooked with about half its weight in potatoes and then mashed. Enriched with butter and cream and nudged by the flavour of garlic, the resulting purée can accompany simply grilled meat, poultry or sausages and turn them into an estimable meal.

1 celeriac, weighing 1 lb (500 g) or more (buy a firm one that is as ungnarled as possible)
½ lb (250 g) potatoes, weighed after peeling
3 fat cloves of garlic, peeled (optional)
3 tbsp cream
2 oz (60 g) butter
salt and generous amounts of freshly ground black pepper

Peel the celeriac which, if it is a knobbly one, takes a bit of energy. Cut it into chunks and drop them immediately into water to stop them browning. Cut the peeled potatoes into pieces of a similar size. In a large pan of salted water, simmer the celeriac, potatoes and peeled garlic cloves until the vegetables are tender. Drain. Mash carefully or, if you have a vegetable mill, turn them through the medium blade. Beat in the cream and butter, and season with salt and pepper. Beat again thoroughly to obtain a smooth mixture and serve as an accompaniment to any simply cooked meat. This can successfully be kept warm in a double boiler.

SERVES 5-6 ISMAIL MERCHANT'S LEMON LENTILS

If, like me, you are a fan of the films of Ismail Merchant and James Ivory – *Autobiography of a Princess, Shakespeare Wallah, The Bostonians, Heat and Dust* to name some – and keen on Indian food you may be interested to know of Ismail Merchant's book

Indian Cuisine. An infectiously keen cook, constrained to prepare food quickly and for large numbers, Mr Merchant's recipes are a delight; original and in some cases intriguingly inauthentic, or anyway demonstrating Indian incursions into Western notions – a reversal of some of the film subjects, you could say. This lentil dish he first prepared for Felicity Kendal just after she had returned to England having starred in *Shakespeare Wallah*. I have halved the quantities of the original recipe. It would make a great accompaniment to take-away or shop-bought tandoori chicken; it is also very good made a day early, so the flavours can blend, and either re-heated or served at room temperature.

5 fl oz (150 ml) vegetable oil
1 medium onion, peeled, halved and thinly sliced
2 in (5 cm) pieces of cinnamon stick
1 lb (500 g) masoor dal (little orange lentils) washed
1 dsp chopped fresh ginger root
1 pt (300 ml) chicken stock
1 pt (300 ml) hot water
salt
pinch of cayenne pepper
1 lemon
1 small onion, peeled and chopped
½ hot green chilli, chopped
2 bay leaves, crumbled
1 tbsp chopped fresh coriander leaves, if available

garlic?

Heat 3 fl oz (90 ml) of the oil in a saucepan. Add the onion and cook until it softens. Add the cinnamon, lentils and ginger. Cook, stirring often, for about 10 minutes. Add the stock and hot water, salt to taste and cayenne pepper. Simmer for 10 minutes. Add the juice and squeezed skin of the lemon, and cook about 40 minutes longer, stirring often. Heat the remaining oil in a small pan. Add the chopped onion, garlic, chilli and bay leaves. Cook, stirring, until the onion is browned. Add this mixture, including the oil, to the lentils. Sprinkle with the chopped coriander leaves and serve.

AUTHENTIC CAESAR SALAD   SERVES 4

Recently a reader wrote complaining bitterly, probably with justification, about an indifferent meal in a restaurant in Covent Garden. The final straw, she said, was the Caesar Salad, which wasn't even made with the fundamental ingredients: mushrooms and advocadoes (*sic*). I can quite see why she had this conviction since so many weird salads are presented under the name. Here are the ingredients and method of the 'classic' salad, made famous by a restaurateur in Tijuana in the twenties. Its simplicity is what makes it so good, provided you take no short cuts in the preparation. Success depends on the coming together of the constituent parts at the last minute.

1 large cos lettuce or 2 smaller ones
juice of ½ a lemon
2 oz (60 g) freshly grated Parmesan cheese
3 slices of good white bread
Worcestershire Sauce or 1 × 2 oz (50 g) tin of anchovies, drained of oil or brine and rinsed
2 fat cloves of garlic
6 tbsp olive oil
sea salt and freshly ground black pepper
2 eggs

Pick over the lettuce and use only the unblemished leaves. Wash them, dry them thoroughly (I often skip this step if they look clean) and put in a plastic bag in the refrigerator. Towards the time of serving, assemble all the other ingredients: squeeze the lemon half, grate the Parmesan if you have bought it in a lump, set the water to boil for the eggs. Trim the crusts from three slices of bread and cut into cubes. Open the anchovies if you are using them (Worcestershire Sauce is apparently authentic). Crush the garlic into 3 tbsp olive oil and fry the croûtons in this, turning and stirring the while to ensure they are evenly browned. Place the lettuce in a large salad bowl and add 2 tbsp olive oil. Toss to coat the leaves. Sprinkle on some sea salt and freshly ground pepper and toss with another 1 tbsp of olive oil, imagining you are a Mexican restaurateur. Pour on the lemon juice, a couple of splashes of Worcestershire Sauce (or the drained and chopped anchovies) and break in the yolks of the eggs that you have plunged into boiling water for 1 minute. Toss once. Sprinkle on the Parmesan. Toss again and add the croûtons, which should first be drained on kitchen paper. Serve immediately.

FATTOUSH
SERVES 4

Fattoush is one of my favourite summer salads. It is a Syrian peasant dish, a salad with an interesting texture and lively flavour, much appreciated all over the Middle East. It can be served as a first course, a light lunch, or as part of a *meze*. It might occur to you that it is a way of using leftover pitta. If that is your plan, do not omit the warming process before incorporating it in the salad. Purslane, sometimes known as continental watercress, is sometimes available in Greek or Cypriot grocers and is an optional, but enhancing ingredient. Try to find the flat-leafed variety of parsley.

1 small cucumber, peeled and chopped into cubes
salt
1 normal or 2 small pittas
juice of 2 small lemons
3 firm tomatoes, skinned, chopped and de-seeded
heart of a cos lettuce, shredded
1 bunch of spring onions, cleaned and finely chopped
2 tbsp chopped fresh mint or 1 tbsp dried mint
2 tbsp chopped fresh parsley
2 tbsp chopped purslane leaves (optional)
1 tbsp chopped coriander leaves (optional)
2 cloves of garlic, peeled and crushed
6–8 tbsp olive oil
freshly ground black pepper

Before beginning the salad, put the cubed cucumber into a colander, sprinkle with salt and leave to drain for about half an hour. If you miss out this step you risk making the salad soggy. Heat the bread under the grill until hot but not stiff. Pull into small pieces and put into a salad bowl. Pour on the lemon juice and let the bread mop it up. If you want a less domineering lemon flavour, use half the amount of juice plus 1 tbsp water. Rinse the salt from the cucumber, pat it dry and place it plus the other ingredients in the salad bowl. Toss very thoroughly. Taste for seasoning, adjusting amounts of lemon juice, oil, salt and pepper to taste.

HOT RUNNER BEAN AND BACON SALAD   SERVES 4

On the day I picked my first crop of runner beans (eight beans) from plants grown up against the garden fence I felt immeasurably proud, even though I knew it was not great proof of green thumb. Also I love runner beans when they are small and snappy, as opposed to long and stringy, and am happy to eat large platefuls of them with just some bacon alongside. Probably because they are so easy to grow they tend to be overlooked by cookery writers. The dish below I have composed along the lines of a 'wilted' salad, as you might make with spinach or dandelion leaves, but with beans they must, of course, be cooked first. Make sure you have warm plates for serving.

2 lb (1 kg) runner beans (avoid the kind which have grown to a foot long)
10 rashers of streaky bacon or
4 oz (120 g) bacon in a piece
2 tbsp vegetable oil
3 tbsp soft fresh white or brown breadcrumbs
2 tbsp red wine vinegar
salt and freshly ground black pepper

Trim the beans at the ends and if there is any suspicion of strings, run your knife down each edge, cutting away a fine strip. Slice them on the diagonal. Put to cook in plenty of salted boiling water. Chop the bacon finely and fry until crisp, add the oil and the breadcrumbs and fry until the crumbs are golden and crunchy. Drain the beans when they are just tender. Pile into a hot dish. Scatter the bacon and crumbs over the beans. Now, into the hot pan where you have been frying the bacon, pour the wine vinegar. Let it bubble and frazzle and when it is reduced to about 1 tbsp, dribble it over the beans. Season.

SERVES 2   # LENTIL SALAD

Full of iron and the Vitamin B group, lentils are nutritious food and ideal as the basis of a winter-time salad which, when composed as below, can be served as a main course. The small slaty-green lentils, *lentilles de Puy*, are the nicest, and many health food shops stock them. If you do not find those, choose brown lentils rather than the large, dull green ones and forget, for the purposes of this recipe, the orange ones. They cook to a slush whereas the others retain their shape. Lentils need no soaking, but they should be washed and inspected for any little bits of gravel or other undesirable elements. They should take between 40 minutes and an hour to cook, but keep checking because you do not want them to fray at the edges.

8 oz (250 g) lentils
1 onion
1 clove of garlic
bouquet garni or 1 bay leaf
3 tbsp olive oil
1 tbsp red wine vinegar
salt and freshly ground black pepper
pinch of dry mustard
2 hard-boiled eggs
2 oz (60 g) black olives, stoned
6 anchovies or 4 rashers of streaky bacon
1 tbsp chopped fresh parsley

Wash the lentils as described above. Cover with water, add the peeled onion, the garlic and bouquet garni or bay leaf, and simmer until the lentils are tender. Drain and remove the onion, garlic and bouquet garni or bay leaf. Make a vinaigrette with the olive oil, red wine vinegar, salt and pepper and dry mustard. Toss the warm lentils in the dressing. Garnish with the hard-boiled eggs cut in quarters, the stoned olives and either anchovies or the bacon, first chopped and then fried until crisp. Sprinkle with chopped parsley and serve.

PUDDINGS

Even mature and well-balanced adults never quite eradicate the notion of pudding as the treat at the end of the meal, the reward for being good about the worthy ingredients that have gone before. Opting for 'just some cheese and fruit' rather sadly misses the point.

Puddings are one of the strong suits of British cooking and, unashamedly, I have included a good number of the traditional ones such as treacle sponge and summer pudding. Bread and butter pudding has enjoyed a renaissance on fashionable restaurant menus and Dorchester chef Anton Mosimann's version is given here; there is also a method for rice pudding that will restore confidence in what might have become a joke or a bad memory. In general, I think it is to the nursery that we should look for inspiration for the last course in the meal – it is not the moment for sophistication or preciousness.

Considerations of seasonality are as applicable to fruit as to vegetables. One delicious way to celebrate a glut of any stewable fruit is to make a crumble, that British mode of pie that is both quicker and crunchier than pastry.

Quantities for the puddings are not for the greedy since in this case it is true that only a little bit of what you fancy does you good. This moral approach was blissfully scuppered by the following story. When the recipe for treacle sponge appeared in the *London Evening Standard*, a misprint occurred that gave 2 lb of golden syrup in place of 2 tbsp. I heard later that a friend of a friend of mine had faithfully put the 2 lb of syrup into the pudding basin and then added the sponge mixture. Her husband and children said she had never made a better dessert and begged her to serve it regularly.

PROPER CUSTARD MAKES 1 pt

La crème anglaise is a name the French give to custard. It brings to mind something a little more silky and seductive than the bright yellow sauce of school days, made with a powder and destined to form a geriatric skin. A proper English custard is a thing of pride. Using only egg yolks, sugar, a vanilla pod and creamy milk or single cream, a custard is easy to make and will add finesse to certain puddings, for example some of the good bottled fruits now available. Once you have mastered the technique of thickening the sauce over a gentle heat, you have a handful of dishes at your disposal. Once cooled and set, the custard can be coated with an even layer of sugar and then grilled under fierce heat, which will result in crème brûlée. Poached meringues perched on top produces floating islands. By caramelising sugar, pouring that into the base of the dish and baking the custard you achieve crème caramel. Whatever other recipe books tell you, it is not necessary to use flour or even the tiniest pinch of cornflour. The yolks themselves will provide the emulsion.

Ironically I took my best custard recipe from an American book and it is perhaps over-rich for some occasions, but it is so good I have known guests to sink their face into it. It makes the ideal base for floating islands.

6 egg yolks
3–4 oz (90–120 g) caster sugar
¼ tsp salt
1 pt (600 ml) creamy milk or single cream
1 vanilla pod

In the top pan of a double boiler, combine the egg yolks, sugar and salt. Set aside. In the bottom saucepan heat the milk or cream with the vanilla pod until it steams but does not boil. Strain the liquid on to the yolks, stirring. Now fill the bottom pan with hot water and cook the custard over simmering water, stirring constantly until the mixture coats the back of a metal spoon. Use as a sauce, or cool and chill in a shallow dish until set.

ECONOMICAL CUSTARD
MAKES ½ pt

This is a more economical and less heart-rending recipe that you can use in the same way.

½ pt (300 ml) milk
1 tbsp sugar
2 egg yolks
a few drops of vanilla essence

Heat the milk and sugar and bring slowly to the boil. Beat the yolks in a bowl. Pour the milk on to the yolks, stirring steadily. Return to the pan and stir over gentle heat until thickened. Add the vanilla essence.

SUMMER PUDDING
SERVES 6-8

August is just about the optimum moment to make summer pudding with red- and blackcurrants, raspberries and strawberries all available. It is one of the most delicious – perhaps the most delicious – English pudding. Make it with respectable white bread, not the pappy, plastic sliced stuff. A whole loaf is easier to slice when somewhat stale. Another tip is to buy extra strawberries and purée them, using the resulting sauce to pour over the pudding should any white patches of bread remain.

1 loaf of good white bread, cut into slices about $\frac{1}{4}$ in (6 mm) thick
2 lb (1 kg) mixed soft fruit e.g. redcurrants, blackcurrants, black-berries, blueberries, raspberries, strawberries
4–6 oz (120–175 g) caster sugar, depending on the sweetness of your choice of fruit
lightly whipped double cream or Jersey cream, to accompany

Remove the crusts from the bread. Cut a circle to fit the bottom of a 2–2½ pt (1.2–1.5 l) pudding basin. Cut wedge shapes in other slices to enable you to line the rest of the bowl. If there are gaps, fill them with small pieces of bread. Simmer your choice of fruit with the sugar, just enough for the sugar to dissolve, and the juices of the fruit to flow. Strain off the juice and reserve. Put the fruit into the bread-lined basin. Add enough juice to moisten well. Place a layer of bread on top, a little more juice if available and then a plate smaller than the circumference of the bowl. Place a weight on the plate and put the bowl in the refrigerator overnight or longer. To serve, remove weight and plate, run a knife round the edge of the pudding and turn out. The bread should be saturated by fruit juice, but if not, use more juice or strawberry purée to colour it. Serve in small slices, as this is an intense pudding. Hand round cream separately.

STICKY TOFFEE AND DATE PUDDING SERVES 4

The Sharrow Bay Hotel in Ullswater is now in its thirty-ninth year and over that time the owners, Francis Coulson and Brian Sack, have made an invaluable contribution to our perceptions not only of hotel standards and English cooking, but of generosity and indulgence and the importance of having your own visions. The fact that this recipe reached me via two other chefs is indicative of their approach. It is a pudding to which to surrender.

2 oz (60 g) softened butter
6 oz (175 g) granulated sugar
8 oz (300 g) plain flour
1 tsp baking powder
1 egg
6 oz (175 g) stoned dates
½ pt (300 ml) boiling water
1 tsp bicarbonate of soda
1 tsp vanilla essence

FOR THE TOFFEE:
2½ oz (75 g) brown sugar
1½ oz (45 g) butter
2 tsp double cream

Turn on the oven to 190°C/375°F/gas mark 5. Cream together the butter and granulated sugar. Sift together the flour and baking powder. Whisk up the egg and beat it with some of the flour into the creamed mixture. After some vigorous beating, add the rest of the flour and make sure that it is well incorporated. Chop the dates finely. Put in a bowl and pour on the boiling water. Mix in the bicarbonate of soda and the vanilla. Add it all to the batter and blend together well. Spread this mixture in a buttered 11 × 7 in (28 × 18 cm) cake tin and bake for 40 minutes.

To make the toffee, heat together the brown sugar, butter and cream. Simmer for three minutes. Pour over the cooked pudding and flash it under the grill until the toffee bubbles, taking care it doesn't burn.

SERVES 4–6 # TREACLE SPONGE

Because steamed puddings take a relatively long time to cook they are thought of as cumbersome to make. With a food processor the actual preparation time is a few minutes and the pudding can bubble away while you divert yourself elsewhere. They are a great treat on a cold day and satisfactorily conclude an otherwise skimpy or thrown together meal.

I managed to put my children in favour of steamed puddings by pointing out that the mixture is the same as that for a cake, and now they think of them as hot cakes and look very pleased to see one being turned out of its bowl. I use lots of lemon juice to cut the sweetness of the syrup.

2 tbsp golden syrup
grated rind and juice of 1 lemon
1 oz (30 g) breadcrumbs
4 oz (120 g) butter, and a little more to grease the basin
4 oz (120 g) caster sugar
2 eggs
5 oz (150 g) self-raising flour, sifted with a pinch of salt
milk, to mix

Mix the syrup with the juice of the lemon and stir in the bread-crumbs. Put this mixture at the bottom of a buttered pudding basin. Cream the butter with the sugar and lemon rind. Add the beaten eggs. Stir in the flour, sifted with a pinch of salt. Add milk until you have a batter that drops slowly from a spoon. Pour into the pudding basin. Tie on a cover of foil or greaseproof paper. Place the bowl in a saucepan which will hold it comfortably, with boiling water coming about halfway up the bowl. Steam with the saucepan lid on for 2 hours, checking the water level from time to time. Serve with cream or custard or more syrup heated and sharpened with lemon juice.

FRUITARIAN CHRISTMAS PUDDING SERVES 6-8

Towards Christmas I noticed that the previous cookery writers for the *London Evening Standard* had always given their own pudding recipes, and that these attracted a loyal following. This recipe, originally from Mrs Beeton, but perfected by my mother, is my favourite because it is light and lively, contains no suet, is studded with pine kernels and can be faced even at the end of an elaborate meal. A friend of mine told me reprovingly that she had her puddings made in September, but if you are not quite so well organised, this pudding will be fine, even if made much closer to Christmas.

8 oz (250g) blanched almonds
4 oz (120g) shelled brazil nuts
8 oz (250g) figs
2 apples
8 oz (250g) raisins
4 oz (120g) currants
4 oz (120g) sultanas
4 oz (120g) candied peel
2 tbsp brandy
4 oz (120g) pine kernels
8 oz (250g) brown breadcrumbs
4 oz (120g) moist brown sugar
1 tsp allspice
pinch of salt
2 lemons
4 oz (120g) honey
4 oz (120g) butter
3 eggs

Chop either by hand, or far more easily in a food processor, the almonds, the brazil nuts and then the figs. Peel, core and chop the apples. Put all the fruit in a bowl and pour on a couple of tbsp of brandy. Put the nuts, breadcrumbs, sugar, allspice, salt and grated lemon rind in another large bowl. Gently melt the honey with the butter and lemon juice. Pour on to the dry ingredients. Add the fruit and the well-beaten eggs. Mix very thoroughly. Fill two greased pudding basins. Tie greaseproof paper and a pudding cloth over them and steam for 4 hours. On Christmas Day, steam the puddings for another 2–3 hours. If you only want to use one pudding, the other will keep for next year.

SERVES 6-8 BREAD AND BUTTER PUDDING

According to the Young Fogey handbook, the grandest YF of them all, Prince Charles, has put this pudding back on the map. I would prefer to credit Anton Mosimann, chef of The Dorchester Hotel, whose recipe appears, more or less, below. It took a Swiss (frightfully fogey nation) to show us how to do it well. I chose this recipe for a Friday on the theory that at the end of the week you would have stale bread to employ. If you do not, it's worth buying bread anyway.

8 fl oz (250 ml) milk
8 fl oz (250 ml) double cream
1 vanilla pod, split
¼ tsp salt
3 size 1 or 4 size 4 eggs
4 oz (120 g) sugar
1 oz (30 g) softened butter
1 lb (500 g) white bread, sliced
1 tbsp fine-shred marmalade
½ oz (15 g) sultanas, soaked in water or whisky
a little icing sugar

Bring the milk, cream, vanilla pod and salt slowly to the boil. Beat together the eggs and sugar and add the milk mixture mixing well. Pour the liquid through a sieve into a bowl. Butter the slices of bread and, a tip from my sister, spread with the thinnest possible coating of marmalade. Butter a shallow ovenproof dish of a size that will only just hold the bread. Arrange the bread slices in the dish. Scatter the sultanas around (soaking in whisky rather than water gives a more dynamic result). Pour in the custard and, if it suits your plans, leave for an hour or two. Cook in a bain-marie in the oven at 160°C/325°F/gas mark 3 for 40 minutes. Remove from the oven, crisp the surface under the grill, sieve on a small amount of icing sugar and serve.

RICE PUDDING SERVES 6

School and other penal institutions have done so much to harm British food, for ever putting us off dishes which are perfectly delicious when correctly, carefully and sometimes extravagantly made. Rice pudding is an example. I can still only *just* manage it when made as below, the way it was served at lunchtime in Hilaire Restaurant under chef Simon Hopkinson. He says it was a sell-out. If you like rice pudding, then this is simply the apotheosis. If you think you don't, then try this recipe when you feel in need of comfort and creaminess. You might think that such a small amount of rice will not absorb the liquid, but it does. Long, slow cooking is the key. The bottom oven of an Aga or a 'crockpot' is ideal.

generous 2 oz (65 g) butter
3 heaped tbsp white sugar
4 oz (120 g) pudding rice (important to get pudding rice)
½ vanilla pod, split lengthways
1½ pt (900 ml) milk
½ pt (300 ml) double cream
pinch of salt

Turn on the oven to 150°C/300°F/gas mark 2. In a roomy, shallow dish – a small fish poacher is Simon's suggestion – melt the butter. Add the sugar and stir around until it froths together. Add the rice and stir until every grain is glistening. Leave on a gentle heat for 5 minutes, stirring occasionally. Although the rice should not colour, the sugar and butter have an effect rather like caramel, apparent in the flavour of the finished dish. Add the vanilla pod, pressing it against the side or bottom of the pan so that it spills its seeds and its flavour. Add the milk and cream carefully and put in a pinch of salt. Bring it almost to the boil and put it on the bottom shelf of the oven for at least 2 hours. If the top seems to be browning too deeply turn the oven down even lower. Serve the pudding warm rather than hot and, if you are being truly indulgent, with some loosely whipped cream.

SERVES 4-6 # BLUEBERRY AND APPLE PIE

Blueberries – your huckleberry friend – are nowadays readily available, fresh, as well as canned or frozen, and they are a lovely ingredient to work into your cooking. The blueberries that are in the greengrocers and supermarkets in autumn most probably come from Dorset or Devon. With sugar, lemon juice and a little cornflour, they will simmer into an excellent sauce for ice-cream or pancakes. They are delicious sprinkled with Cointreau or Grand Marnier and a little granulated sugar for crunch, and they make a great treat when folded into lightly sweetened whipped cream – aiming to cram as many blueberries as possible into the cream. To extend them, you can mix them with apples, which they partner well, and either make a crumble or a pie as suggested below. I have suggested a pâte sucrée, but equally you could use shortcrust pastry or another favourite recipe.

2 lb (1 kg) cooking apples
8 oz (250 g) blueberries
about 6 oz (175 g) soft brown sugar
1 oz (30 g) butter
rind of 1 small lemon
1 tbsp water

FOR THE PASTRY:
8 oz (250 g) flour
4 oz (120 g) butter
3 egg yolks
3 oz (90 g) caster sugar
pinch of salt

Peel, core and slice the apples. Put them in a pan with the blueberries, sugar, butter and lemon rind, and water. Cook very gently
until the apples break down. Taste for sweetness and adjust if
necessary. If you are using home-made pastry, ensure that it has
rested for at least 30 minutes after the mixing. Roll out and line a
23 cm (9 in) pie plate or flan ring with half of it. Bake blind in an
oven heated to 190°C/375°F/gas mark 5 for 20 minutes. Fill the
pie with the apple and blueberry mixture, first of all pouring off
any excess juices. Cover the pie with the remaining pastry and
bake again for about 30 minutes, or until the pastry is crisp and
lightly gold. Serve hot or warm with cream.

TARTE TATIN SERVES 4-6

Evidently the two spinster sisters Tatin – or *les demoiselles* Tatin
to put it more prettily – were an impoverished pair and cooked
this tart, a favourite of their father's, to earn a living. The point
about it is that the pastry is cooked on top, which keeps it light
and crisp, while the apples caramelise beneath. To serve, you can
turn it out of its pan and hand round with it either whipped cream,
crème fraîche or thick Greek yogurt.

The choice of pastry can be a matter of preference – either puff
pastry, a sweetened shortcrust, or pâte sablée, which is basically
a shortbread mixture. It is important to have a round pan, which
you can first heat on the stove and later transfer to the oven. An
enamelled iron pan would be ideal. The recipe is traditionally
made with apples, but pears work too.

6–7 dessert apples
juice of 1 small lemon
4 oz (120 g) butter
6 oz (175 g) sugar (brown or white)
pinch of cinnamon
8 oz (250 g) bought or home-made pastry of your choice

Turn on the oven to 200°C/400°F/gas mark 6 (hotter if you are using puff pastry). Peel the apples, core and quarter them and sprinkle with lemon juice to prevent them browning. Spread the butter over the base of your pan and then sprinkle on the sugar, mixed with the pinch of cinnamon, in an even layer. Arrange the apples on top. Roll out your choice of pastry, having given it a chance to rest for 20 minutes or so if it is home-made. Lay the pastry over the apples and trim off any excess, leaving a generous border. Set the pan over fairly high heat on top of the stove and cook until the butter and sugar caramelises. You can peek under the pastry to check, but the smell should tell you when this is happening and if it is starting to burn. The process should not take much longer than 15 minutes. Now bake in the pre-heated oven for 20 minutes or until the pastry is golden. When it is cooked, remove and carefully invert the tart on to a large round serving dish. Eat hot or warm, but not cold.

SERVES 4   LIGHTNING APPLE TARTS

I had one of these apple tarts at Pierre Martin's London brasserie/restaurant Lou Pescadou. It was small, light and delicious; an ideal dessert. When I rang him later for the recipe, he described the process – simplicity itself – and added that three-star French restaurants do exactly the same sort of thing, call it 'tarte fine' and charge a great deal of money for it. Use one of the dessert apples – Cox's or Laxton's – and do not be tempted to put more than one layer of paper-thin slices on the pastry rounds. Pierre said, in a satisfied restaurateur's voice, 'One apple will do four tarts.' Too many layers and it would not cook in the time.

8 oz (250 g) packet puff pastry
1 dessert apple
2 tsp butter
a little caster sugar
dash of Calvados (optional)

Make the oven very hot, 240°C/475°F/gas mark 9. Roll out the defrosted pastry very thinly. Cut out four rounds using a saucer as a guide. Place these on a wetted baking sheet (puff and flaky pastry rises evenly and crisply, oddly enough, with the help of the rising steam). Peel the apple and cut paper-thin slices. Lay them on the pastry rounds, making a layer of slightly overlapping apple pieces. Dot each tart with about half a teaspoon of butter and sprinkle with caster sugar. Cook for five to eight minutes. Remove from the oven and serve immediately. A dash of Calvados on top is a nice thought, and the tarts go well with whipped cream.

GRAPES

Grapes are plentiful in autumn and less expensive than at other times of the year. For dessert, I love the combination of chilled black grapes and a white soft cheese like ricotta or an incredibly mild, almost chalky, creamy cheese. Grapes are also good accompanied by soured cream or thick yogurt (as in the Greek variety now generally on sale). The small seedless variety can be tossed in a mixture of 3 tbsp Cognac, 2 tbsp honey and a splash of lemon juice, chilled thoroughly, and, again, served with yogurt or soured cream. There is another quick dessert, based on not dissimilar principles, which uses fresh double cream and the crème brûlée technique: a layer of grapes, de-seeded if applicable, in a shallow gratin dish, covered completely by a layer of stiffly whipped cream, chilled, a layer of demerara sugar sifted evenly on top and the whole flashed under the grill until the sugar caramelises and subsequently hardens. Grape tart serves 4. If you find muscat grapes (often called Italia), a large green variety sometimes flecked with brown spots, which have a very distinctive scent and flavour, try this grape tart for a special occasion when you can be bothered to peel and seed the grapes. The pastry is taken from Frances Bissell's most excellent book, *A Cook's Calendar*. She, in turn, took the idea from a friend.

5 oz (150 g) butter
2½ oz (75 g) sugar, or less, to taste
about 8 oz (250 g) plain flour
4 fl oz (120 ml) whipped cream, yogurt or fromage blanc
about 12 oz (375 g) muscat grapes, peeled and seeded

Pre-heat oven to 200°C/400°F/gas mark 6. Melt the butter gently in a heavy saucepan. Add the sugar; let it melt and amalgamate but not cook. Remove from the heat. In the pan work in the flour. Eventually you will have a stiff dough. Press it with your fingers or the back of a wooden spoon into a buttered baking dish or pie tin. Prick all over and bake for 12–15 minutes, moving it to a lower shelf if it show signs of burning. When the base is cool, spread it with very cold whipped cream, yogurt, or fromage blanc and cover with the peeled and seeded muscat grapes, preferably chilled. Serve with a chilled muscat wine, such as Muscat de Frontignon.

SERVES 4 ## CLAFOUTIS

'Can she bake a cherry pie?' has always struck me as a rather odd qualification for marriage, if indeed it was marriage that was sought after by Billy Boy. But it is probably as good as any and better than some. Clafoutis is not exactly a pie, though the texture of the batter after cooking should be such that it can be sliced. It is one of the best ways of using cherries if you want to go a step further than eating them raw. A cherry stoner is quite a useful gadget to possess – it can also be used on olives – and arguably has more of a function in your life than a lemon zester, butter curler or any other of those sort of implements that hide in the back of kitchen drawers.

3 tbsp plain flour
pinch of salt
3 tbsp caster sugar, preferably vanilla sugar (i.e. stored with a vanilla pod in it)
2 whole eggs
1 egg yolk
1 tbsp vegetable oil
½ pt (300 ml) milk
1 lb (500 g) dark sweet cherries
icing sugar or caster sugar, to sift over the top

Turn on the oven to 180°C/350°F/gas mark 4. Sift the flour with a pinch of salt and the sugar into a mixing bowl. Make a well in the centre and add the eggs and egg yolk. Work in the flour slowly with a wooden spoon, as if making pancake batter, which is more or less what you are doing. When smooth, beat in the oil. Gradually beat in the milk until you have a thin batter. Set aside while you stone the cherries, doing it over a bowl to save the drips of juice. Butter an ovenproof dish of about 10 in (25 cm) diameter or an equivalent oblong size. Put the cherries and their juice on the bottom. Pour on the batter, tipping it over the back of a spoon to avoid jostling the cherries. Bake for 40–45 mins or until a knife blade slipped in comes out clean. Dust with icing sugar or caster

sugar and serve warm. Alternatively, let the clafoutis cool,
unmould and cut into wedges.

APRICOPITTA SERVES 6-8

On disappointingly grey days in early summer, the nearest thing
to sunshine is the sight of apricots in the shops. They inspire me
to make this pie using filo pastry, which you should be able to
buy in a Greek or Cypriot bakery, delicatessens and the more
enterprising branches of some supermarkets. Do not forget that
once you have removed it from the packet, you should keep it
covered with a damp tea-towel to prevent it becoming brittle. If
you fail to find it and have not yourself mastered the art of making
strudel pastry, which it resembles, then use bought puff pastry
rolled out extremely thinly. The meringue incorporating ground
almonds makes a nice, surprising layer that you can glimpse
through the slashes in the pastry.

2 lb (I kg) fresh apricots
5 cardamom pods
3 oz (90 g) demerara sugar, or more or less to taste
3 oz (90 g) butter, melted
I lb (500 g) filo pastry
3 egg whites
3 tbsp demerara sugar
4 oz (120 g) ground almonds
a sprinkling of icing sugar

Bake the apricots in a medium oven with a little water, the seeds
from the cardamom pods and about 3 oz (90 g) sugar, to taste (do
not make it too sweet), until the fruit is softened and a little syrup
has formed. Brush the base of a small roasting tin with melted
butter, lay in a sheet of the pastry, brush that with butter and
repeat in this fashion for four layers. Purée the fruit after removing
the stones and any thick skin. Spread the purée on the pastry.
Cover with another sheet, brush it with melted butter and continue
for two more sheets. Set the oven to 190°C/375°F/gas mark 5.
Whisk the egg whites until stiff. Whisk in the 3 tbsp sugar and
fold in the ground almonds. Spread this layer of meringue on the
pastry. Cover gently with three to four more sheets of pastry,
brushing each one and the top one with melted butter. Using a
very sharp knife, criss-cross the pie down to the meringue layer,
creating diamond shapes on the pastry. Dust with icing sugar and
bake for about 50 minutes. Serve warm or cold.

SERVES 4   # PLUM CRUSTS.

Plums in season beckon you to make jam and chutney; so satisfying to look at the gleaming jars with carefully written labels, so handy to give away as presents ... But should your mood not be helping-hands-at-home, here is something more immediate to do with plums.

4 thick slices of crusty new white bread, cut from a loaf
3 oz (90 g) butter
2 lb (1 kg) ripe plums
4 oz (120 g) brown sugar
thick cream to serve

Pre-heat the oven to 180°C/350°F/gas mark 4. Butter the slices of bread on both sides. Halve the plums and winkle out the stones. Press plums with cavities upwards neatly on to the slices of bread. Into each hollow put a dab of butter and a teaspoon of brown sugar. Place the bread in a baking dish, cover with foil or buttered paper and cook near the top of the oven for 30 minutes. The bread should be golden and crispy, the fruit syrupy. If not, remove foil or paper and cook a little longer. Serve hot with cold, thick cream.

SERVES 6   # DAMSON COBBLER

'Blessed be he that invented pudding! For it is manna that hits the palates of all sorts of people better even that that of the wilderness. Ah! what an excellent thing is an English pudding! To come in pudding-time is as much as to say to come in the most lucky moment in the world.'

These words, written by a French visitor to Britain in 1690, introduce *The National Trust Book of Traditional Puddings* by Sara Paston-Williams, an excellent collection of recipes for that course at which we British excel. Creams, flummeries, fools, snows, syllabubs, custards, trifles, tarts and flans; how evocative pudding vocabulary is.

The recipe below is from a Cumbrian source. If damsons are not available, other fruits like plums or blackberries can be substituted.

2 lb (1 kg) damsons
9 oz (275 g) caster sugar
¼ pt (150 ml) water
2 oz (60 g) butter, and a little more to grease the dish
8 oz (250 g) self-raising flour
pinch of salt
1 egg
1–2 tbsp milk
granulated sugar, for sprinkling

Wash the damsons and cook slowly in a heavy saucepan with 8 oz (250 g) of sugar and water until just tender. Remove the stones and turn the fruit into a buttered ovenproof dish. Leave to cool. Sieve the flour and salt together into a mixing bowl. Stir in the remaining sugar and rub in the butter. Beat the egg and add to the mixture with enough milk to make a soft dough. Roll out on a lightly floured board to about ½ in (1.5 cm) thick. Cut out dough into rounds with a 2 in (5 cm) cutter and arrange them in a ring around the edge of the dish of fruit, with the rounds overlapping each other. Brush the scone topping with a little milk and bake near the top of a hot oven (220°C/425°F/gas mark 7) for 10 minutes. Reduce the oven temperature to 190°C/375°F/gas mark 5. Sprinkle the top generously with granulated sugar and bake for a further 5–10 minutes until well risen and golden brown.

PLUM CRUMBLE SERVES 4-6

Plums are one of the few fruits, I think, that are improved by cooking and, even though stewed plums has a horrid institutional ring to it, if carefully done and served with thick Jersey cream rather than packet custard, they can be a dessert that brings pleasure. The tartness of the fruit lends itself admirably to a crumble with its sweet crunchy topping. I like to include a good brand of muesli in the crumble mixture, partly because it lends a fairly spurious air of healthiness, but also because there is usually a good mixture of grains and various kinds of dried fruit. If you can be bothered, crack open the plum stones and remove the kernels and add them to the crumble. The flavour is good and they are supposed to be frightfully beneficial.

2 lb (1 kg) dessert plums
about 4 oz (120 g) sugar, to taste

FOR THE CRUMBLE:

4 oz (120 g) self-raising flour
3 oz (90 g) demerara sugar
6 oz (175 g) butter
3 tbsp muesli
the plum stone kernels (optional)

Wipe the plums with a damp cloth. Split in half and remove the stones. Place the plums in a heavy-bottomed saucepan, add a few tablespoons of water and sugar to taste (how much will depend on the tartness of the fruit). Set on a low heat, cover and cook gently until the plums are just softened. Pour off the juices and reserve. Turn on the oven to 200°C/400°F/gas mark 6. Place the plums in a shallow baking dish. Mix the flour and sugar together for the crumble. Rub in the butter until you have a mixture that resembles large breadcrumbs. Stir in the muesli and the plum stone kernels. Spread the mixture over the fruit. Bake for 20 minutes and then lower the heat to 180°C/350°F/gas mark 4 and leave for another 20 minutes. Watch that the top browns but does not burn. Serve with whipped cream or soured cream or Greek yogurt. Into any of these you can stir the reserved plum juices, which you have boiled up and reduced to a syrup. Stir it in only enough to marble the cream or yogurt.

SERVES 4-6   BLACKBERRY AND APPLE CRUMBLE

Apart from wild mushrooms, which smug people will tell you are there for the picking without telling you where, my favourite free food is blackberries. Even if you have not had the pleasure of blackberrying this year to procure enough booty to make that best of all spreads, sloppy bramble jelly, you can still buy cultivated blackberries in the shops or use frozen ones which retain their flavour well. A crumble always strikes me as preferable to a pie because of the texture.

1 lb (500 g) cooking apples
2–4 oz (60–120 g) sugar, to taste
2 in (5 cm) strip of lemon peel
1 lb (500 g) blackberries

FOR THE CRUMBLE:

4 oz (120 g) flour, or 3 oz (90 g) flour and 2 tbsp muesli
4 oz (120 g) demerara sugar
2 oz (60 g) ground almonds
4 oz (120 g) butter

Peel, core and chop the apples. Put in a saucepan with a splash of water and cook gently with a little sugar (it must be judged to complement the sweetness of the fruit) and the lemon peel. When the apples are softened, add the blackberries and simmer very gently until they are heated through. Put into a pie dish, keeping back any excess of juice. Rub together the crumble ingredients until you have a mixture with the texture of breadcrumbs – the crunchiness of muesli is a good addition. Sprinkle over the fruit and bake in a hot oven until the crumble is browned and crisp. If you are planning to serve it with double cream, add some of the reserved juice as you beat the cream, to slightly flavour and colour it.

PECAN PIE SERVES 4

That Americans are particularly hot on baking is not always apparent in American restaurants here, where the cheesecakes, chocolate cakes, apple pies and pecan pies often taste as if they are all delivered from a ropy central source of supply. This recipe, which comes from an American living in Britain, is delightfully simple and also delicious. Try to buy pecans in their shells and shell them yourself as the ready-to-use kind sold in plastic containers often seem to have a mustiness about them. Corn syrup is usually used for pecan pie, but a good substitute is the golden syrup that is now sold in bottles for pouring.

about 8 oz (250 g) bought or home-made shortcrust pastry to line a
9 in (23 cm) pie dish
3 eggs
2½ oz (75 g) butter, melted
5 oz (150 g) sugar
½ tsp salt
6 oz (175 g) corn syrup or pouring golden syrup
5 oz (150 g) shelled and halved pecan nuts

Set the oven to 190°C/375°F/gas mark 5. Roll out the pastry, let it rest for 15 minutes and then line the pie dish. Beat together the eggs, butter, sugar, salt and syrup. Stir in the pecan halves. Pour into the pastry case. Bake for about 35 minutes or until the filling is set and the pastry golden brown.

GUILT-FREE TREACLE TART

SERVES 4-6

By almost no stretch of the imagination could you think of treacle tart as being beneficial to your system, but it is one of those simple and simply delicious desserts that should not be brushed aside in the current upsurge of culinary moral fervour. By using *brown* breadcrumbs, incorporating the *zest* of lemons and dwelling on the Vitamin C content of oranges you can almost convince yourself that treacle tart is germane to fitness. To make matters worse, enjoy this with whipped cream.

8 oz (250 g) plain flour
pinch of salt
4 oz (120 g) butter or margarine
2 oz (60 g) lard
1 egg yolk
grated rind of 2 lemons
juice of 2 lemons
5 tbsp golden syrup
4 oz (120 g) fresh brown breadcrumbs
1 thin-skinned orange, washed but not peeled and thinly sliced

Turn on the oven to 200°C/400°F/gas mark 6. Sift the flour into a mixing bowl and sprinkle on the salt. Cut in the fats with a knife and then work the mixture with your fingertips until you arrive at the consistency of uneven breadcrumbs. Using the knife again, mix in the egg yolk, and rind and juice of one lemon. To get a cohesive mixture you may need a little cold water. Gather into a ball and, if possible, leave in the fridge for an hour. Roll out the pastry on a floured board. Line an 8 in (20 cm) pie tin and prick the base of the pastry. Mix together the syrup, breadcrumbs and rind and juice of the other lemon. Pour into the pastry case. Arrange the orange slices, overlapping, on the surface. Bake for 25–30 minutes. Serve lukewarm.

PROFITEROLES WITH CHOCOLATE SAUCE

SERVES 4

Making choux pastry – the basis for profiteroles and also éclairs and cream buns – is one of the more magical aspects of cooking. The way you tip the flour in with one rash gesture, the way the mixture leaves the side of the pan, the way the eggs make it glossy and, finally, the way it rises into light and airy spheres (we trust) is all satisfying and almost ennobling. If at first you don't succeed, try again, making sure you cook the profiteroles long enough.

8 fl oz (250 ml) water
3 oz (90 g) butter
4 oz (120 g) sifted plain flour
3 size 1 or 4 size 4 eggs
whipped cream or ice-cream, to serve

FOR THE CHOCOLATE SAUCE:
8 oz (250 g) soft dark brown sugar
3½ tbsp cocoa powder
3 oz (90 g) butter
2 tbsp instant coffee powder
3 tbsp golden syrup
½ pt (300 ml) boiling water

Turn on the oven to 200°C/400°F/gas mark 4. Put the water and butter together in a heavy saucepan and bring slowly to the boil so that by the time the water is boiling the butter is melted. When it is properly bubbling, immediately tip in the flour and remove the pan from the heat. Beat the mixture vigorously with a wooden spoon until it thickens and leaves the side of the pan. Beat in the salt. Cool the mixture – standing the pan in a bowl of cold water speeds things up. Beat in the eggs one by one until the dough is shiny. Put small teaspoons of the mixture on to a wet baking sheet (the steam helps the rising) about 3 in (8 cm) apart. Bake for about 25 minutes or until the profiteroles are puffy and brown. Remove from the oven. Switch off. Make a hole in each profiterole for the air to escape and return them to the warm oven, upside down, for 5 minutes or until dry. With a piping bag fill with whipped cream, or spoon in ice-cream and serve with the hot chocolate sauce. To make the sauce, put all the ingredients in a saucepan, adding the water last. Stir over a medium heat until smooth and then bring to the boil. Simmer gently for five minutes, giving the odd stir. Any leftover sauce can be kept in a jar in the fridge and warmed gently when needed.

FRUIT FRITTERS

I remember as a child always being extremely pleased when my mother made apple or banana fritters for pudding, but I realise that I have never done that for my children. Perhaps the current obsession with healthy eating is causing us to forget agreeable old-fashioned ideas. You can usually assemble fritters from what is available in the house, which makes them a good spur-of-the-moment idea for a dessert. I have given two recipes for batter below, one rather more ambitious than the other, both lighter than an ordinary pancake batter.

BATTER 1:
4 oz (120 g) flour, sifted with a pinch of salt
2 tbsp vegetable oil
¼ pt (150 ml) tepid water
1 egg white

Sift the flour and salt into a bowl. Add the oil and then the water, beating it in with a wire whisk and keeping going until you have a smooth mixture. Let sit for about an hour, then, just before using, whisk the egg white until stiff and fold in.

BATTER 2:
3½ oz (100 g) flour, sifted with a pinch of salt
1 egg, separated
5 tbsp tepid beer
about 2 tbsp water
1 oz (30 g) melted butter
1 tbsp Cognac or similar (Calvados would be good with apples)

Sift the flour into a bowl. Add the egg yolk, beer and water and slowly incorporate the flour into the liquid. Stir in the butter and your choice of alcohol. Let rest and, before frying, beat the egg white stiffly and fold it into the mixture.

To make the fritters, cut your choice of fruit into bite-size pieces and sprinkle with a little lemon juice and sugar if it needs it. Go beyond apple and banana; try apricots or plums. Bring vegetable oil for deep-frying to a high temperature, coat the pieces of fruit in batter and fry until golden, turning over once. Drain on kitchen paper. Sprinkle with sugar and serve immediately.

SERVES 4   # FRUIT KEBABS

There is a sort of person eternally on a diet – I am one – who, when it comes to the time for dessert, mutters, 'Oh I'll just have some fruit.' It is annoying to entertain such types and usually, since they can't be bothered to peel and cut the fruit, they ingest hundreds of calories eating bread and cheese and looking smug. With these kebabs the work is done. They are met with enthusiasm by 'dieters' and non-dieters alike. Use a mixture of interesting fruit. The list below is but a guideline. Prepare them in bite-size pieces. Fruits that discolour, such as apples and pears should have lemon juice or lime juice squeezed liberally over them.

1 apple or pear
1 small bunch of grapes
½ melon, shaped into balls or cubes
1 mango
8 oz (250 g) strawberries
2 kiwi fruit, peeled and sliced
½ pineapple
lemon or lime juice, as required for squeezing over the fruit

FOR FLAMBÉED KEBABS:
granulated sugar, to sprinkle over
2 tbsp brandy, Grand Marnier or fruit-based alcohol

Thread the prepared fruit on to kebab skewers, the slender wooden kind sold for satay are best. Squeeze on the lemon or lime juice and chill in the refrigerator. Leave only an hour or so before serving as you do not want the fruit to become flossy. For a more dramatic presentation, sprinkle the fruit with granulated sugar, grill them quickly under a hot grill and place on a heated plate. Heat the alcohol gently in a small pan. Pour on to the fruit kebabs and flame them. Serve immediately.

RHUBARB FOOL   SERVES 4

Early rhubarb has a nice slender delicacy which, whilst not quite justifying the name Champagne (one of the varieties), can be a far cry from the Quatermass Experiment sort of slime that might have been forced on you in the past on the grounds that it would do you good. Medicinal rhubarb is a main constituent of Gregory's Powder. Rhubarb fool can, and in my view should, be made just of the carefully stewed fruit with perhaps a little orange or ginger as flavouring and thick cream stirred in not too thoroughly so as to achieve a marbled effect. If you wish you can use custard in place of cream. If so, make the custard with ½ pt (300 ml) of single cream and 3 egg yolks. For a less rich dish, stew the fruit as directed and serve with soured cream or thick Greek yogurt sprinkled with a little demerara sugar. The nicest accompaniment to rhubarb fool is slices of plain sponge cake gently fried in butter. A slightly stale sponge cake is all to the good. Gooseberries also lend themselves admirably to fooling, but should you use them, omit the flavouring of Pernod and substitute elderflower wine or Frontignan.

2 lb (1 kg) young rhubarb
4–6 oz (120–175 g) demerara sugar, depending on how tart you like your dessert
finely grated rind of 1 small orang ̄
9 fl oz (275 ml) thick cream
2 tsp Pernod (optional but good)
a little preserved ginger in syrup, chopped small (optional garnish)

Trim the rhubarb stalks of any leaves or brown roots. Chop into 2 in (5 cm) lengths. Put into a heavy saucepan or ovenproof dish with the sugar, just a little water and the orange rind. Simmer or cook in a low oven for about 5 minutes or until the fruit is tender. Drain off excess juice. Either sieve, blend or leave the fruit whole – the last would be my choice. When cold, stir in the cream or custard and the Pernod if you are using it. Serve in a china or pottery bowl rather than a glass one. Garnish, if you like, with preserved ginger.

SERVES 4–6 # BLACKBERRY AND APPLE SHAPE

I have a childish fondness for jellies and this shape, a recipe taken from Mrs Hilda Leyel's *The Gentle Art of Cookery*, first published in 1925, has a comforting nannying quality.

1 lb (500 g) blackberries
1 lb (500 g) apples
4 oz (120 g) sugar
2 cloves
½ oz (15 g) packet of gelatine

TO SERVE: *whipped cream*

Cook the blackberries and apples with the sugar and cloves. When the fruit is thoroughly soft, either liquidise, whizz in a food processor or push through a sieve. Dissolve the gelatine in a little hot water. Stir into the purée, fill a mould and chill. Turn out when set and serve with whipped cream.

PEARS IN CIDER WITH CARAMEL CHIPS SERVES 4

A bad pear, a flossy pear, is such a cruel disappointment that I almost hardly dare to eat one fresh. One way round this problem is to buy the fruit under-ripe and hard and poach it. Pears in red wine, or 'pears in wine gravy' as one hostess put it to me, has become a sort of dinner party cliché. Pears in cider is, I think, a more elegant notion as apples and pears belong together, not only in rhyming slang but also botanically. If you happen to see quinces being sold, one of them, peeled and cored, can also be added for a perfect *ménage à trois* of flavours. If the pears are not rock hard and the cider is sweet, you should be able to do without the added sugar. The caramel is quick and easy to make and provides a welcome crunch.

1 lb (500 g) hard pears
1¾ pt (1 l) bottle of cider, preferably dry vintage cider
1 cinnamon stick
2 cloves
1–2 in (3–5 cm) strip of lemon peel
granulated sugar to taste and 2 heaped tbsp for caramel

Peel the pears, leaving whatever remains of the stalk attached. Bring the cider to the boil with the cinnamon stick, cloves and an inch or two of lemon peel for flavour. Use your own judgement about adding the granulated sugar – I am on the side of under-sweet desserts. Simmer the pears in the cider until they are tender – the time will vary according to the hardness of the pears. Bullet-like varieties can take over an hour. Remove the pears to a pretty dish and reduce the poaching liquid by half with fierce boiling. Pour on to the fruit. Close to the time of serving, put two heaped tbsp of white sugar into a small, heavy-bottomed saucepan with enough water to wet it thoroughly. Put on to a low heat until the sugar dissolves and then boil, watching like a hawk. When the syrup colours and is golden remove from the heat. Quickly drip blobs of it from a wooden spoon on to the pears in their reduced cooking liquid, remembering the caramel is extremely hot. It will harden to caramel immediately. Serve with perhaps some single cream.

The sugar pan, which will fill you with gloom, is easily cleaned after leaving it to soak in water.

SERVES 4 # MANGO TREAT

The arrival of a box of Alfonso mangoes sent by a friend in India made me think of ways of handling them beyond peeling and eating – really the best way with this particularly delicious variety of mango. I made a fruit salad using just mangoes and halved and pipped black grapes, which looked pretty, thought it might benefit from a bit of a crunch and remembered, or thought I remembered, a sort of Chinese nut brittle incorporating crushed black peppercorns. After experimenting and fooling around with the inclusion of bicarbonate of soda and butter, which had a chewy result, I found the method below to work the best. Be brave about the pepper. It is surprisingly agreeable. Try to buy flaked, rather than whole, almonds.

2 ripe mangoes, preferably Alfonso
8 oz (250 g) black grapes, halved and seeded
4 oz (120 g) granulated or caster sugar
1 generous tbsp golden syrup
2½ oz (75 ml) water
2 oz (60 g) flaked almonds
freshly ground black pepper

Peel and slice the mangoes. Mix with the grapes and put in a pretty bowl. Leave to chill in the refrigerator. Combine sugar, golden syrup and water in a thick-bottomed saucepan and heat until the sugar dissolves. Boil the mixture, stirring until it spins a thread when dropped from the tip of a wooden spoon. By this time it will be a deep golden colour. Stir in the nuts and remove from the heat. Grind in four or five twists of black pepper. Stir again and pour on to a metal tray or marble surface that you have lightly greased with vegetable oil. When cold and set, smash into shards. Sprinkle these on the fruit and serve.

SERVES 4-6 # DRIED FRUIT SALAD

My godmother, Margot, makes this salad. It provides an excellent ending to a meal. Because she works hard her dinner parties have a plan of campaign. This dish is easygoing about being prepared up to three days ahead. In a sense, the longer the fruit steeps, the better. What I like about her mixture is the colours, the combination of fresh and dried, the cushiony softness of the apricots and prunes contrasted with the crack of almonds and the piquancy of soured cream (or yogurt) against the sweetness of the juices. A crisp, fresh pear, or a Tientsin Ya pear, that fruit which looks as if it is somewhere between an apple and a pear and is sold in Chinese and other supermarkets, is a nice addition. Although the notion of seasonality of foods has more or less faded from our lives, a dish like this, designed for winter, is all the more gratifying for being eaten at the appropriate time.

8 oz (250 g) dried apricots
4 oz (120 g) dried pears and 1 fresh pear (optional)
2 fl oz (60 ml) port
8 oz (250 g) stoned prunes
2 fresh oranges
2 fl oz (60 ml) white wine (optional)
2 oz (60 g) blanched almonds, slivered
sugar
soured cream or Greek yogurt

Soak the apricots and the dried pears overnight in enough water to cover, or put them to soak in the morning for the evening. Pour some port over the prunes and leave them to swell. Simmer the apricots and pears in their soaking water plus the juice of one orange plus a little white wine, if you have some open, until they are tender – about 15 minutes is average. With a vegetable peeler take thin strips of rind from the other orange. Cut into threads. Peel and section the orange. Peel and slice the fresh pear. Drain the apricots, keeping the juices. Take the prunes from the port. Mix the dried and fresh fruits, the orange rind and the nuts. Simmer together the apricot soaking juices and any remaining port. Taste and add sugar if you want it sweeter. When you have just enough liquid left to cover the fruits, pour on. Leave to cool. Serve cool, but not chilled, with soured cream or Greek yogurt.

CHOCOLATE MOUSSE   SERVES 4

I want you to know how easy it is to make a wonderful chocolate mousse. There are recipes that fool around with milk and cream and gelatine and all kinds of unnecessary ingredients. What you need for a quick and perfect chocolate mousse is 1 oz (30 g) of dark, bitter chocolate per person and one egg. Melting the chocolate in strong coffee is the only flourish I will allow. I would be against adding brandy or rum. I have been known to grate orange rind on top at the last moment but sometimes, often, simplicity is the best course.

4 oz (120 g) plain chocolate (Menier is a good choice)
1 heaped dsp instant coffee
3 tbsp boiling water
4 eggs

In either a bowl that fits over a saucepan without touching its base or a double boiler, place the squares of chocolate with three tablespoons of strong hot coffee that you have made by pouring not too much boiling water on to the instant coffee. Let it melt very gently, preferably in one layer so that you don't have to disturb it; overheating chocolate makes it grainy. The water in the lower saucepan should just shudder. To be really safe bring the water to the boil and then turn off the heat. The chocolate will eventually melt. Remove the pan containing the chocolate from the heat source and stir to blend. Separate the eggs. Beat the yolks one by one into the chocolate. In a clean bowl whisk the egg whites until they stand in stiff, dry peaks. Add a quarter of the volume of the beaten whites to the chocolate mixture and fold in with a light hand. Pour this on to the egg whites still in the bowl and fold again, blending carefully so that there are no white 'islands' but not hammering the air out of the mousse. Pour into small ramekins or cups. Chill in the refrigerator for a few hours. The chocolate hardening will set the mousse to just the right consistency. If you must serve cream, serve single cream.

SERVES 6 ## HONEYCOMB MOULD

Obviously there has been some dreadful slip 'twixt cup and lip in the upbringing of my children, for they do not feel that a meal is a meal without something sweet to conclude it. We all particularly like this nursery confection, which has a clear, singing, palate-refreshing flavour of fresh lemon and a diverting appearance (particularly if you use a fancy mould) of three layers; a summit of lemon jelly, a band of creamy mousse, and a faintly crackling golden base. Actually, all grown-ups to whom I have given it love it.

3 size 1 or 4 size 4 eggs
grated rind and juice of 2 lemons
½ oz (15 g) powdered gelatine
3 oz (90 g) sugar
6 tbsp single or double cream
¾ pt (450 ml) creamy milk

Separate the eggs. Whisk the yolks in a basin and add the lemon rind, gelatine, sugar and cream. Heat the milk to scalding point and whisk it into the eggs. Don't fret if it looks grainy – it will smooth out. Put the basin over simmering water and cook, stirring, until you have a mixture as thick as double cream that coats the back of the spoon. Mix in the lemon juice. Taste to see if you want more sugar, but try to resist. Beat the whites into stiff peaks and strain the lemony custard on to them, folding it in carefully and with a light hand, using a metal spoon. Pour into a 2 pt (1.2 l) jelly mould and chill until set. To unmould, slip a knife round the edge, put a plate on top and turn over. It should plop out pretty as a picture.

PORT AND CLARET JELLY   SERVES 8–10

I have a childish love of jellies, wibbly-wobbly on the plate. Making one with such grown-up ingredients as port and claret seems a wickedly good idea. It strikes me that this dessert would be a good alternative to Christmas pudding. The colour is jewel-like and the effect easily as tipsy as brandy butter. The recipe comes from a book by John Tovey, chef at Miller Howe in the Lake District, where desserts are the grand finale to meals that are extravaganzas. He points out that the jelly requires little or no effort of digestion.

$\frac{3}{4}$ pt (450 ml) cold water
8 oz (250 g) granulated sugar
2 tbsp redcurrant jelly
$\frac{1}{2}$ stick of cinnamon
$\frac{1}{2}$ pt (300 ml) port
$\frac{3}{4}$ pt (450 ml) claret
2 tbsp brandy
just under 1 oz (30 g) powdered gelatine

In a clean saucepan put the water with the sugar, redcurrant jelly and cinnamon. Bring to the boil. In another saucepan put the port, claret and brandy (obviously don't use your best vintages in a jelly). As the alcohol mixture comes to the boil, sprinkle on the gelatine. Leave both pans to simmer for 10 minutes, then pour the contents through a fine sieve into a jug. Stir swiftly and, as it is cooling, pour it into small dishes or glasses. It should make about 12 restrained portions. Shortbread is a good accompaniment.

COEURS À LA CRÈME

SERVES 4-6

It seems to me that the French have always understood cream and soft cheeses rather better than we have. Now it is possible to buy tubs of fromage blanc or fromage frais with varying fat contents and the slightly acid crème fraîche, but there is still not the general availability nor range that you find in the shops and market stalls of France. All three accompany soft fruit or compôtes of fruit better than does whipped double cream with its rather vapid taste. For the recipe below you need a dish with holes in it for the cheese to drain. You can buy sweet little glazed porcelain heart-shaped moulds in good kitchen shops or, more prosaically, you can pierce holes in small plastic tubs. You can make coeurs à la crème with a mixture of cream and fromage frais, but I have stipulated unsalted double cream cheese because it is easier to find. Make sure you beat the cheese and sugar until absolutely smooth.

8 oz (250 g) unsalted double cream cheese
1 tbsp caster sugar
3 egg whites, stiffly beaten
¼ pt (150 ml) single or double cream
muslin, for lining the moulds

Beat the cheese until smooth and then thoroughly beat in the sugar. Gently fold in the stiffly beaten egg whites. Rinse squares of muslin in water and wring out. Line the moulds and spoon in the cheese mixtures. Leave in the refrigerator for a couple of hours or longer. Turn out carefully. Pour the cream over the top and serve with soft fruit, with a bowl of sugar to add to taste.

BROWN BREAD ICE-CREAM

SERVES 4-6

I had this lovely ice-cream at a dinner party and it reminded me what a good idea it is to mix toasted caramelised crumbs into a creamy base and freeze it. To the uninitiated it sounds perhaps a daft idea but recipes for it have been on the go since the late nineteenth century. Even without an ice-cream maker this recipe works successfully and although you could, if you felt like it, stir it halfway through the freezing process, it should not be necessary. What is important is to remove the ice-cream from the freezer at least an hour before you mean to eat it so that it is cold and creamy and firm but not a numbing block. Jane, the friend of mine who served this, accompanied it with an apricot mousse.

3 oz (90 g) wholemeal breadcrumbs
2 oz (60 g) butter
4 oz (120 g) brown sugar
$\frac{1}{2}$ pt (300 ml) double cream
$\frac{1}{2}$ pt (300 ml) single cream
2 eggs, separated
1 tbsp sherry, rum or brandy (all optional)

Fry the breadcrumbs in the butter until crisp. Add half the sugar and cook gently until the sugar caramelises and coats the crumbs. Whisk the double cream until thick and then beat in the remaining half of the sugar, the single cream, the egg yolks and sherry, rum or brandy if you are using it. Whisk the egg whites in a clean bowl until stiff and gently fold them into the ice-cream mixture. Freeze in a suitable container.

INSTANT RASPBERRY SORBET   SERVES 4

This elegant idea, which delights with its almost outrageous simplicity, was given to me by Prue Leith, a canny cook and restaurateur and a person to be applauded for supplying *British* food at the conference centre near Westminster, so scuppering the notion that to be good or grand you must, in gastronomic terms, imitate the French.

This method works well with raspberries, the fruit I tried, and also with strawberries. I see no reason not to apply it to currants either when they are in season. I am afraid it is predicated on the ownership of a food processor. A liquidiser might work but you would have to do the fruit in batches. What is wonderful is not only the speed in the making but the immediacy of flavour that shines through. The proportion of one-third sugar to two-thirds fruit is the one that makes sorbets successful. However, since, for me, this gives a fairly sweet result, I would advise the addition of lemon juice to tone it down.

1 12 oz (340 g) packet of frozen raspberries (most supermarkets sell polythene cartons)
4 oz (110 g) sugar or $\frac{1}{3}$ the weight of the fruit
juice of $\frac{1}{2}$ a small lemon

Empty the frozen fruit into the bowl of the food processor. Sprinkle the sugar on top and leave for about 20 minutes until the fruit is beginning to soften around the edges. Turn on the motor and whizz, either using a pulse button or switching on or off, until you have a purée the consistency and temperature of sorbet. Add lemon juice to taste and whizz again. Serve it immediately or freeze until wanted.

BUTTERSCOTCH SAUCE

This recipe was given to me by Bill Blackburn, the man behind New England Ice-cream. Having been made a member of his Ice-cream Academy, a body that meets sporadically for tastings, I discovered that one of the benefits was delivery of every variety of New England ice-creams and sorbets. My children, who given half a chance will always sniff out and prefer the synthetic product, much to my surprise adored these ice-creams made with only the best and the purest and absolutely no dubious ingredients. Every supper time became a tasting which I joined in – before going out to eat in a restaurant. If you can tear yourself away from the mint-chocolate-chip and the maple-pecan, then the vanilla suits this sauce admirably.

4 oz (120 g) butter
8 fl oz (250 ml) single cream
6 oz (175 g) soft brown sugar
2 tbsp brandy
4 drops of vanilla essence

Melt the butter in a double boiler or over very low heat. Add the cream and blend, then stir in the sugar. Cook gently for about 30 minutes. Add the brandy and vanilla essence (try and find the real thing rather than ersatz flavouring). Stir and remove from the heat. The sauce will thicken as it cools. This recipe makes a considerable amount of sauce, but extra can be stored in a screw-top jar in the refrigerator.

BAKING

It is no coincidence that most of the recipes here have been supplied by friends and relations. Baking seems to me properly a hand-me-down business and passing on a method or an idea is just part of the spirit of giving and caring that is implicit in the smells and sights of home-made biscuits, cakes and breads. There is an American influence which only underlines the fact that the key to American cooking is not fast food or California dreaming but a solid tradition of baking that has thrown up some classics, such as brownies, beloved by children.

The most hastily assembled meal can be lifted into another class by the addition of something home-baked, such as cornbread or oatcakes, preferably served warm. Both cornbread and soda bread, needing no yeast, can constitute spur-of-the-moment cookery and such trouble taken will always be noticed.

EGGIE'S BISCUITS

My mother, who is my Auntie Eggie's sister, passed this recipe on to me under the title of American Cookies. I don't like that name but I am extremely fond of my Auntie Eggie (her name is Meg but I couldn't say that when I was little) and although she must have got the recipe from somewhere, I always think of these ultra-crisp, delicious and not over-sweet biscuits as hers. My mother, who says that they are much better than anything you can buy, often makes them for my children and the inclusion of bran flakes makes me feel that they can only be doing them an immense amount of good. They are also something that children can make themselves.

4 oz (120 g) hard margarine, not butter
4 oz (120 g) caster sugar
1 dsp milk
1 dsp golden syrup
6 oz (175 g) plain flour
1 tsp bicarbonate of soda
2 oz (60 g) bran flakes

Set oven to 190°C/375°F/gas mark 5. Cream together the margarine and sugar. Add the milk and syrup. Mix together the sifted flour and bicarbonate of soda and stir into the mixture. Fold in the bran flakes. Roll heaped teaspoons of the mixture into walnut-sized balls. Place quite far apart on greased baking sheets and bake for 15 minutes. Cool on a wire rack.

HEIDI'S COOKIES

This recipe, given to me by an American acquaintance, is quick and easy to make and goes down as a treat with children. Once bitten, the cookies are likely to be made by the children themselves. the mixture is not a million miles away from a brownie recipe and the result should have a similar stickiness. Also like brownies, the mixture puffs up in the oven and then sinks upon cooling, but don't let this alarm you – it is the correct procedure.

4 tbsp vegetable oil
3 oz (90 g) butter
3 oz (90 g) caster sugar
3 oz (90 g) brown sugar
1 egg
1 tsp vanilla essence
7 oz (200 g) self-raising flour
½ tsp bicarbonate of soda
½ tsp salt
4 oz (120 g) shelled walnuts, roughly chopped
6 oz (175 g) plain chocolate chips

Turn on the oven to 190°C/375°F/gas mark 5. Cream together the oil, butter and two sugars. Beat in the egg and vanilla. Sift together the self-raising flour, bicarbonate of soda and salt. Stir the flour into the mixture, add the walnuts and the chocolate chips and blend them in fairly evenly. Spread the mixture in a 13 in × 9½ in (33 × 24.5 cm) baking tin. Cook in the pre-heated oven for 15–20 minutes until the surface is puffy. Let cool and then cut into squares. These are very good with a decent make of vanilla ice-cream.

BRANDY SNAPS

When I was due to write a recipe for Valentine's Day I thought hard about seductive food. My own choice was potato omelette because someone I loved once cooked it for me when I was tired and put upon, and I didn't even know until then that he could fry an egg. This anecdote explains why I did not choose a recipe for an oyster dish, a phallic array of asparagus or a heart-shaped mousse: whom you eat with, not what you eat, is the key to romance. Finally, I gave a recipe for brandy snaps, a decision predicated on the assumption that loved ones would be touched by something home-made that you might easily have bought or not even bothered with at all.

generous 4 oz (125 g) butter
4 oz (120 g) caster sugar
4 fl oz (120 ml) golden syrup
4 oz (120 g) plain flour (sifted)
½ tsp ground ginger

Turn on the oven to 190°C/375°F/gas mark 5. In the top pan of a double boiler, heat together the butter, sugar and syrup over simmering water until all is melted. Remove from the heat and stir in the flour gradually. Add the ginger and stir again. Oil two baking sheets. Spoon small rounds of the mixture on to one baking sheet, spacing them well apart. Put in the oven. Five minutes later, put in the second baking sheet. Five minutes later check the first sheet and if the mixture has spread into lace mats, is bubbling and a deep golden brown, remove it. Here is the only mildly tricky part. Wait until the biscuits seem to solidify but are still bendy, and then roll them round the handle of an oiled wooden spoon or something similar. As they cool they will become crisp. Slide them off and let rest on a wire tray. Continue alternating the baking sheets until the mixture is all cooked.

LIBBY SILVER'S CHOCOLATE ACORNS

Not everyone has fully grasped the fact that baking is the basis of American food. Hamburger and spare rib restaurants do not seem to have realised it. This recipe has been given to me by an American friend living in London. It is his mother's recipe. She lives, he says, in Hollywood, Florida, a notorious centre of baking excellence. It is important to find unsweetened cooking chocolate, such as Baker's. It gives these 'flavour bombs' particular resonance and a quality that can enable them to be served as petits fours. For this purpose, make them on the small side.

8 oz (250 g) blanched almonds
8 oz (250 g) unsweetened cooking chocolate (e.g. Baker's)
3 egg whites
1 tsp vinegar
8 oz (250 g) caster sugar
1 tsp vanilla essence
4 oz (120 g) semi-sweet chocolate
2 oz (60 g) chopped pistachio nuts (optional)

Turn on the oven to 135°C/275°F/gas mark 1. Grind the almonds and the unsweetened chocolate, using a mouli-légumes or the grating blade of a food processor. Put the egg whites and vinegar into a large clean bowl. Add a pinch of salt and beat the whites until stiff. Gradually add the sugar, beating all the while until you have shiny peaks of meringue. Fold in the almonds, unsweetened chocolate and the vanilla essence. Grease two baking sheets. Drop teaspoons of the mixture on to the sheets about 1 in (3 cm) apart. Bake for 30 minutes. Remove and cool on wire racks. Melt the semi-sweet chocolate gently. Dip half of each cookie into the melted chocolate (so that it resembles an 'acorn'). If you are using the pistachio nuts, sprinkle them on the dipped ends. Leave to set.

THE RICHEST BROWNIES KNOWN TO MAN

This idea has been taken from the appropriately named book *Food as Presents* by Patricia H. White. Now working in London as a literary agent Ms White grew up on a farm in America and, as Americans understand brownies profoundly, I am happy to take her words for this recipe. The high proportion of sugar among the ingredients is what gives brownies their characteristic stickiness and fragile, flaky crust.

4 eggs
8 oz (250 g) soft butter
2 tsp vanilla essence
6 oz (175 g) unsweetened baking chocolate, melted and cooled to room temperature, or 4½ oz (135 g) unsweetened cocoa powder and 3 oz (90 g) butter
10 oz (300 g) plain flour
¼ tsp baking powder
½ tsp salt
1 lb (500 g) white sugar
6 oz (175 g) chocolate chips and/or 4 oz (120 g) chopped walnuts (optional additions)

Pre-heat the oven to 180°C/350°F/gas mark 4. In a bowl combine the eggs, butter and vanilla essence and beat either with an electric mixer at highest speed or with a wooden spoon until light and fluffy. At medium speed, slowly add the chocolate, continue beating for 1 more minute, or 3 minutes by hand. Sift together the dry ingredients and fold them in thoroughly. Mix in the chocolate chips and/or walnuts if desired. Divide the mixture between two greased and floured baking tins about 7 in (18 cm) square and spread evenly. Bake for about 40 minutes or until the brownies begin to shrink away from the side of the tin. Cool before cutting into squares. Because brownies should be gooey, it is best to wrap each one in cellophane or greaseproof paper before storing or packing. This way they will keep for at least a week.

BANANA BREAD

When my children were babies mashed banana was one of the easiest meals to make without feeling quite as slovenly as I did after simply opening a tin or jar. So easy was it, that now only one of the children will countenance bananas and, even then, only occasionally. However, it was my eldest child who made this banana bread – and ate it enthusiastically, substantiating one of my arguments for getting children interested in cooking, which is that they will always at least try the things they have made.

This is a useful recipe to have at hand when bananas begin to grow too brown and spotty. They are, as you know, immensely nutritious, easily digestible and high in vitamins and minerals. One book I have read advise them as a face pack. But try this bread first, hot and buttered, for tea.

6 oz (175 g) sugar
4 oz (120 g) butter
2 eggs
2 tbsp milk
8 oz (250 g) mashed ripe banana
8 oz (250 g) self-raising flour
2 tsp baking powder
1 tsp salt
4 oz (120 g) chopped walnuts

Turn on the oven to 180°C/350°F/gas mark 4. Cream together the sugar and butter. Beat in the eggs and the milk. Fold in the bananas, which you have mashed slightly but not so much as to remove all texture from the loaf. In another bowl sift together the dry ingredients and mix in the nuts. Blend the dry mixture into the creamy one. Bake in a greased loaf tin 9 × 5 × 3 in (23 × 13 × 8 cm) for 30 minutes. Test with a skewer to see if done and, if the skewer comes out tacky, cook a little longer.

CHRISTMAS CAKE

I have a childhood memory of coming out of the sea at Westward Ho! in Devon, blue and shivering as is the way on English sea-side holidays, and sitting on the pebble-ridge having tea with slices of this wonderfully rich cake that my mother had baked. Now she makes it only at Christmas time and it is my children who love it – and help themselves to secret slices. When my mum gave me the recipe she said that I should stress that the funnel shaped tin (like an angel cake tin) that she bakes it in probably contributes to even cooking. I think she is right. It also makes it easy to slice.

8 oz (250 g) glacé cherries
8 oz (250 g) currants
8 oz (250 g) sultanas
6 oz (175 g) raisins
4 oz (120 g) mixed candied peel
2 oz (60 g) muscatel raisins (optional)
3 tbsp brandy
12 oz (375 g) butter
12 oz (375 g) caster sugar
4 eggs
1 lb (500 g) flour
1 tsp baking powder
1 tsp ground cinnamon

Pre-heat the oven to 135°C/275°F/gas mark 1. Cut half of the glacé cherries into two, keeping the others whole for decoration. Mix together the halved cherries with the rest of the dried fruit, pour on the brandy and leave to steep for a while. Cream the butter and sugar. Beat the eggs. Add alternately and in stages, the flour, sifted with the baking powder and cinnamon, the fruit and the eggs. Line your cake tin with greaseproof paper. Pour in the mixture and smooth the surface. Dot with whole cherries. Wrap brown paper around the outside of the tin and tie with string. Bake for 3 hours at the above temperature, then at 110°C/225°F/gas mark $\frac{1}{4}$ for a further half hour. Cool the cake on a rack, then store in a tin with a tight-fitting lid.

BROWN SODA BREAD

Despite the dismal fact that *nouvelle cuisine* is now all the go in Ireland – it seems particularly inappropriate there – I noticed when I visited that mercifully there was no shortage of the delicious salty Irish brown soda bread. A request for breakfast in the hotel brought plastic white sliced bread; a request for bread summoned up the real thing. The great plus about soda bread is the speed with which it can be made; none of that diddling around waiting for it to prove itself. From start to finish it can be made in less than an hour and it will make any meal, even a shop-bought one, feel wholesome.

10 oz (300 g) wholemeal flour
6 oz (175 g) plain white bread flour
3 tsp baking powder
1 tsp bicarbonate of soda
2 tsp salt
1 pt (280 ml) buttermilk or milk soured with lemon juice
1 egg, beaten, and another to glaze (optional)

Turn on the oven to 190°C/375°F/gas mark 5. Sift together the two flours, baking powder, soda and salt. If you are using a coarse brown flour, do not bother sifting it. Mix together the buttermilk or sour milk and the eggs and stir them into the dry ingredients. Mix roughly with a spoon or knife and then knead on a floured surface for a few minutes until smooth. Shape into a round, flat cake and put on to a greased baking sheet. Using a knife, make a deep cross on the round and bake for 35–40 minutes. If you wish to glaze the bread, brush with a beaten egg and return to the oven for a few minutes.

CORNBREAD

Cornbread, much loved in the Southern states of America, is reasonably quick to prepare and once you accept, as Americans readily do, a sweetish carbohydrate accompaniment to a savoury main course, you and your guests will appreciate the cakey consistency and the Scarlett O'Hara graciousness of warm cornbread served alongside, say, a microwaved frozen chicken fricassee.

The recipe below comes from James Beard's book on American Cookery. He got it from a Mrs Jeanne Owen, 'a stalwart disciple of the art of good living'. I have converted the quantities from those maddening cup measurements the Americans go in for, so use your judgement over consistency. Leftover cornbread mixed with sautéed onions, crumbled fried sausage meat and perhaps a chicken liver or two, enlivened with seasoning, makes a splendid stuffing for a bird.

$2\frac{1}{2}$ oz (75 g) plain sifted flour
7 oz (200 g) corn meal or polenta
1 tsp salt
1 tsp sugar
2 tsp baking powder
2 eggs, well beaten
8 fl oz (250 ml) milk
2 fl oz (60 ml) cream
$2\frac{1}{2}$ tbsp melted butter

Sift the dry ingredients together into a mixing bowl. Add the eggs and milk and beat with a wooden spoon. Beat in the cream and lastly the melted butter. Pour into an $8\frac{1}{2} \times 11$ (21.5 × 28 cm) buttered cake tin. Bake at 200°C/400°F/gas mark 6 for 15–20 minutes. Cut into squares while still hot and serve wrapped in a cloth napkin.

WATER BISCUITS AND OATCAKES

The recipes below for water biscuits and oatcakes take only minutes, but if you serve hot biscuits with cheese, a pot-luck supper becomes almost sumptuous.

WATER BISCUITS

8 oz (250 g) plain flour
1 tsp baking powder
2 oz (60 g) butter or margarine
$\frac{1}{2}$ tsp salt
sea salt
poppy seeds, or sesame seeds or caraway seeds (depending on the cheeses these will accompany)

Turn on the oven to 150°C/300°F/gas mark 2. Sift together the flour, baking powder and $\frac{1}{2}$ tsp salt. Rub in the fat and add enough water to make a firm dough. Roll out thinly on a floured surface. Prick all over with a fork and cut out circles with a cup or biscuit cutter. Sprinkle just with sea salt or with your choice of seeds as well. Bake on a lightly oiled sheet for about 20 minutes or until crisp and faintly brown. If you store them, crisp in a low oven when you need them.

OAT CAKES

1 oz (30g) lard, dripping or bacon fat
½ pt (300 ml) hot water
1 lb (500g) medium oatmeal – extra for the rolling
½ tsp bicarbonate of soda
½ tsp salt

Turn on the oven to 150°C/300°F/gas mark 2. Melt your chosen fat (bacon fat is good) in the hot water. In a bowl mix the oatmeal with the bicarbonate of soda and salt. Make a well, pour in the melted fat and water and mix with a knife to a fairly moist dough. Dust a surface with oatmeal and roll out the dough, using plenty of oatmeal to prevent any sticking. Cut into rounds. Bake for about 20 minutes on an ungreased baking sheet, turning several times, until they are crisp.

PRESERVES

The task of getting a meal on the table can be much facilitated by an interesting store cupboard containing some items, such as preserves and pickles, that you have put up when you had time on your hands or just felt in the mood. There is little in life more satisfying than the sight of gleaming glass jars with labels inscribed in your own handwriting. A cache of these is also a godsend when you need a present to take with you when visiting.

Pickled and preserved vegetables can enliven a meal and nudge a bored palate. Once the methods are understood they are easily applied to different ingredients. Brine and oil give predictably quite different results. Once you have used your own pickled lemons when cooking rice or poultry, you will never want to be without that particular form of sunshine.

The two preserved meats – chicken legs and chicken livers – are ideal for sophisticated snacks and both keep well in the refrigerator. Traditionally, when evenings lengthen with the approach of winter, it is the time to think about preserves and this fits well with the need for presents on hand at Christmas time.

PICKLED CAULIFLOWER AND RED CABBAGE

The asperity of pickled vegetables is particularly welcome after bouts of eating too much rich food. In the East and Middle East the role that these sharp, crunchy condiments can play is properly understood. In Japan pickles are much relied upon to enliven what is still often a fairly rudimentary diet of rice and fish. Koreans would not consider a meal a meal without *kimchee* – Chinese leaf cabbage. Kimchee ought to take several weeks to prepare, but there are many quicker pickles put up in water, brine or vinegar. Madhur Jaffrey's *Eastern Vegetarian Cooking* has a good chapter on pickles, chutneys and relishes. The recipe below, taken from Claudia Roden's *A Book of Middle Eastern Food*, might stir sluggish systems.

1 cauliflower
½ red or white cabbage
about 3 oz (90 g) salt
1½ pt (900 ml) water
½ pt white wine vinegar
1 small dried chilli (optional)

Trim, wash the cauliflower and separate it into florets. Chop the cabbage roughly. Do not shred or grate it. Pack alternate layers of cauliflower and cabbage chunks into a large clean glass jar. Mix salt, water and vinegar in a glass or china container. Pour the liquid over the vegetables and bury the chilli pod in them if you wish. If you use white cabbage, colour the pickle with a few slices of raw beetroot. Close tightly, with a glass top if possible, for example in a Kilner jar. Store in a warm place for about ten days, by which time the vegetables will be mellow and ready to eat.

SERVES 4   PUGLIA (PRESERVED SWEET PEPPERS)

When I am asked about my best meals every, I find it hard to disassociate them from romance. One memorable meal, coloured by emotion, was on a cold bright November day on the island of Torcello where there was a church to be seen. No restaurants appeared to be open. We asked a local young man if there was any place to eat and he took us to his house and grilled some steaks. As a first course he produced some aubergines preserved in oil, evidently made by his mother. We drank thin, red wine. It remains a milestone meal. In England we put up jellies and jams but pay little mind to preserving vegetables; a shame because the bottles are so decorative and the results delicious, lending potency to many a meal. The recipe below comes from *The Illustrated Book of Preserves*, an Italian book published in England. It is a fund of good recipes.

5 sweet red, green or yellow peppers, or preferably a mixture
about 1 pt (300 ml) white wine vinegar
pinch of salt
3 cloves of garlic, peeled and slivered
2 oz (60 g) salted capers
5 oz (150 g) tinned anchovy fillets
1 small bunch of parsley
1 small bunch of fresh basil
olive oil, to cover

Wash the peppers, dry them, cut in half and discard the stalk, seeds and membrane. Cut into fairly wide strips. Bring the vinegar with a pinch of salt to the boil. Sprinkle in the peppers gradually to prevent the liquid from cooling. Boil for about 10 minutes. Remove with a slotted spoon and dry on a cloth. In a glass preserving jar lay a layer of pepper strips, sprinkle with a few slivers of garlic, a few capers, pieces of anchovy fillet, several parsley sprigs and washed basil leaves. Continue layering the ingredients to within ¾ in (2 cm) of the top of the jar. Pour in enough oil to cover the peppers. Seal the jar and leave for a day, then check the oil level and top up. Seal again and keep in a cool dark place for one month before using as part of an hors d'oeuvre or as a garnish.

PICKLED LEMONS

My store-cupboard always has a glass preserving jar with these pickled lemons, for which Claudia Roden gives a recipe in her *A Book of Middle Eastern Food*, a book I use a great deal. They could hardly be easier to make, but add a note to your cookery quite different from the use of fresh lemon: they add a richness and tanginess to dishes of boiled rice, roast chicken, baked fish, casseroled lentils and to the Moroccan stews called tagines. Don't make this pickle in huge quantity (unless you plan on giving some away); just assemble it when lemons are looking good in the shops, as they are now. I use the large size of Kilner jar and find that this amount lasts well for a few months, both in terms of preservation and quantity needed.

8 thin-skinned, firm lemons
sea salt
paprika
vegetable oil, to cover the fruit

Scrub the lemons well and slice them. Arrange the slices on a large plate or plastic tray and sprinkle them with sea salt. Arrange the plate at an angle so that the juices produced can run off. Leave that way for 24 hours. The slices will become soft and limp and lose their bitterness. Arrange the slices in a glass jar, sprinkling a little paprika between each layer. Cover with vegetable oil. Close the jar tightly and leave for three weeks before using, when the lemons will have mellowed and taken on the role of sunshine in your larder. If you wish to speed the whole process, freeze the lemon slices and leave until rigid. Take them out, sprinkle with salt and leave for about an hour. Pot up as above. They will be ready to use after only a few days. Because I believe in everything taking its own time, I prefer the slower method.

PICKLED ORANGE RINGS

One answer to the problem of Christmas presents is to make them yourself. Everyone appreciates home-made goodies and they are a particularly appropriate little something to take when visiting friends. You could even put together edible presents, enhanced by the odd bottle of wine, Christmas cake and so on, to make a hamper; much cheaper and better than the commercially prepared hampers. Wrapping the presents prettily is part of their allure and jam jars can be made lovely by the addition of a 'hat' made from a circle of material fixed on with an elastic band. Once you are really into this activity, you will try to match the fabric with the contents of the jars.

For the recipe below, which does a great job in cheering cold meat such as cold turkey, choose small, thin-skinned oranges. Proper preserving jars, such as the smaller size of Kilner jar, are best for this confection and also become part of the present as they are reusable.

8 small oranges
1½ pt (900 ml) cider vinegar
2 lb (1 kg) sugar
12 cloves
2 cinnamon sticks

Scrub the oranges quickly. Cut them into slices, rejecting the end pieces that have no flesh attached. Remove any pips. Put them in a large pan and barely cover with water. Simmer for about 30 minutes, watching that the water does not boil or the slices will disintegrate. With a slotted spoon, remove the orange slices to a plate. Add the other ingredients to the cooking water and boil spiritedly for 10 minutes. Reduce the heat, carefully return the orange slices and slowly bring back to the boil. Remove the slices again and pack into hot jars. Boil the remaining syrup until it thickens slightly and then fill the jars to the brim. The cloves, but not the cinnamon sticks, can be allowed in to the jars. Press the fruit to release any air bubbles and seal the jars. When cool, label them and add a cover made from cutting out a fabric circle, allowing a large overhang.

LEMON CURD

This recipe continues the notion of putting up preserves to give
as presents at Christmas. Lemon curd will keep about six weeks,
but should be kept in the refrigerator. Its sharp citrus flavour cuts
through the richness of Christmas food and so should be much
appreciated for use as the base of a pie or just as a spread.

4 juicy thin-skinned lemons
4 oz (120 g) unsalted butter, at room temperature
12 oz (375 g) sugar
4 eggs

Grate the lemons, taking off only the yellow part (the white pith
is bitter). Squeeze the lemons and strain the juice into the top part
of a double boiler, or use a bowl that fits into a saucepan. Add the
rind, the butter and the sugar to the juice and stir occasionally
over simmering water until the butter and the sugar have melted.
Beat the eggs in a bowl and pour them through a strainer on
to the lemon juice mixture. Stir enthusiastically to blend well.
Continue to cook the curd over the simmering, water, stirring
occasionally, until it is thick and glossy and coats the back of a
spoon. It will take about 20 minutes. On no account let it boil or
the eggs will curdle. Don't despair if it does not seem much
thickened as this will happen as it cools. Pour into hot jars and
cover them when the mixture has cooled. Label and store in the
refrigerator.

CHICKEN LEGS PRESERVED WITH PEPPERCORNS

I went to a reception for the British launch of something called
the Farm Verified Organic (FVO) Programme, an internationally
linked body which sets out to earmark products that have been
grown and farmed organically, in other words without the use of
chemical fertilisers and pesticides. Such products, at the moment
mostly dried foods such as muesli, are stamped with a distinctly
unrural looking symbol in green, red and orange that says Farm
Verified Organic. Cynic and fatalist that I am, I found my attention
wandering to the buffet prepared by chef Nicholas Blacklock of
the restaurant La Bastide, where the gathering was held. The
recipe below was one of the best dishes – made, of course, with
free-range chicken and, I trust, organic parsley and peppercorns.

Although the preparation may seem lengthy, the dish will keep in the refrigerator for eight weeks and is absolutely delicious.

4 whole chicken legs
salt
5 sprigs of fresh parsley or chervil
5 sprigs of fresh tarragon
5 fl oz (150 ml) dry white wine
5 fl oz (150 ml) dry vermouth (Cinzano is good)
2 tsp powdered gelatine
1 pt (600 ml) chicken stock (use a good stock cube if necessary)
8 very thin slices of unsmoked streaky bacon
20 green peppercorns

EQUIPMENT:
1¾ pt (1 l) capacity wide-neck preserving jar or saucepan at least 3 cm (1 in) taller than the jar

Divide each chicken leg in two by cutting across at the joint. Expose about ¾ in (2 cm) of bone at the bottom end of each piece. This will act as a 'handle'. Salt each leg lightly, rubbing the salt in with your hands. Roll the legs in the finely chopped herbs, place in a dish, cover with the wine and vermouth and marinate overnight in the refrigerator. Next day dissolve the gelatine in the warm chicken stock. Remove the chicken pieces from the marinade, brush off any excess herbs back into the marinade and wrap each piece of chicken in a slice of bacon. Pack the legs in the preserving jar. Sprinkle in the peppercorns and pour in the marinade and chicken stock. Seal the jar. Place a cloth at the bottom of a large pan of water filled to the level of the top of the contents of the jar. Place the jar on the cloth, bring the water to the boil and simmer gently for 2 hours. Take off the heat and leave in the water until cold. Refrigerate.

When the stock has jellied it is ready to serve. Remove the small amount of fat from the top; spoon the chicken and jelly on to a serving plate. Eat like Henry VIII.

SERVES 4   # CONFIT OF CHICKEN LIVERS

This is not a handy supper dish, but something that can be made with the minimum of preparation. It lasts well in the refrigerator, to be resorted to whenever you feel like a delicious bite or a rich first course. Confit refers to meat preserved in its own fat and is a term and process often applied to duck or goose when the joints of the bird are then eventually either cooked in the oven and served with potatoes or become part of a cassoulet. The idea for cooking and storing chicken livers in this style came from Rita Masseron, my mother-in-law, and it is symptomatic of her inventive cooking. All good Jewish mommas have quantities of chicken fat on hand but, if you do not, and do not feel like rendering it from the fat of a boiling fowl, use butter, lard, duck fat or whatever dripping you feel appropriate. Although at the end of the cooking time the livers may look too rosy, they will only be a gauche pink when you come to mash them on your toast.

8 oz (250 g) chicken livers
salt and freshly ground black pepper
1 large onion, peeled and thickly sliced
4 oz (120 g) chicken fat or alternative (see above) or enough to cover the livers
3 cloves of peeled garlic (optional)

Pick over the chicken livers and discard any gristle or green bits which, on account of a taint from bile, will be bitter. Separate the livers into their natural portions, pieces about 1 in (3 cm) wide. Find a glass Kilner jar about the right size to hold the livers or, failing that, seek out a clean jam jar. Pack in the livers, interspersing the layers with salt and freshly ground pepper. Top up the jar with the onion slices. Melt the fat you are using and heat the cloves of garlic in it. Pour it on to the livers. Turn on the oven to 180°C/350°F/gas mark 4. Bring a kettle of water to the boil. Put the glass jar into a larger ovenproof dish. Add boiling water to come at least halfway up the jar. Place in the pre-heated oven for one hour. Remove the jar and let cool. Refrigerate. Fish out a liver when you want a snack and spread it on some brown toast with a little of the garlic-flavoured fat and some browned onion (the onion will almost have charred in the cooking process).

CHEFS' CONTRIBUTIONS

Since chefs have recently taken to writing cookery books much as ducks take to water, there is no shortage of the 'secrets' of restaurants. The chefs in this section are friends I met as restaurant critic for the *London Evening Standard* who kindly agreed to fill the gap when I was on holiday. Chefs' recipes seemed particularly applicable to a column aimed at suggesting speedy ideas for evening meals, for chefs like to cook quickly and, indeed, in the restaurant most dishes are prepared to order with only the *mise en place,* the preparation, done beforehand.

None of the chefs is French. Two, I am pleased to say, are women. The eclectic style of the recipes strikes me as symbolic of the way restaurant food is going – away from rigidity and towards simplicity and clarity of flavours.

Sally Clarke, who did some of her training in California at Michael's Restaurant in Santa Monica, is chef and owner of Clarke's, 124 Kensington Church Street, W8 (01 221 9225). There she serves a menu which changes each day and features a small choice at lunchtime and no choice in the evenings. Hers is inventive, lively food with productive attention to details.

Simon Hopkinson wrote his recipes for the column while working as chef at Hilaire in South Kensington. By the time this book is published, he will be running the Bibendum restaurant and bar at Sir Terence Conran's and Paul Hamlyn's newly renovated Michelin building in Fulham Road, SW3. It is a peculiarly fitting match, in my view, given the quality of Simon's cooking and his utter dedication to the art.

Carla Tomasi is chef at Frith's, 14 Frith Street, W1 (01 439 3370), a small Soho restaurant that offers 'new British cuisine'. Italian in origin, Carla Tomasi loves English food, a predilection that was ushered in by our puddings. Set-price menus at Frith's keep prices in check and, again, details like the breads, the vegetables, the oils and the petits fours are all *comme il faut.*

Brian Turner made his mark when chef at the Capital Hotel in Knightsbridge, a hotel known for the excellence of its dining room. He also supervised there the opening of Le Métro, a particularly chic wine bar that features a Cruover machine facilitating fine wines by the glass. Turner now has his own restaurant, Turner's, 87–89 Walton Street, SW3 (01 584 6711), a notably pretty place where his way of making the food taste wholly of itself can be tried.

GRILLED RADICCHIO LEAVES WITH ANCHOVY AND WALNUT DRESSING

When a waiter suggests a particular item on the menu, is he genuinely showing his approval for the dish? Or is he under pressure from the chef to 'Get rid of it or else ...'? In a London Italian restaurant one night, a waiter suggested a warm salad of radicchio leaves grilled with a garlic and walnut sauce. It sounded so extraordinary to me that I felt that it had to be tried.

2 large heads of radicchio leaves, separated and washed
roughly chopped parsley leaves, to garnish

FOR THE DRESSING:
8 anchovy fillets
½ clove of garlic (optional)
3 tbsp walnuts
1 small handful of parsley leaves
freshly ground black pepper
about ¼ pt (150 ml) olive oil

To make the dressing place all the ingredients except the olive oil in a food processor and purée until just smooth. Do not overmix. Alternatively finely chop the ingredients together. Place the mixture in a bowl and gradually whisk in enough olive oil to form a consistency like double cream. Taste for seasoning. Pre-heat the grill to its highest temperature. Arrange the leaves, slightly overlapping one another, either on four heat-resistant serving dishes or on one platter small enough to fit under the grill. Make sure that the stems of the leaves are at the centre of each dish so that the result resembles a fully-blown rose. Drizzle the dressing here and there over the leaves, making sure that puddles are not created. Place under the grill and cook for 30–90 seconds, or until the leaves have wilted slightly and have begun to turn brown. Sprinkle with the parsley and serve immediately with good warm bread.

SERVES 4
MINIATURE STEAK TARTARE ON GARLIC TOASTS

A few years ago I visited Holland for the first time. An English friend was to marry a Dutch girl and thirty of us travelled across to be there. During the welcoming supper party, I was introduced to a style of food unfamiliar to me. Among the various smoked

meats and delicious cheeses I was surprised to find miniature steak
tartare about the size of walnuts. They nestled into a wonderful
mustard mayonnaise sitting on crisp pieces of dark bread. We
consumed them by the handful!

FOR THE MAYONNAISE:
1 egg yolk
1 dsp strong mustard
salt and pepper
¼ pt (150 ml) olive or other good vegetable oil

FOR THE STEAK:
½ chilli, finely chopped
2 tbsp chopped fresh coriander leaves
1 tbsp chopped parsley leaves
½ tsp salt
8 oz (300 g) lean rump steak

FOR THE TOASTS:
8 small slices of good bread
1 clove of garlic
fresh parsley, to garnish

In a small bowl mix the egg yolk, mustard, salt and pepper with
a wooden spoon. Add the oil, drop by drop, beating continually,
until an emulsion is formed. Taste for seasoning and leave on one
side. Mix the chilli, coriander, parsley and salt together. Trim the
steak with a small sharp knife, removing any fat or sinew. Mince
the meat and place in a large bowl, adding three-quarters of the
chilli mixture. Mix with a fork and taste for seasoning. Remembering that the flavours will increase on standing, add more chilli
if desired. Shape into eight balls, then flatten slightly with the
back of a teaspoon. Cover and refrigerate. Pre-heat the grill to a
high heat. Brush the bread slices with olive oil and grill until crisp.
While still warm, rub the garlic clove over the surface of each
toast. To serve, spread a spoonful of mayonnaise on each toast,
place the steaks on top, garnish with parsley sprigs and serve.

TOMATO, FENNEL AND BASIL TART   SERVES 6-8

We all know that Real Men do not eat quiche, but have any of
them tried a Real Quiche Lorraine? Probably not. Nevertheless,
the original idea has provided the basis for an infinite number of
savoury tarts and, although this recipe bears little relation to the
Quiche Lorraine, it is light, creamy and quite delicious. It is best

served straight from the oven, but on the rare occasion when a tepid slice or two remains uneaten, it is amazing how quickly it vanishes later.

1 × 8–9 in (20–23 cm) uncooked pastry shell
10 oz (300 g) tomatoes, preferably baby
salt and freshly ground black pepper
1½ oz (45 g) butter
1 large onion, finely sliced
2 small bulbs of fennel, finely chopped
1 bunch of basil, cut into fine strips
2 eggs
¼ pt (150 ml) single cream
2 tbsp choppped fresh herbs (such as basil, thyme, parsley)
salt and pepper

TO SERVE: ¼ pt (150 ml) soured cream

Bake the pastry case blind until golden all over. Without removing from the tin, place on to a baking sheet. Halve the baby tomatoes and place them in a bowl. Sprinkle with salt and pepper. If using large tomatoes, slice them thinly. Heat the butter in a frying pan and, when foaming, add the onion and fennel. Stir over a medium heat until the onion begins to soften. Add half the basil. With a slotted spoon, leaving the juices in the pan, spread the onion mixture into the tart shell. Again with a slotted spoon, place the tomatoes over the top. If using large tomatoes, arrange the slices neatly to cover the onion. Lightly beat the eggs and cream with salt and pepper. Pour into the tart to just below the pastry rim. Do this with care as the tart may not need all the liquid. Bake for 10 minutes, sprinkle with the remaining basil and return to the oven for a further 15 minutes or until the egg mixture has set and the top has a light golden appearance. Serve as soon as possible with the soured cream and a salad of various lettuce leaves.

LIGHT FISH BROTH WITH CHILLI AND FRESH CORIANDER

The world offers us a wonderful plethora of fish soups and stews. In Provence we find fish heads and garlic in bowls brimming with broth. From Thailand comes shellfish infused with coconut milk, chillis and lemon grass.

FOR THE BROTH
1 lb (500 g) fresh clean fish bones and trimmings (head and skin)
1 large leek, washed and finely chopped
1 bulb of fennel, finely chopped
fresh coriander and parsley stalks
1 bay leaf
2 slices of fresh ginger
½ pt (300 ml) double cream

FOR THE FISH
8 oz (250 g) various fish fillets (e.g. brill, monkfish, salmon, plaice)
½ red chilli, seeds removed
1 walnut-sized piece of ginger, finely chopped
juice of 1 lime
salt
coriander leaves, to garnish

Place the fish bones in a large saucepan with all the broth ingredients except the cream. Cover with 2 pt (1.2 l) of cold water. Bring to the boil and then simmer for 25 minutes, skimming from time to time. Strain into a large, clean pan and boil steadily to reduce the liquid by about half. Meanwhile, prepare the fish. Cut the fillets into even-sized cubes and place in a bowl. Add the chilli, ginger, lime juice and a little salt. Mix carefully together and leave to marinate. Add the cream to the broth and boil gently for 1–2 minutes. It will thicken slightly. Add a little salt and taste for seasoning. To serve, warm four serving bowls and divide the fish mixture evenly between them. Spread the fish over the bottom of each bowl and pour in the hot broth. Garnish with a sprig of coriander. The fish will 'cook' as it sits in the bowls while going to the table. Serve immediately with chunks of hot garlic and parsley bread.

PARSLEY SOUP WITH CRISP NUGGETS OF CHICKEN

SERVES 4

This is an adaptation of a soup created by a most special and extraordinary chef, Fredy Girardet. His restaurant sits in the centre of a small industrial town near Lausanne; a modest location for this modest man. For me, he stands apart from the others: godlike, as if from another planet. No dish emerges from his kitchen unless perfect. So simple in its presentation, but so meticulous in its preparation. On one occasion I ate at the restaurant on three consecutive days; dinner, lunch, dinner and dinner! Not once did I feel disappointed or let down.

I remember a parsley soup sprinkled with crisp chunks of frogs' legs arriving at the table. The purée beneath was a most brilliant green, smooth and fabulous to taste. His secret was to cook, purée and strain the soup to order. Nothing had been pre-cooked except the vegetable stock. This is our version of the soup, using chicken breasts instead of frogs' legs. It may be made in advance!

$1\frac{1}{2}$ oz (45 g) butter
1 medium onion, finely diced
1 medium potato, finely diced
1 large bunch of parsley, washed and stalks chopped
1 clove of garlic
1 bay leaf
1 pt (300 ml) chicken or vegetable stock
3 tbsp olive oil
2 large chicken breasts without skin, cut into 1 in (3 cm) cubes
salt and pepper
$\frac{1}{4}$ pt (150 ml) single cream

Melt the butter in a heavy-based saucepan and add the onion and potato. Cook over a gentle heat until soft but not coloured. Add the parsley stalks, garlic and bay leaf and cook gently for a further three minutes. Add the stock and simmer until the ingredients are soft. Then add the parsley leaves and bring to the boil. Liquidise and strain into a clean pan. In a frying pan (preferably non-stick) heat the olive oil. Add the chicken pieces and stir constantly until crisp on the outside, but juicy on the inside. Remove to a bowl with a slotted spoon. Season lightly and keep warm. Add the cream to the soup and taste for seasoning. Re-heat gently without allowing it to boil. Serve in warm bowls sprinkled with the chicken pieces.

SERVES 4 VARIOUS FISH WRAPPED IN WAFER-THIN PASTRY WITH SPINACH AND SHALLOTS

I think I can safely say that at Clarke's we make everything ourselves – everything, that is, except the filo pastry. I remember making filo pastry years ago. Its preparation was time-consuming and awkward, and the thought of making enough for seventy is rather daunting! We have always achieved good results with bought filo pastry.

8–10 oz (250–300 g) various fish fillets (e.g. salmon, monkfish, plaice or cod)
3 fl oz (90 ml) white wine
freshly ground black pepper
2 oz (60 g) butter
2 shallots or 1 small onion, peeled and finely sliced
1 lb (500 g) spinach leaves, washed but not dried
4 oz (120 g) flat black mushrooms
1 tbsp chopped fresh dill or parsley

FOR THE PASTRY:
4 oz (120 g) butter
4 sheets of filo pastry

TO SERVE: soured cream mixed with chopped fresh dill and black pepper (optional)
lemon mayonnaise (optional)
tender fresh spinach leaves

Cut the fish fillets into evenly sized cubes of approximately 1 in (3 cm). Place in a bowl and add the wine and pepper. Mix gently together. In a large saucepan, melt half the butter and add the shallots. Cook them until they begin to soften, but do not brown them. Add the spinach leaves, stirring gently until they begin to wilt. Remove to a plate with a slotted spoon and leave to cool. When cool enough to handle, squeeze in small handfuls until quite dry. Chop roughly. Wipe the pan dry, add the remaining butter and fry the mushrooms until soft. Drain on absorbent paper, then slice in thin strips. Gently melt the butter for the filo pastry. Lay one filo pastry sheet on a clean dry tea-towel. Brush with a thin film of butter. Cover three-quarters of this sheet with the second sheet, brush again and continue in the same way with the last two sheets. Leaving any juices in the bowl, place the fish mixture in a strip along the short edge of the pastry, leaving about 1 in (3 cm) at each end uncovered. Cover with the spinach and top with the mushroom slices. Lightly sprinkle with salt and dill. Lifting the tea-towel gently, roll the pastry, starting at the fish side, until it resembles a neat 'log' shape. Tuck the end under the roll to seal in the filling. With a palette knife, lift the roll to an ungreased baking sheet, brush with butter and bake for 15–20 minutes or until the pastry is crisp and evenly brown. Remove from the tray and cut into four equal slices slightly on the bias. Serve as its sauce soured cream mixed with chopped dill and black pepper or a lemon mayonnaise, plus a small spinach leaf salad.

SERVES 4 # MARINATED CHICKEN SALAD

This salad brings back many memories of California, where I lived
for four years. If you have the patience and the time, set up your
barbecue to cook the chicken for this recipe.

2 sweet peppers, preferably 1 red and 1 yellow
8 oz (250 g) asparagus or green beans
3 lb (1.5 kg) chicken, cut into portions
¼ pt (150 ml) best quality olive oil
finely grated rind of 1 lemon
*1 small chilli, finely chopped with seed (BEWARE: wash hands
thoroughly after preparing this)*
1 small bunch of fresh coriander, roughly chopped
salt

Cut the peppers into quarters; de-seed and devein. Place them
over an open gas flame or under a grill until the skin blackens.
Remove to a plate, cover with an upturned bowl and leave to steam
as they cool. Peel away the skin and discard it. Cut the flesh into
½ in (1.5 cm) diamond shapes. Trim the asparagus or beans and
blanch for 30 seconds in boiling salted water. Drain, spread on to
a clean tea-towel and leave to cool. Poach, fry or grill the chicken
pieces until just done. It is important that the chicken is not
overcooked, as it will continue to cook while cooling. Remove the
bones (and soft skin if poached) and cut the meat into 1 in (3 cm)
cubes. Place in a stainless steel or ceramic bowl and drizzle over
the oil, grated lemon rind, chilli, coriander, a little salt and the
sweet peppers. Toss gently together and cover. Leave to marinate
for one hour. Toss again, just before serving, with the asparagus
or beans and taste for seasoning. Serve with a salad of various
leaves tossed with a good olive oil, salt and pepper.

SERVES 4 # GRILLED PROSCIUTTO HAM, MOZZARELLA CHEESE AND BASIL 'SANDWICH'

I wonder how many American visitors we shock every year as we
continue to serve them bleached white slices, smeared with
'butter', enclosing a preserved pink wafer described as 'ham'. To
them, a sandwich is 5 inches tall and bursting at the seams. This

is the style of sandwich that we offer at the restaurant. The recipe, which places a strong emphasis on flavours and aromas, could easily be used as a source of inspiration for creating other versions with a variety of different ingredients, carefully paying particular attention to colour, texture and taste.

1 large bunch of basil
2 cloves of garlic
1 oz (30 g) toasted pine kernels or almonds
½ pt (300 ml) good olive oil
salt and freshly ground black pepper
1 loaf of good wholemeal or granary bread
8–12 thin slices of prosciutto ham
2 mozzarella cheeses, preferably buffalo milk (from any good Italian delicatessen)

Reserve a few basil leaves to garnish. Make a sauce by placing one clove of garlic, the basil leaves and nuts in a food processor or pestle and mortar. Grind the ingredients together until smooth and gradually add half the olive oil until an emulsion is formed. Add salt and pepper to taste. Pre-heat the grill to a medium/high heat. Crush the second clove of garlic and place in a small pan with the remaining olive oil. Warm gently, then leave on one side to infuse. Slice the bread into thin slices, allowing one to two slices per person, depending on the size of the loaf. Lay the bread on a baking tray and brush with half the garlic olive oil. Grill until crisp and golden. Turn grill to a high heat. Place the proscuitto ham in a loose, crumpled fashion over the toasts, thus giving the sandwich 'height'. Cut the mozzarella balls in half, then into slices and place them in and around the folds of ham. Drizzle with the remaining garlic olive oil and sprinkle with pepper. Grill for about one minute or until the cheese begins to melt. Arrange the 'sandwiches' on serving dishes and spoon over the basil sauce. Garnish with the whole basil leaves and serve immediately.

CHOCOLATE AND ROASTED PEANUT TART

SERVES 8

Mother to daughter, chef to apprentice ... recipes have been handed down for generations. This recipe is one 'borrowed' from a chef in New York who 'borrowed' it from a chef in France. The result is fabulous. Serve it with lots of whipped cream.

1 sweet pastry shell
3 oz (90 g) shelled peanuts
4½ oz (135 g) good dark chocolate
4 oz (120 g) unsalted butter
4 eggs
5 oz (150 g) sugar
2 oz (60 g) flour

Pre-heat the oven to 180°C/350°F/gas mark 4. Bake the pastry shell blind until it is a pale golden colour all over. Place the peanuts on a baking sheet and bake until the skins begin to peel away. Rub them gently in a clean cloth to remove the skins. Melt the chocolate and butter together over a low heat, stirring continuously to prevent the chocolate from burning. Whisk together the eggs, sugar and flour until thick and creamy. Add the chocolate and butter and continue beating until the mixture is thick enough to leave a trail when the whisk is lifted above the bowl. Place the peeled peanuts in the tart shell and pour the chocolate mixture over. Bake in the oven for 20–25 minutes or until the chocolate has risen slightly. Test the tart by placing a wooden cocktail stick in the centre. When removed it should have a slightly sticky appearance. Take the tart from the oven and allow it to cool before serving. The centre should be moist.

SPICED PLUMS, NECTARINES AND PEACHES

SERVES 4

In the summer, when the selection of fruits and salads in the markets is at its best, we make lots of fresh fruit tarts using plums, peaches, nectarines and apricots. They are made very simply: just good sweet pastry filled with the sliced fruit, baked with a touch of sugar to bring out the juice. No sugar or jam to glaze as the natural juices make them shine. The result is heavenly.

8 medium ripe purple plums
4 medium ripe nectarines
4 medium ripe peaches
1 pt (600 ml) water
½ pt (300 ml) red wine
8 oz (250 g) sugar
1 walnut-sized piece of fresh ginger
1 chilli, split in two
2 cinnamon sticks
1 dsp black peppercorns
6 cloves
1 small blade of mace
juice of 1 lemon

Holding the fruit over a bowl to save any juices, cut around the circumference of the stone with a small sharp knife. Gently twist the fruit halves apart in opposite directions to release the stone. Cut the fruit into neat quarters or halves, depending on their size. Place the water, wine, sugar and fruit juices (if any) in a stainless-steel saucepan and stir over a gentle heat until the sugar has dissolved. Add the other ingredients, cover and simmer for 15–20 minutes. Strain and pour into a wide-based pan (a well scrubbed frying pan would be fine). Bring the liquid to a simmer and gently poach the fruit, one type at a time, removing each slice with a slotted spoon as they soften. They should not lose their shape. Place them in a glass serving dish. Reduce the liquid by boiling for a few minutes until it has thickened slightly. The syrup should not become at all sticky or caramelised. Pour this over the fruit and allow to cool. Chill for at least one hour and serve with lots of vanilla ice-cream.

SALAD OF RED PEPPERS SERVES 4

This is a very pure and colourful first course. The ingredients are of prime importance and all should be of the finest quality available. The skinning of the pepper is essential and the dish should not be made if this very simple procedure is not undertaken – the texture of the pepper is so soft and succulent in contrast with its leathery quality when the skin is left on.

This dish always comes first to mind when there is a vegetarian eating at the restaurant.

4 shiny red peppers
6 tbsp finest extra virgin olive oil
sea salt and coarsely ground black pepper
chopped chives or spring onion tops
1 lemon

The easiest way to skin the peppers is to place them under a very hot grill. Keep an eye on them as they can burn quite easily. You will find that the skin 'blisters'. When this has happened on one side, turn them by one quarter and grill again. Continue this process until all the sides are well blistered. Remove and allow to cool. Taking a sharp knife, top and tail the peppers so that you have a floppy hollow cylinder. Cut in half lengthways and flatten each half out on a chopping board. With your knife, scrape off all the inside pith and seeds and trim up the edges so that you are left with eight squarish slices of pepper. I find that the simplest and most attractive presentation is to leave them in this form, slightly overlapping on a plain white plate. But it's up to you. When arranged on four individual plates, dribble the olive oil over, sprinkle with the salt and coarsely ground black pepper and the chopped chives or chopped spring onion tops. Cut the lemon into four wedges and serve separately. The only accompaniment needed is warm crusty French bread and some really good unsalted butter.

SERVES 4   # FISH WITH A HERB CRUST

The best fish to use for this is an inherently moist one as the oven cooking could dry out species such as cod or haddock. Hake is my preference but salmon would do well and sea bass would be ace as long as you can run to the considerable cost of it. The crisp herb crust provides a good contrast to the yielding nature of the fish and you can serve this dish with just wedges of lemon for garnish. If, however, you want a richer meal you could offer a Hollandaise sauce or Beurre Blanc alongside. Lightly cooked fresh spinach dressed with olive oil and boiled new potatoes are suitable accompanying vegetables. Another idea would be batons of steamed cucumber sautéed in butter with a splash of wine vinegar added at the end to provide a kick.

2 lb (1 kg) hake fillet (or other fish; see above)
salt and freshly ground black pepper
1 tbsp plain flour
4 tbsp fresh breadcrumbs
a handful of chopped fresh herbs, e.g. parsley, chives, tarragon
1 large clove of garlic, peeled and finely chopped
grated rind of ½ a lemon
1 egg beaten with 1 dsp milk
2 oz (60 g) butter

Turn on the oven to 220°C/425°F/gas mark 7. Cut the hake into four equal pieces and season them on both sides with salt and pepper. Dust one side of the fish pieces with flour. Don't worry if it starts to look sticky; that is all to the good. Mix together in a bowl the breadcrumbs, herbs, garlic and lemon rind. Spread them on to a large plate. Using a pastry brush, coat the floured side of the fish with the egg beaten with milk. Press the floured and egged side of the fish pieces firmly into the herb mixture.

Using 1 oz (30 g) of the butter, grease a baking sheet or roasting pan. Arrange the fish on the pan, herb crust side up. Dot with remaining butter. Bake for 10 minutes or until the crust is golden. For serving suggestions, see above.

LAMB'S KIDNEYS WITH CABBAGE   SERVES 4

Kidneys should be fresh and in their suet; in this condition they are guaranteed to be succulent and tender. If you give your butcher twenty-four hours' notice he should be able to deliver. The kidneys need to be trimmed of the bulk of their suet. You should leave yourself with just a thin coating of fat. The best cabbage is a good green Savoy variety. Use the best quality olive oil you can afford for the vinaigrette.

1 large cabbage (preferably Savoy)
2 oz (65 g) butter
8 lamb's kidneys in suet
2 tbsp red wine vinegar
2 tbsp Dijon mustard
1 large shallot, peeled and finely chopped
1 clove of garlic, finely chopped
¼ pt (150 ml) best olive oil
1 handful of parsley, finely chopped

Quarter the cabbage and trim off the hard core. Shred as thinly as possible. Heat the butter in a roomy saucepan till melted. Throw in the cabbage and season with salt and pepper. Set on a gentle heat and put on a lid. Let stew, stirring occasionally until soft, but a little crunchy. Keep warm. Take a frying pan large enough to take eight kidneys and set on a high heat. Don't grease the pan – leave it empty and let it get very hot. Season the kidneys all over with salt and pepper. When the frying pan is good and hot, throw in the kidneys, which will immediately throw off their own fat. Turn the heat down a little and leave to cook for a couple of minutes before turning over. Cook them for a similar amount of time on the other side. Pop them in a warm oven on the bottom shelf, for five minutes if you want them to be pink, longer if you like them well cooked. During this time take a bowl and put in it the vinegar, mustard and some salt and pepper. Add the finely chopped shallot and garlic. Whisk together and add the olive oil in a thin stream. This can be even more easily done in a liquidiser. Chop the parsley as finely as possible. To serve, pile the cabbage evenly on to four plates. Slice the kidneys and arrange on top of the cabbage. Dribble the vinaigrette generously over each serving and sprinkle with the chopped parsley.

SERVES 4   STEAK AU POIVRE

This is the only steak that I serve at the restaurant. It is very simple, but to my mind that is the key to its success. I am not fond of the method using all types of peppercorns – pink, green and so on – or using cream or, in some cases, using mustard too. For me rump has the best flavour and the steak is best if cut thick. If you wish to add more flavour to the juices that constitute the sauce, then you can add some meat jelly – the sort that you might find hidden underneath some dripping.

4 thick rump steaks
1 dsp white peppercorns
1 dsp black peppercorns
4 tbsp good olive oil
3 oz (40 g) butter
4 generous tbsp 3-star Cognac
2 dsp meat jelly, if available

Trim the steaks if they are too fatty or untidy. Crush or grind together the peppercorns. If grinding, use a small electric coffee grinder for the best results. Otherwise, use a pestle and mortar. Place the peppercorns in a sieve and shake around until there is no fine powder left. This is important as the steak will be too hot otherwise. It is worth pressing the peppercorns into each side of the steak an hour or so before you cook it so that the flavour of pepper permeates the mat. Place the steaks in a roomy shallow dish and sprinkle over and below some good olive oil. Take a good roomy frying pan, melt the butter and heat until just starting to brown. Place the steaks in it and salt on one side only. Turn them only once and, depending on how you like your meat cooked, prod them with your finger to determine their readiness. They should be soft and just resistant for rare; a bit bouncy for medium; firm and with no resistance for well done! Place steaks on four hot plates. Keeping the cooking fat hot but not burning add the Cognac, which will froth up fiercely. Flame it if you wish. The combination of the liquid and butter should amalgamate into a buttery sauce. At this moment add your meat jelly if you have some – a couple of dessertspoons should do. Pour the sauce over the steaks and serve with fried potatoes and a good green salad.

ALMOND TART   SERVES 4-6

The secret of this rich and buttery tart lies in the very gentle cooking temperature so that the filling does not rise too much and is just set when the cooking has finished. The crispness of the pastry is also important; to achieve this you must bake the pastry blind.

4 oz (120 g) flour
pinch of salt
2 oz (60 g) sugar, preferably icing sugar
2½ oz (75 g) butter, chopped
1 egg yolk

FOR THE FILLING:
4 oz (120 g) unsalted butter
4 oz (120 g) caster sugar
2 eggs
4 oz (120 g) ground almonds
2 tbsp best quality raspberry jam

Put the first four ingredients in a large bowl, work together with your fingers gently until the mixture is like large breadcrumbs. Add the egg yolk, bind together with a fork and finally with your hands. You can use a food processor. Leave to rest in the fridge for an hour or so. Roll out the pastry and line a 9 in (23 cm) ring

with a loose bottom. Bake blind, having pricked the base of the
pastry and lined it with greaseproof paper filled with rice or lentils,
for example. Cook till dry and crisp, with a honey-coloured look.
The oven should be quite hot – about 195°C/385°F/gas mark 5 or 6.

For the filling, cream together the butter and sugar until white
and fluffy. Add the eggs one by one and beat again. Beat in the
almonds. Spread the raspberry jam on to the base of the tart case
and pour in the filling. Cook very gently in a moderate oven
180°C/350°F/gas mark 4, for about an hour on the lower shelf until
pale golden and just firm to the touch. Serve warm, not hot, with
loosely beaten cream.

SERVES 4 # LITTLE MUSHROOM CAKES

Mushrooms, underrated vegetables, are now found in abundance
in various shapes and varieties. We import vast quantities of wild
mushrooms every week from France, although they grow, and
could be easily picked – by experts at least – in the woods all over
Britain. Last year one expedition to Esher Forest proved most
unfortunate.

The more exotic ones have a most distinctive flavour, enabling
you to create a dish with identity. As always the better the ingredients, the better the results. So do try to get a few types, one of
them being oyster mushrooms. However, this recipe will equally
satisfy with a mix of readily available flat cap and button mushrooms.

1½ lb (750 g) assorted mushrooms, washed if necessary
2 oz (60 g) onion, peeled and finely chopped
4 tbsp olive oil
2 oz (60 g) ricotta or fresh goat's cheese or any other soft cheese, to
taste
3 egg yolks
1 tbsp finely chopped fresh parsley

Reserve some of the nicest mushrooms to use as a garnish for each
individual cake, and chop the rest. Fry the onion gently with the
oil until soft but not coloured. Add the mushrooms and garlic and
cook on a high heat for five minutes, stirring continuously, till the
mushrooms have just gone soft. Season and tip the contents into
a bowl. Cream the cheese of your choice with the egg yolks; stir
into the cooked mushrooms together with the parsley. Lightly oil
four 3 in (8 cm) ramekins, fill them with the mixture and cook in
a bain-marie, with the water reaching two-thirds of the height of

the ramekins. Cook at 180°C/350°F/gas mark 4 for 20–30 minutes – the cakes should feel firm when lightly pressed. While the cakes are cooking, clean – or wash – and slice the reserved mushrooms. Cook them for a few minutes with a little olive oil, salt and pepper.

Warm four small plates. Run a knife around the ramekins to free the cakes, then turn out on to the plates, arranging a few of the sliced mushrooms around each one. To follow a first course with such a distinctive flavour, I would suggest something like hare or kidneys.

TOMATO AND ORANGE SOUP FLAVOURED WITH FRESH THYME

SERVES 4

Tomato soup is certainly one of the most popular soups of all time. This one tastes very fresh and can be served hot or cold since it benefits from the absence of cream and butter. To make this soup with fresh tomatoes is the best method; however, in this country you may not get as much flavour in tomatoes because there is no substitute for the sun to ripen any kind of fruit. The most satisfactory tomatoes come from Guernsey so it is worth asking for them. A way to add excitement is the addition of fresh orange juice and thyme.

I always use vegetable stock for soups because all you have to do is to scrub and chop some vegetables, cook them gently with some herbs, and add water. Then you can just forget about it.

2 oz (60 g) onion, peeled and chopped
1 fl oz (30 ml) olive oil
1 clove of garlic, peeled and chopped
2 lb (1 kg) tomatoes, quartered
2 sprigs of fresh thyme
1 tsp caster sugar
salt and freshly ground pepper
juice of 3 large oranges
grated zest of 1 orange

FOR THE VEGETABLE STOCK:
1 large potato
1 carrot
1 stick of celery
1 bay leaf
1 tbsp olive oil
1½ pt (900 ml) water
1 clove of garlic

Make the vegetable stock. Scrub all the vegetables and chop them with the onion in large pieces. Lightly fry the vegetables and herb in the oil. Add the water and garlic, bring to the boil and simmer for 30 minutes in the covered pan. Strain and reserve the liquid. Soften the onion in the oil without colouring it. Add the garlic, tomatoes and thyme. Lower the heat, cover the pan with a lid and cook until the tomatoes are very soft. Add most of the stock, bring to the boil and simmer for a further 15 minutes. Cool a little, then blend and rub through a sieve. Add the sugar and seasoning; re-heat or chill the soup, adding the juice and zest at the last minute.

SERVES 6 SALMON POACHED WITH OLIVE OIL AND ROSEMARY

Salmon is without doubt the king of British fish. It is now making a marvellous comeback and, since numerous fish farms are now supplying our markets, there should be a considerable drop in price. Personally, having tasted both wild and farmed varieties, I cannot tell the difference. I have gradually become quite fond of salmon, since I have started eating it 'my way'. Many times I have had it offered in restaurants with either a butter or a cream sauce. Is this because the majority of people associate eating out with rich and elaborate food? I really like this recipe because cooks in general have preconceived ideas for salmon, so I have gone about it with a continental or, rather, a Mediterranean approach.

$1\frac{1}{2}$ pt (900 ml) water
6 tbsp olive oil
1 lemon, cut in half
2 cloves of garlic, crushed
a few leaves of parsley
2 sprigs of rosemary
$1\frac{1}{2}$ lb (750 g) salmon – ask your fishmonger to fillet and scale the fish, but leave the skin on
1 large cucumber
salt and freshly ground pepper

Pour the water into a shallow pan, add the rest of ingredients (apart from the salmon and cucumber) and bring slowly to the boil. Simmer the water till you can taste the lemon, then strain the contents into a bowl discarding everything except the rosemary. Pull the soft needles from the stems of rosemary and put them in a blender together with 8 fl oz (250 ml) of the poaching liquid. Run the blender until the rosemary has broken down into tiny specks. Pour everything back into the pan. Cube the salmon into bite-size pieces and, with the aid of a metal peeler, slice the cucumber lengthwise into thin ribbons.

Bring the poaching liquid back to the boil, adding salt and freshly ground pepper, drop the salmon in and poach for 5 minutes. Lift the fish out and arrange in warmed soup bowls. Cook the cucumber ribbons in the same pan for 1 minute, or less if you like it quite crunchy in texture. Lay the poached cucumber on top of the salmon, adding a few tablespoons of the flavoured stock to each bowl.

ROAST RACK OF LAMB WITH MINT AND HONEY

SERVES 6

Lamb is one of my favourite meats since it has a distinctive flavour and can be served fairly plainly without being bland. Here is a way of improving traditional roast lamb with mint sauce. Ask your butcher to chine the rack, to facilitate the carving, and to trim some of the fat. For extra flavour you can marinate the meat for a few hours by rubbing it with salt and freshly ground pepper, olive oil and the herb of your choice, in this case mint. What could easily accompany the roast lamb are some new potatoes, boiled with the skin on, tossed while still warm in olive oil, and a few toasted and chopped hazelnuts.

1 rack of lamb, about 8 cutlets

FOR THE MARINADE:
salt and freshly ground pepper
2–3 tbsp olive oil
4 sprigs of fresh mint

FOR COOKING:
2 cloves of garlic, unpeeled but crushed
4 sprigs of fresh mint
8 tbsp white wine
4 tbsp clear honey, for example orange blossom honey, gently warmed

Season and marinate the lamb as described above. Remove from the refrigerator at least three hours before roasting; chilled meat tends to burn on the outside before the inside is cooked. Pre-heat the oven to 220°C/425°F/gas mark 7. Put the meat in a shallow roasting pan. Add the garlic and mint – reserving one sprig – and roast for 45 minutes for rarish lamb. Shortly before the end of the cooking time, pour the wine and honey mixture on the rack. Remove the meat from the oven and let it rest for 10 minutes. Skim the fat from the roasting pan; if you do not have enough juices left, you will have to add some more wine. Bring the contents of the pan to the boil, add the chopped leaves from the reserved sprig of mint and adjust the seasoning. Slice the rack into cutlets and serve with a little sauce on warmed plates.

SERVES 8-10 ## LEEK AND GRUYÈRE TART

Having lived in the north of England my mother used to concoct all types of dishes around onions and cheese that I still remember with affection.

Somehow, however, the images of Spanish onions and Cheddar cheese do not have the same qualities as the images of leeks and Gruyère cheese. Leeks are of the onion family yet have a delicate and rather sweet flavour, while we all love the 'nuttiness' of Gruyère. One word of warning – please wash the leeks two or three times as they are often very sandy and gritty when cooked. To remove the grit, stand them upside down in a big jug of cold water between washings.

4 oz (120 g) unsalted butter
6 leeks, trimmed and well washed
2 eggs and 2 yolks
½ pt (300 ml) double cream
½ pt (300 ml) milk
salt and pepper
a little grated nutmeg
1 lb (500 g) home-made or bought puff pastry
4 oz (120 g) grated Gruyère cheese

First melt the butter and add the sliced leeks. Cook slowly in a covered pan until soft – do not allow them to colour. Stir regularly and, when soft, remove and cool. Whisk the eggs, eggs yolks, cream and milk together, add the seasoning and the nutmeg. Line a 10 in (25 cm) flan case with the pastry and bake it blind in the oven – around 150°C/300°F/gas mark 2 for about 10 mins. Remove from the oven and cool slightly. Add the leeks to the egg mixture, check the seasoning and pour into the flan case. Sprinkle the top with the Gruyère. Bake in the oven – 150°C/300°F/gas mark 2 for 35–45 minutes – until the top is browned and the filling is set. Cool for five minutes, serve warm with salad.

BRILL STEAKS WITH SMALL GLAZED ONIONS AND SWEET PEPPERS

SERVES 4

There's not a day that passes without at least one phone call from someone trying to sell me Scotch salmon. As most chefs these days enjoy fish cookery more and more it is nice to be able to enjoy the great availability of fresh salmon. We are very fortunate that varieties of fish available have multiplied over the past few years, especially now the English fish markets are trying to compete with the French in this direction. Recently I have fallen in love again with the traditional English fish and have found that this brill dish is very tasty as well as colourful.

4 oz (120 g) butter
24 pickling onions, peeled
salt and pepper
2 fl oz (60 ml) home-made or tinned consommé
2 sweet red peppers
4 brill steaks, cut through the bone and with the black skin removed, each weighing 8 oz (250 g)
24 small cooked potatoes
juice of 1 lemon
1 bunch of chives, chopped

Take 2 oz (60 g) of the butter, melt it, sauté the pickling onions, season, add the consommé and cook until soft. Reduce the cooking liquor until a glaze is formed, then roll the onions in this until the onions are coated. Blanch the peppers to remove the skins and then cut them into large batons. Lightly sauté in 2 oz (60 g) butter and put to one side. Pre-heat the oven to 190°C/375°F/gas mark 5. Sauté the brill steaks in the remaining butter until golden and then put in the oven to bake, white skin side down. When cooked – about 10 minutes – remove from the pan. Place on a dish. Take the cooked potatoes, onions and peppers and whirl round in the pan with lemon juice, pour over the fish, cover with chopped chives and serve.

TWO WAYS WITH SCALLOPS

Twice a week, weather permitting, I receive a sack of beautiful scallops from the west coast of Scotland. To me these are perhaps the finest seafood produced around this island of ours. They are wonderful eaten raw and have a delicate flavour and texture when very lightly cooked. To overcook scallops is a crime, so please be very careful. If you can buy the scallops in the shell, do so; to open them, just place a pan on the stove, put the scallops in and watch them open quickly. Here are two of my favourite quick scallop recipes.

SCALLOP AND BACON SALAD
SERVES 4

12 scallops
12 small radishes
4 rashers of bacon
1 clove of garlic, peeled
2 slices of good white bread
2 oz (60 g) butter
salad leaves of your choice

FOR THE SALAD DRESSING:
½ tbsp sherry vinegar
1 tsp grainy mustard
3 tbsp walnut oil
salt and pepper
1 clove of garlic

Prepare the scallops: clean and slice them in half, separate the roes. Chop the radishes. Cut the rashers of bacon and the peeled clove of garlic into thin strips. Cut the bread into strips.

Fry the bread in the butter until golden brown. Fry the bacon in butter until golden brown. Arrange the salad leaves nicely on a plate. Quickly sauté the seasoned scallops, then mix with the bacon and radishes and lay on top of the salad leaves. Sprinkle with salad dressing and garlic and then with the crisp bread croûtons.

MARINATED SCALLOPS AND GINGER ON A BED OF AVOCADO SALAD
SERVES 4

20 scallops
salt and pepper
2 tbsp walnut or hazelnut oil
juice of ½ lemon
4 small radishes
½ oz (15 g) piece of fresh ginger
2 avocados
1 tbsp chopped chives

Clean the scallops, cut into thin slices crossways, lay on a tray and season with salt and pepper. Sprinkle with nut oil and lemon juice. Grate the radishes and ginger over the scallops and place in the fridge for four hours. Peel and chop the avocados, lay on a plate and sprinkle with salad dressing. Lay the scallops over the avocados, sprinkle with chives and the nut oil and lemon juice.

CALF'S LIVER WITH HERBS, GARLIC AND GRAINY MUSTARD SAUCE

SERVES 4

Calf's liver is generally found in Italian restaurants, but here is an adaptation of a dish I once ate in a bistro in Paris. There is no doubt that calf's liver is an expensive item, but in my view it is well worth the expense. However, if one can buy good fresh English lamb's liver – that has not been frozen – then this can make an admirable substitute.

1 clove of garlic
1 tbsp fresh herbs such as tarragon, chervil, chives, parsley
4 thin slices of calf's liver
a little flour
2 oz (60 g) unsalted butter
3 fl oz (90 ml) Madeira
¼ pt (150 ml) home-made or tinned consommé
1 tbsp grainy mustard

Cut the garlic into thin strips and chop the herbs. Dip the liver into the flour, taking care to shake off all the excess. Melt 1 oz (30 g) of butter in the frying pan. Sauté the liver very quickly till golden brown on either side. Do not overcook. Remove and keep warm. Rinse the frying pan with the Madeira, being careful as the pan is hot and the Madeira will evaporate very quickly; the steam caused can be very dangerous. Add the consommé and reduce by half. Take the remaining 1 oz (30 g) of butter and shake this into the sauce. Add the garlic, herbs and then stir in the mustard. Pour this over the liver, and serve immediately.

SURPRISE DES FRAISES ET POMMES
(Apple and Strawberry Pudding)

In early summer the talk among many of our suppliers is all about the quantities of produce that they have to find for the coming London season. Ascot, Henley and Wimbledon are now almost

upon us. These events always make me think of English strawberries, although increasingly there is also a good supply of foreign
ones. Here is a dish that must be eaten immediately. I like this
pudding on a Sunday or in the evening when I need something
really sweet to finish my dinner.

3 dessert apples
water acidulated with lemon juice
8 oz (250 g) strawberries
4 oz (120 g) sugar
4 oz (120 g) butter
2 eggs
3 oz (90 g) plain flour
3 oz (90 g) ground almonds
½ oz (15 g) baking powder
1 fl oz (30 ml) milk
2 oz (60 g) strawberry jam
a little icing sugar
cream, to serve

Peel and slice the apples; keep them in the water and lemon juice.
Clean and slice the strawberries. Make a sponge mixture. Cream
the sugar and butter until white; slowly beat in the eggs; sieve the
flour, almonds and baking powder together; add to the creamed
mixture and fold in; soften the mixture with milk. Butter an oval
serving dish and spread the base with jam. Add two sliced apples.
Pre-heat the oven to 200°C/400°F/gas mark 6. Fill up the sponge
mixture with half the strawberries mixed into it. Place the last
apple in slices around the top of the pudding. Bake for 10 minutes,
turn down the heat to 180°C/320°F/gas mark 4 and bake for another
30 minutes. Place the rest of strawberries in the centre of the
pudding, sprinkle with icing sugar and serve with cream.

BIBLIOGRAPHY

James Beard, *American Cookery*, Hart-Davis MacGibbon Ltd, 1974
James Beard, *Beard on Pasta*, Macmillan, 1985
Frances Bissell, *A Cook's Calendar*, Chatto & Windus, 1985
Caroline Blackwood and Anna Haycraft, *Darling, You Shouldn't Have Gone To So Much Trouble*, Jonathan Cape, 1980
Paul Bocuse, *The Cuisine of Paul Bocuse*, Granada, 1985
British Trout Association, *Take Two Trout*, 1986
Vincento Buonassisi, *The Classic Book of Pasta*, Futura, 1985
Anna del Conte, *Pasta Perfect*, Conran Octopus, 1986
Cornwall Historic Churches' Trust, *Men's Menus*, 1986
Nicola Cox, *Nicola Cox's Good Food from Farthinghoe*, Gollancz, 1986
Elizabeth David, *A Book of Mediterranean Food*, John Lehmann, 1950
Elizabeth David, *An Omelette and a Glass of Wine*, Robert Hale, 1984
Elizabeth David, *French Provincial Cooking*, Michael Joseph, 1960
Elizabeth David, *Summer Cooking*, Penguin, 1969
Alan Davidson, *North Atlantic Seafood*, Macmillan, 1979
Josceline Dimbleby, *A Traveller's Tastes*, Sainsbury's, 1986
Theodora FitzGibbon, *Irish Traditional Food*, Gill & Macmillan, 1983
Dr Jack Gillon, *Le Menu Gastronomique*, Macdonald, 1981
Victor Gordon, *The English Cookbook*, Jonathan Cape, 1985
Jane Grigson, *English Food*, Macmillan, 1974
Jane Grigson, *Vegetable Book*, Michael Joseph, 1978
Nathalie Hambro, *Particular Delights*, Jill Norman & Hobhouse, 1981
Nathalie Hambro, *Visual Delights*, Conran Octopus, 1986
Marcella Hazan, *The Classic Italian Cookbook*, Macmillan, 1980
Madhur Jaffrey, *Eastern Vegetarian Cooking*, Jonathan Cape, 1981
Tom Jaine, *Cooking in the Country*, Chatto and Windus, 1986
George Lang, *The Café des Artistes Cookbook*, Jonathan Cape, 1981
George Lang, *The Cuisine of Hungary*, Penguin, 1985
George Lassalle, *The Adventurous Fish Cook*, Macmillan, 1976
Ranse Leembruggen, *Easy Eastern Cookery*, Macdonald, 1986
Mrs Hilda Leyel, *The Gentle Art of Cookery*, Chatto & Windus, 1925
Kenneth Lo, *Healthy Chinese Cooking*, William Collins, 1984
Lady Macdonald of Macdonald, *The Harrods Book of Entertaining*, Ebury Press, 1986
Richard Olney, *Simple French Food*, Penguin, 1983
Sara Paston-Williams, *The National Trust Book of Traditional Puddings*, Penguin, 1969
Princess Pamela, *Soul-Food Cookbook*, New American Library, 1979
Claudia Roden, *A Book of Middle Eastern Food*, Thomas Nelson, 1968
Helen Saberi, *Noshe Djan, Afghan Food and Cookery*, Prospect Books, 1986
Nancy Shaw, *Food for the Greedy*, Cobden Sanderson, 1936
The Three Course Newsletter, available by subscription from Tom Jaine, Allaleigh House, Blackawton, Nr Totnes, Devon TQ9 7DL
John Tovey, *Entertaining with Tovey*, Macdonald, 1979
Roger Vergé, *Cuisine of the Sun*, Macmillan, 1979
Clare Walker with Keryn Christiansen, *A Taste of American Cooking*, Penguin, 1986
Alice Waters, *Chez Panisse Menu Cookbook*, Chatto & Windus, 1984
Patricia H. White, *Food as Presents*, Penguin, 1982

INDEX